modest claims

*Dialogues and Essays on
Tolerance and Tradition*

ADAM B. SELIGMAN

University of Notre Dame Press

Notre Dame, Indiana

"The Place Where We Are Right" from *The Selected Poetry of Yehuda Amichai*,
edited and translated from the Hebrew by Chana Bloch and Stephen Mitchell,
rev. ed. (Berkeley: University of California Press, 1996), copyright © 1996
The Regents of the University of California, is reprinted by permission
of the Regents of the University of California and the University
of California Press.

Library of Congress Cataloging-in-Publication Data
Seligman, A.
Modest claims : dialogues and essays on tolerance and tradition /
Adam B. Seligman.
p.   cm. — (Erasmus Institute books)
Includes bibliographical references and index.
ISBN 0-268-04106-7 (hardcover : alk. paper)
ISBN 0-268-04107-5 (pbk. : alk. paper)
1. Religious tolerance.   2. Religions—Relations.   I. Title.   II. Series.
BR1610.S46   2004
201'.723—dc22
2003024639

∞ *This book is printed on acid-free paper.*

modest
claims

Erasmus Institute Books

The Place Where We Are Right

From the place where we are right
Flowers will never grow
In the spring.

The place where we are right
Is hard and trampled
Like a yard.

But doubts and loves
Dig up the world
Like a mole, a plow.
And a whisper will be heard in the place
Where the ruined
House once stood.

————Yehuda Amichai

CONTENTS

PREFACE AND
ACKNOWLEDGMENTS

In April of 1999 a group of scholars from different disciplines and countries met in Vienna, at the Institute for the Study of Human Sciences, to discuss issues of tolerance from a religious perspective. The scholars represented the three monotheistic religions and ranged in places of origin from Turkey, Egypt, Israel, and Bosnia to Spain, India, the United States, and Germany. The meetings were funded by the Ford Foundation.

The meetings were taped, transcribed, and edited. They provide a unique window into the opportunities for establishing dialogues of tolerance predicated on religious assumptions rather than on secular ideas of self and society. This is an increasingly important undertaking as more and more policy makers, religious leaders, and concerned citizens are coming to realize that the challenge of tolerance, especially at the point of its intersection with religious beliefs and practices, is one of the critical issues of our times. Globalization has meant a higher degree of interaction with people and civilizations who are different, who are "other." Many of the burning political issues of our time, from the Balkan Wars of 1992–1995 to the continuing crises in the Middle East to the role of Muslim immigrants in Western Europe, turn around issues of religion and tolerance. An awareness of the importance of these issues appears in a growing allocation of funds and programs dealing with the topics of religion and of tolerance (the Ford Foundation has, for example, only recently added religion to its portfolio of programs, and the United Nations has declared a year of Tolerance in Education. Even the American military is contracting out for programs that will teach tolerance among people of different religions and ethnic backgrounds). There is thus a widely felt need among policy makers, religious leaders, and concerned congegrants in the multiple and diverse religious communities of this country and worldwide, who realize how imperative it is to address these issues from a new perspective.

As one cannot, in the final analysis, argue Thomas Jefferson with the Muslim *ulema* or the Orthodox Rabbinate in Israel, other bases and arguments for tolerance and pluralism must be found. This book provides the beginnings of such a set of arguments. In doing so, it draws on existing work that has touched on some of the themes discussed. There exist, for example, philosophical studies of the problem of tolerance, as well as historical works on religious toleration, works on religion and conflict resolution, and works on religion and Human Rights.[1] All these works have been critical in raising the issue of tolerance and putting it back on the contemporary agenda. They have also contributed to clarifying the historical record about not only the complicated relation between religion and toleration, but that between liberalism and toleration as well. Our own argument here, which draws on the dialogues and develops further in the essays, makes the case for the contemporary need to find explicitly religious arguments for tolerance and then attempts to provide the beginnings of such arguments in three religious contexts. In so doing it seeks to uncover the sources of tolerance and pluralism that exist within the traditions of the three revealed religions: Judaism, Christianity, and Islam. Our contemporary and modernist stress on tolerance as rooted in a secular consciousness has left these sources unexplored and often marginalized in current debates and social agendas. And yet, these sources are crucial if we are to deal with the growing saliency of religious identities worldwide, as well as the renewed calls within the different religions for a recognition of their own internal, pluralist components.

The dialogues are structured around the different interlocutors' brief presentations, followed by general discussion. They are meant to encourage the reader to go beyond his or her own tradition and engage with other and perhaps more unfamiliar modes of being in the world. Dialogue is thus used as both a heuristic device and, as will be made clear in the following, a substantive principle that stands at the root of all forms of tolerance.

Here perhaps is the place to note that little attention is paid to any rigorous distinction between toleration and tolerance in the following, though other texts sometimes make much of the difference. Here "toleration" is, on the whole, used when indicated by the historical context (following the Wars of Religion in Europe, say) while "tolerance" is the preferred term for what I am trying to get at, as specific virtue. So too, as will become clear, it is tolerance rather than pluralism that is the subject of this inquiry, as it is tolerance that preserves the element of substantive difference and even disapproval that I find so necessary to engage with. The reader will see that not all the interlocutors agree with this principle (Fisch, Wolfteich) or with my usage (Stone).

The chapter following the dialogues, "Towards a Phenomenology of Religious Tolerance," takes the very structure of dialogue and of translation as metaphors for the tolerant act and views their connection to the religious consciousness and to the play of symbol systems that are necessitated by a tolerant approach. Taking off from the dialogues and developing the more analytic aspects of some of the themes raised in the dialogues, this chapter, together with the concluding "Languages of Tolerance," makes the claim for the uniqueness of a tolerance based on religious assumptions and views its fundamental difference from modern, secular, and liberal versions of tolerance—which are, inter alia, subjected to critique.

In editing the dialogues and writing the accompanying chapters, I have acquired many debts. First and foremost I want to thank all of our interlocutors for their time and contributions to this volume. I especially wish to thank Shlomo Fischer and Rusmir Mahmutćehajić for contributing so much to the real development of religious tolerance, beyond these published dialogues. David Gordis, Robert Weller, John Holmwood, Chris Winship, and Bennett Simon all read much of this volume. Their sagacious comments have helped form this book in more ways than I can here recount. The comments of the reviewers at University of Notre Dame Press were also enormously helpful in turning a set of discussions into an accessible and cogent argument, with the potential to reach beyond the small circle of interlocutors who first met and discussed the issues of religious tolerance. I further extend my thanks to David Montgomery for his help in preparing the book for publication. I also wish to express my gratitude to the Ford Foundation for funding both the meetings that gave birth to this book and the accompanying research. The Pew Charitable Trusts have supported the Toleration Project at Boston University for the past three years. It is my pleasure to acknowledge their ongoing commitment.

ABOUT THE
INTERLOCUTORS

Nasr Abu Zayd is one of the most respected and well-known Islamic commentators on the Qu'ran. His works of interpretation are published throughout the Arabic-speaking and Muslim world. He was Professor of Islamic Thought in Cairo and now resides in Leiden, in exile after multiple attacks by Islamic extremists in his home country.

Peter Berger is University Professor Emeritus at Boston University and Director of its Institute for the Study of Economic Culture. His many books include *The Social Construction of Reality* (with Thomas Luckman, 1966); *The Sacred Canopy: Elements of a Sociological Theory of Religion* (1967); *The Homeless Mind: Modernization and Consciousness* (with Brigitte Berger and Hansfried Kellner, 1973); *The Heretical Imperative* (1979); *A Far Glory: The Quest for Faith in an Age of Credulity* (1992); *Redeeming Laughter* (1997).

Joan Estruch is Professor of Sociology and Director of the Center for the Study of Sociology and Religion at the Autonomous University of Barcelona. He has written extensively on politics and religion in the Spanish context. His major works include *La innovación religiosa* (1972); *La secularización en España* (1972); *Sociología de una profesión: los asistentes sociales* (1976); *Plegar de viure: un estudi sobre els suïcidis* (1982); *Saints and Schemers: Opus Dei and Its Paradoxes* (1995).

Menachem Fisch is Associate Professor of History and Philosophy of Science at Tel Aviv University, and Senior Fellow of the Shalom Hartman Institute for Advanced Jewish Studies in Jerusalem. His published works deal chiefly with confirmation logic, rationality theory, the history of nineteenth-century British science and philosophy, and the nature and significance of Talmudic discourse. He has written the following books: *William Whewell, Philosopher of Science* (1991); *Lada'at Hokhma / To Know Wisdom* (1994); and *Rational Rabbis: Science and Talmudic Culture* (1997).

Shlomo Fischer is the Founder and Director of Yesodot (Centre for Torah Research and Democracy) in Jerusalem. He supervised the production of textbooks on Jewish history for Israeli secondary state schools. He teaches at the Hebrew University and in colleges for teachers of religion (Beit Morasha). He is a member of the Forum for Research into Israeli Culture and Society at the Van Leer Jerusalem Institute. Among his best-known books and articles are *History of the Jews in Islamic Lands in the Modern Period* (1990); *Collective Exile and Individual Redemption: Hasidism and the Jewish Enlightenment* (1988); *Jewish Society in the Second Temple Period* (1985).

Nilüfer Göle is Professor of Sociology at Ecole des Hautes Etudes en Sciences Sociales in Paris. Formerly she was at Bogazici University in Istanbul. She is concerned with Islamic movements, gender issues, public space, and non-Western modernism. Her book on Islamic veiling is published in English as *The Forbidden Modern: Civilization and Veiling* (1996), and also in Turkish, French, German, and Spanish.

Friedrich Wilhelm Graf is Professor of Systematic Theology in Ethics at the University of Munich, a position he assumed in 1999. Prior to this, he held two chairs in Systematic Theology at the University of Augsburg, one from 1996–1998, and one from 1988–1992, when he established the Ernst-Troeltsch-Forschungsstelle. He was Professor at the University of Hamburg (1992–96) and a Fellow at Max-Weber-Kolleg at the University of Erfurt (1997–99). In 1999 he was the first theologian to receive the Leibniz Prize, Germany's highest research prize. Professor Graf is a regular contributor to the *Neue Züricher Zeitung* and the *Frankfurter Allgemeine Zeitung*.

Sohail H. Hashmi is Alumnae Foundation Associate Professor of International Relations at Mount Holyoke College. He has written on the Islamic ethics of international relations, including articles on jihad, sovereignty, and international society. He is currently completing a book entitled *The Islamic Ethics of War and Peace: An Interpretative Essay with Historical References*. He is the editor of several works, including *Bound-*

aries and Justice: Diverse Ethical Perspectives (with David Miller, 2001) and *Islamic Political Ethics: Civil Society, Pluralism, and Conflict.*

Rusmir Mahmutćehajić is Professor of Applied Physics and Islamic Phenomenology at the University of Sarajevo and President of International Forum Bosnia. He is former Deputy Prime Minister of Bosnia and Hercegovenia. Among his many works are *Živa Bosna: politicki eseji i intervjui* (1995); *O Nauku Znaka* (1996); *Dobra Bosna* (1997); *Kaligrafski Listovi Cazima Hadzimejlica* (1997); *Kriva Politika: Čitanje historije I povjerenje u Bosni* (1998); *Bosnia the Good: Tolerance and Tradition* (2000); *The Denial of Bosnia* (2000); *Sarajevski eseji: Politika, ideologija i tradicija* (2000); *Sarajevski Eseji: Politika, ideologija i tradicija* (2000); *Prozori: Riječi i slike* (2001); *Bosanski Odgovor: o modernosti i tradiciji* (2002); *Sarajevo Essays: Politics, Ideology and Tradition* (2002).

Adam B. Seligman is Professor of Religion and Research Associate at the Institute for the Study of Economic Culture at Boston University. His best-known works are *The Idea of Civil Society* (1992); *Innerworldly Individualism: the Institutionalization of Charismatic Community* (1994); *The Problem of Trust* (1997); *Modernity's Wager: Authority, the Self and Transcendence* (2000), *Market and Community: The Bases of Social Order, Revolution and Relegitimation* (with Mark Lichbach, 2000).

Suzanne Last Stone is Professor of Law at Cardozo Law School, Yeshiva University. She has published numerous articles on Jewish legal and religious thought and on contemporary legal theory. Among her best-known articles are "Sinaitic and Noahide Law: Legal Pluralism in Jewish Law," 12 *Cardozo Law Review* 1157 (1991); "The Transformation of Prophecy," 4 *Cardozo Studies in Law and Literature* 167 (1992); "In Pursuit of the Countertext: The Turn to the Jewish Legal Model in Contemporary American Legal Theory," 106 *Harvard Law Review* 813 (1993); "Justice, Mercy and Gender in Rabbinic Thought," 8 *Cardozo Studies in Law and Literature* 139 (1996); "Comment: Cultural Pluralism, Nationalism and Universal Rights," 21 *Cardozo Law Review* 1211 (2000); "Commentary on Prophecy," in *The Jewish Political Tradition*, ed. Michael Walzer (2000); "The Jewish Tradition and Civil Society," in *Alternative Conceptions of Civil Society*, ed. Will Kymlicka (2002).

Dorothee C. von Tippelskirch is a Protestant theologian and psychoanalyst. Her current research focuses on the works of Emanuel Lévinas and Karl

Barth. Her published works include: "The Reason of War—Reason beyond Unreason?: Emanuel Lévinas' Reading of Bava Kamma," *European Judaism* 31, no. 2 (1998), Issue no. 61, ed. Leo Baeck College and Michael Goulston Educational Foundation; "Jenseits der geraden Linie des Gesetzes das unendliche, unerforschte Land der Güte," in *Torah-Nomus-Ius: abendländischer Antinomismus und der Traum vom herrschafts-freien Raum*, ed. Gesine Palmer and Dorothee C. von Tippelskirch (1999); "Fundamentalismus in der Bibel," in *Fundamentalismus in der Moderne*, ed. Rolf Hanusch and Dorothee C. von Tippelskirch (1999); "Lévinas' Beitrag zur Entwicklung einer zeitgemäßen Ethik," in *Existentialismus heute*, eds. Peter Knopp and Vincent V. Wroblewsky (1999); "Das Juden-tum einer Vaterreligion—das Christentum eine Sohnesreligion?" and "Nach Vernichtung und Umarmung—Zeit für die Auslegung," in *Das christlich-jüdische Gespräch. Standortbestimmungen*, ed. Christina Kurth and Peter Schmid (2000).

Claire Wolfteich is Associate Professor at Boston University School of Theology. She teaches and conducts research in the areas of religion and public life, practical theology, American Catholicism, and spirituality. She has published *American Catholics through the Twentieth Century: Spirituality, Lay Experience, and Public Life* (2001). Her forthcoming book, *Navigating New Terrain: Work and Women's Spiritual Lives* (2003) traces the theological and spiritual implications of women's changing work roles, from 1940 to the present. She also is writing a cross-national case study book on public religious engagement.

My daughters go to an intentionally pluralistic Jewish day school. This means that children from Orthodox, Conservative, and Reform Jewish families attend the school, as well as children from families who have very little religious (as opposed to cultural or historical) identification as Jews. Even though the school has won an award for pluralism from the Jewish community, no one is quite sure just what pluralism means. Consequently, every few months we have endless discussions long into the night on the sense and meaning of pluralism. During one of these discussions, I presented some of the ideas developed in this book on tolerance and was immediately subjected to a barrage of criticism. One parent was quick to point out that tolerance of difference was not at all what was needed, but rather to embrace difference, engage with it and grow and develop together with those who are different. Tolerance, he claimed, was much too modest a virtue, not robust enough, and ultimately lacking in moral fiber.

This was at the beginning of the evening, before many of the different views, complaints, and grudges had been aired. By the end of the evening however, after quite a few parents had given vent to their feelings on how the curriculum did not adequately express their religious commitments and needs, this parent, and others, came to think that perhaps tolerance was not such a bad thing after all. Perhaps a minimalist virtue was in fact precisely what was called for. As they came to realize just how long the way was to actually embracing difference, they came around to the idea that until such time as this could be realized—if it could be realized at all—it might not be such a bad idea to promulgate the virtue of tolerance: a second-best solution to be sure, but one that was, it seemed, realizable and one that would contribute to the conduct and culture of the school.

This exchange in the relative quotidian context of a parochial day-school brings us to the heart of some critical issues connected to tolerance. For on the one hand, as Bernard Williams once remarked, tolerance is an "impossible virtue."[1] It is impossible because it involves accepting, abiding, or accommodating views that one rejects. It calls us to live in cognitive dissonance and presents contradiction as a sought-after goal. We are obliged to "bear" what in fact we find unbearable. And of course if we did not find this, that, or the other word or deed objectionable, there would be no call to tolerate them. The whole issue of tolerance arises only when some act or speech is deemed objectionable. Viewed from one perspective then, tolerance is indeed a virtue so demanding as to be "impossible" of realization, perhaps even logically untenable, involving us in the laws of contradiction.

Yet, from another perspective, that of my fellow day-school parent and as we shall see, of Menachem Fisch in the dialogues below, tolerance is far from being sufficient. It is deemed too vapid, too thin, and far from adequate to the construction of a civil order or civil society of mutual appreciation and recognition. Tolerance with its historical associations of *suffering* the presence of what is detestable (in the eyes of God and mankind) is, in this reading, too feeble a thing to promote. Pluralism and the celebration of difference and otherness is what is called for rather than the insipid call to tolerance.

Complicating this picture even further is that whether we view tolerance as either impossible or insipid, argument can be made that in neither case does it take us very far. For almost all would agree that there are actions (and perhaps words as well, though that is much debated at present) that are beyond any moral compass and should not be tolerated. Many of the horrors of the twentieth century encompassing genocide and other crimes against humanity would fall under this rubric. And so, if certain sets of acts clearly are beyond what can be tolerated, we are left with the need to define the boundary of what can and cannot be tolerated. And it is far from clear what criteria would be used to define such a boundary. Such a task seems then to push the problem of tolerance up one analytic level, but not to solve it.

Despite these problems and the logistical conundrums to which they give rise, this book will make the argument for tolerance, as a minimalist position, albeit not easy to attain (though not impossible either). In addition, it will claim that what passes for tolerance (let alone more robust virtues) in contemporary modern societies is often not tolerance at all, but rather some mixture of indifference, realpolitik, and the denial of difference (that is, the denial that there is really something else, other, different, and thus perhaps threatening that I must engage with in a tolerant manner).

The denial of difference comes in many forms, most often as what may be termed the aesthetization of difference (differences are a matter of tastes, not morals; as there is no accounting for tastes, no real tolerance of difference is called for, rather a recognition of each individual's "right" to their own opinion). The aesthetization of difference is often accompanied by a trivialization of difference. Here the differences or the arenas of difference are not deemed important enough to merit a principled tolerance. Your rather poor taste in neckties is not something which demands of me a tolerant attitude, though I find the ties both offensive and in bad taste. Precisely because they are a matter of taste (aesthetics) and of no great significance (trivial), tolerance does not effectively enter the picture.

These moves of aesthetizing difference or trivializing it are, of course, ways to avoid having to engage with difference, or what has so fashionably come to be called alterity. By trivializing what is different, one makes a claim to the essential similarity or sameness of the nontrivial aspects of selfhood and shared meaning. What makes us the same (as Jews, Episcopalians, Americans, or radical feminists) is much more essential to our definitions of who we are than what divides us (your horrendous taste in bathroom fixtures). This is a form of denying difference rather than engaging with it. And we do it all the time; it is of the very stuff of our social life.

In a certain sense such denial of difference (relegating it to the aesthetic or trivial) is itself a form of indifference towards what is other and different. By framing our difference from alter's position or action in terms of tastes or the trivial, we are not forced to engage with it and can maintain an attitude of indifference. I may find your religious beliefs foolish and your sexual appetites objectionable, but they are neither illegal nor hurtful to others. They do not affect me in my relation to you (as, say, member of the same university department) and so, in the long run, are matters of indifference to me.

As we push this argument one step further, we come to realize that indifference, at least in liberal-individualist societies, is not simply a psychological state or form of social etiquette. It is in fact ensconced as a fundamental aspect of the social order, in the form of our legal and principled separation of public and private spheres. For what is deemed private is removed from public scrutiny and ceases to become a subject for tolerant or intolerant attitudes on the part of others in society. Defining a realm of privacy is tantamount to defining a realm of principled indifference where issues of tolerance are not to be broached and are indeed rendered irrelevant. Not surprisingly, the freedom of conscience—which historically was in fact the freedom of religion—went hand in hand with its privatization, a fact to which we shall return again and again in the pages that follow. We must note as well that the privatization of religion, together with a politics of rights rather than a politics of the good and a secularized public sphere are all, in some sense, the hallmarks of a liberal vision of modernity (though this is less so in more republican versions of the Enlightenment project).[2] Moreover, and according to popular wisdom, if only those intractable and fundamentalist Jews, Christians, or Muslims could accept these principles, which are reasonable and accessible to all, we would have solved the problem of tolerance. And of course precisely here is the rub. For accepting these principles essentially means accepting as well a certain liberal, post-Protestant vision of selfhood and society that is not shared across the globe and across human civilizations.

More to the point is that these different attitudes, while seen uncritically to be of a tolerant nature, are in fact less than tolerant in that they disengage with difference rather than practice the "impossible" virtue. They are perhaps more than anything a way to elide the whole problem of tolerance in modern society, rather than realize it. Critically, they would not necessarily be effective in societies that did not share liberal-individualist assumptions on self and society, and it is in fact far from certain that they will continue to work in those that do. For what is understood as tolerance in modern Western European and North Atlantic societies has much to do with the liberal synthesis, as this has evolved in these societies (with all their differences) over the past two hundred years. And this synthesis, as we shall see, is not without its contradictory elements.

Foremost in their construction was, as just noted, the public/private distinction. For if not really indifference, the liberal distinction between public and private realms is, among other things, a distinction in realms and types of toleration—certain beliefs and practices are deemed private and therefore beyond the realm of what even enter a calculus of tolerance. Here then, it is not quite indifference *simpliciter* but more a principled indifference. For one has no *right* to intervene in private matters, or even to judge them. In this reading, all conflicting views are reduced to an almost aesthetic realm of different matters of taste (or as the current popular imagery has it of lifestyles—as they say so tellingly in the U.S.A., "different strokes for different folks"). As is clear from the above, I would in fact query whether this is tolerance at all. For if liberalism is neutral towards different conceptions of the good, can we then say it is tolerant of them? Principled indifference is not the same as tolerance.

Similarly, the politics of rights rather than the politics of the good, of individual autonomy over shared public conceptions of the good, sometimes lead to tolerance not in principle, but simply as a temporary expedient, until such non-autonomy-valuing subgroups come to share the assumptions of liberalism.[3] Liberalism's much-vaunted toleration may then well be more complicated and problematic than we often take it to be, tending in fact to constantly be in the danger of slipping into either indifference or intolerance.

There is, however, one critical basis of toleration within the liberal tradition: the basis of individual autonomy. Toleration as a practice flows from autonomy as a virtue or a good. This is fine, except that at this point the supposedly liberal indifference to an idea of the good becomes untenable. As Bernard Williams has stated: "Only a substantive view of goods such as autonomy can yield the value expressed by the practice of toleration."[4] Moreover and more crucially, the positing of a good always involves us in that familiar situation of a "conflict of goods," which as we have seen liberalism cannot really avoid even though the practice of toleration is one of its central premises.

A liberal foundation for tolerance seems, then, either (1) to be not tolerance at all but indifference, or (2) to involve us in a contradiction—that between the practice of tolerance predicated on a politics of rights rather than the good and the very principle of individual autonomy as a prime good upon which such toleration is to be based.[5] This contradictory situation involves refusing to advance a politics of the good while at the same time resting on at least one very clearly defined principle of the good, that of individual autonomy. The very practice of toleration from this perspective thus contradicts the basis of the practice itself—or at very least leads us into a discussion of conflicting goods that we had hoped to avoid. Within such a conflict of goods, moreover, a good other than that of individual autonomy may become accepted as of greater value, as "trumping" autonomy (e.g., the view that abortion is murder and the prevention of murder trumps individual choice, because it is of greater good).

The concern of this book, however, is not to rescue liberalism from its own contradictions (however worthy a project that surely is). Moreover, the very principle of individual autonomy upon which so much of liberal thought rests is being increasingly questioned in different ways in different societies and at different levels of social praxis (from the so-called "Southeast Asian" model of development to evangelical Protestantism in Korea to the postmodern politics of English professors in Berkeley). If tolerance is to continue to exist as a virtue, it would thus seem that a foundation must be found for it other than that of individual autonomy. And this is precisely where this book hopes to make a contribution by returning the issue of tolerance to its first historical context, that of religious belief and practice. From the realm where tolerance and religion intersect and from an exploration (in the dialogues) of contemporary voices analyzing tolerance from within a religious perspective we will be in a much better position to review the subject as a whole.

For in truth the issue of pluralism and tolerance in religion takes us quite beyond the confines of religion per se. The problems of religious identity, of sacred or "truth communities" and their boundaries, take us immediately to some of the defining issues in current political practice—to what can be termed the current crises in models of community and participatory membership as these have come to be accepted in the West for the past three centuries. The essentially liberal vision of community founded on the radical autonomy of the individual moral agent is currently being questioned from a host of sources and perspectives. From the Christian Coalition to the communitarian movement, from family to neighborhood to nation, there is a sense among some that American society is no longer a "moral community" with shared ideas of justice and of the public good. Rather, received beliefs in the social good and its relation to individual rights, responsibilities, and freedoms seem to be unraveling and, in the process, eroding many commonly held beliefs of what a community itself may mean. The search for new models of the Public Good, for new criteria of communal identity and of trust, are all expressions of that crisis in models of community and of self that we have come to identify with modernity. Whether other such models of solidarity, trust, and the Public Good are possible in a pluralistic society and whether such may gain from knowledge of religious traditions is an issue deeply tied up with the idea of tolerance itself. To a great extent the position we are attempting to articulate here can be described as a midpoint between nihilism and postmodern relativism on the one hand and diverse absolutist claims on the other. Such a perspective, we are claiming, is one that can best be approached through the oft-invoked, but just as often misunderstood, principle of tolerance.

Beyond this, however, arguments made both in the ensuing dialogues as well as in the more analytic sections claim that religious traditions have something unique to contribute to an understanding of tolerance. It is not only that secular and Western liberal models of tolerance and pluralism are contradictory and circumscribed in their applicability, but that if approached properly, religious understandings of self and society have a substantive contribution to make in their own right. The seemingly intractable nature of religion in the modern world points to an aspect of human existence not easily assimilated into modernist epistemologies and sociologies.[6] What is all too often seen as a motley of parochial and particular religious identities, between which no mediation, discourse, or rapprochement can be maintained, points in fact to aspects of human life in the world not adequately addressed by modernist philosophies. Moreover, as religious dictates come more and more to shape the personal, social, and political behavior of men and women in many parts of the world, it becomes more and more absurd simply to marginalize them analytically and shunt them off under the broad and inexact rubric of fundamentalism, with the inherent antimodern, totalistic, repressive, and authoritarian connotations that fundamentalism has to modern, secular, Western ears. To do so is to deny a significant aspect of human life in the world. And as will be explored in the following chapters, a huge price is paid for that denial.

Hence, and given the continuing salience of religious ideas, identities, and modes of social order in different parts of the world, it would seem imperative to explore the potential of religions to reach beyond their own terms of meaning and significance and exist within and as part of pluralistic social structures. The all too facile identification of religion with fundamentalism that we so often witness must be countered with a more nuanced and sophisticated inquiry into the religious consciousness and the sources of tolerance it can provide. Doing so will lead to a broader understanding of what is one of the most important transnational developments at the dawn of the twenty-first century.

This book, with its combination of dialogue and analysis, offers a tentative beginning to such a project. It focuses on the monotheistic religions in order to keep the analysis manageable and accessible to a Western audience of nonspecialists. The book begins with a series of dialogues that touch on many themes: from pluralism and religious liberty to the meaning of revelation and the context of belief. The didactic purpose of the dialogues is to illustrate what is one of the most significant claims of our endeavor: that the religious apprehension of human existence provides a basis for translation and dialogue and ultimately for that recognition of the other, without which no robust form of tolerance can be procured.

The dialogues thus broach the possibility of alternative forms of tolerance not rooted in the liberal understanding of individual autonomy, nor in the separation of public and private realms, nor—following Michael Ignatieff—in an "idolatry of human rights" (as the sole basis of human mutuality).[7] In fact, one position that they explore in great detail, one that for a period shared the stage with what became the liberal argument for autonomy, but then retreated to the background, is an argument for tolerance based on *skepticism*. Both arguments, that predicated on individual autonomy (then termed conscience, though for sure they are not the same thing) and that predicated on skepticism, emerged out of the Protestant Reformation and the wars of religion and the challenge that the Reformation posited to the faith and practices and criteria of justification of Catholic Europe.

The path that eventually led to the liberal argument of individual autonomy is of course one which has been studied by generations of historians and sociologists, and by philosophers from Ernst Troeltsch and Max Weber and George Jellinek down to Louis Dumont, Benjamin Nelson, Hans Blumenberg, Wolfgang Schluchter, J. G. A. Pocock, and others.[8] It is, briefly, the path of the secularization of the ideas of inner light or Holy Spirit, the internalization of the idea of grace and, by the eighteenth century, its secularization into more contemporary notions of morality and civic virtue and often romantic nationalism as well. Anyone whose work or interests has touched on this body of scholarship knows just how rich it is in insights into the historical, religious, and most especially Protestant sources of modernity as a civilization, some of which have been noted above.[9]

The other path, that of skepticism, has been perhaps less studied and less well marked, especially outside the history or sociology of science. The early work by Richard Popkin, now almost forty years old, still stands as a monument to this mode of inquiry.[10]

Very briefly, what Popkin argued is that the Protestant Reformation, in challenging the Church's infallibility, challenged as well existing ideas of certitude. (What constituted probability reasoning in the seventeenth century was nothing close to what we consider probability today, but only the veracity of received authorities). The sixteenth and seventeenth centuries were also characterized by arguments over sufficient evidence. Ultimately, the failure to justify faith on the basis of knowledge led to pure fideism (that is, belief by faith alone) on one hand and a sort of mitigated skepticism on the other. The latter was the position taken by Sebastian Castellio in his condemnation of the burning of Miguel Servetus in Calvin's Geneva—a reasonable belief that, since we cannot be sure of truth, we cannot be sure of the nature of heresy and therefore cannot go to such extremes as the burning of heretics.[11]

This debate and others took place in an atmosphere characterized by the revival of classical Pyrrhonism (i.e., the doubting of all propositions, including those of doubt itself), which was itself called up by the search for justification for an infallible truth via a self-evident criterion: while the Protestants contested papal authority, the Catholics made short work of inner conscience. François Véron was one of the masters of the Counter-Reformation polemic which showed how: (1) the Protestant claim that Scripture was self-evidently clear was manifestly false and in need of interpretation; and (2) predicating interpretation on individual conscience opened the floodgates to endless sectarianism and antinomian potentialities. It was, as one early-seventeenth-century Congregationalist described his more enthusiastic neighbors, a "search for heaven and their lusts as well."[12]

The one side claimed that the Catholic demand for infallible knowledge led to the discovery that no such knowledge exists and so to complete doubt and Pyrrhonism; the other side claimed that the very proliferation of opinions created by Protestantism ended in compete uncertainty in religious belief and hence total doubt.

From this debate certain rather interesting positions emerged. One was fideism, faith justified by no structure of knowledge, which itself would provide a very interesting way into the issue of toleration via a diffusion of those realms ruled by faith and those ruled by rational knowledge—an opening perhaps to a reconceptualization of the public/private distinction without incorporating the liberal idea of self and society which has come to define these distinctions in the West.

Another position was of a faith that, as advocated by Montaigne, arose out of Pyrrhonist principles and was as a lived nature and custom—a Christian *Sittlichkeit*. This is an interesting position from which to develop tolerance. Certainly this was the position advocated by Montaigne, who understood the issue of tolerance with the most modern of sensibilities. The thought and personhood of Miguel de Montaigne can themselves be understood as a paradigm of such a position of contextualized belief, embedded within the practical experience of life itself. Having, as Montaigne teaches us in his *Apology for Raimond Sebond*, "no intercourse with being," we must forever be vigilant against both the vanity of our reason and the self-certitude of faith, which is but the play of chance.[13] As he reminds his readers: "Another country, other testimony, similar promises and menaces might, by the same means impress on us a very different belief. We are Christians by the same title that we are Perigordins or Germans."[14]

Historically, the emergence in the West of the argument for a tolerance based on skepticism was overtaken by two developments: the liberal argument for autonomy and the process of secularization itself, which obviated the very need for a religious tolerance. To these was added the Cartesian revolution, which reoriented the whole issue of certitude as well as the position of the knowing subject.[15]

The contingency of history aside, a principled tolerance is indeed a difficult position to maintain, as it would seem that people have a marked preference for certitude, even if it is of a tremendously circumscribed horizon. To maintain a position of belief while at the same time maintaining a position of skepticism as to its truth-claims—indeed a skepticism so great that one is tolerant of other such claims—is a truly stoic position. But it is one that, first and foremost, rests on some belief; otherwise the whole issue of tolerance becomes moot. At the very end of this book we shall return to the problem of certitude and control not in the matter of knowledge and belief, but in the context of boundaries of self and community—and see just how critical its questioning is to the construction of tolerance.

There has yet to appear for other religious traditions the type of history of skepticism that Popkin has provided for Western Christian thought. Yet some preliminary efforts are in evidence that this skepticism developed in other traditions as well. The work of Menachem Fisch, for example, on the role of counterfactual evidence in talmudic discourse and the tension, as he terms it, between reason and received authority in the redaction of the Babylonian Talmud is a case in point.[16] The paradigm case of this is the excommunication of Rabbi Eliezer ben Hyrcanus, described in the Babylonian Talmud (T. Baba Mezia 59a.b) as follows:

> We learned elsewhere: If he cut it into separate tiles, placing sand between each tile: R. Eliezer declared it clean, and the Sages declared it unclean and this is the oven of Aknai. . . . On that day R. Eliezer

brought forward every imaginable argument but they did not accept them. Said he to them: "If the *halachah* agrees with me, let this carob tree prove it!" Thereupon the carob tree was torn a hundred cubits out of its place—others affirm four hundred cubits. "No proof can be brought from a carob tree," they retorted. Again he said to them: "If the *halachah* agrees with me, let the stream of water prove it!" Whereupon the stream of water flowed backwards. "No proof can be brought from a stream of water," they rejoined. Again he urged: "If the *halachah* agrees with me, let the walls of the school house prove it," whereupon the walls inclined to fall. But R. Joshua rebuked them, saying: "When scholars are engaged in *halachic* dispute what have you to interfere?" Hence they did not fall, in honor of R. Joshua, nor did they resume the upright, in honor of R. Eliezer; and they are still standing thus inclined. Again he said to them: "If the *halachah* agrees with me, let it be proved from Heaven!" Whereupon a Heavenly Voice cried out: "Why do you dispute with R. Eliezer, seeing that in all matters the *halachah* agrees with him!" But R. Joshua arose and exclaimed: *"It is not in heaven."* What did he mean by this? Said R. Jeremia: That the Torah had already been given at Mount Sinai; we pay no attention to a Heavenly Voice, because Thou hast long since written in the Torah at Mount Sinai, *After the majority must one incline.*

R. Nathan met Elijah [the prophet] and asked him: What did the Holy One Blessed be He, do in that hour?—He laughed (with joy), he replied, saying, "My sons have defeated Me, My sons have defeated Me."

To understand the full import of this story one must realize: (1) that Rabbi Eliezer was *the* expert on laws of purity and impurity (upon which this dispute turned); (2) that he was reputed to be an almost superhuman storehouse of received wisdom and would not utter a pronouncement on law that was of his own making, but all his wisdom was received wisdom that could be traced to the revelation of Moses on Sinai; and (3) the quote from the Pentateuch noted at the end (Exodus 23:2) is in fact torn from its context and used here to make a point quite at odds with the clear meaning of the text. All of these together with the story itself have lent it its rather paradigmatic place in the Jewish corpus as a defense of the use of reason (through the debates and decisions of the majority) over against a simple appeal to received authority in the practicalities of moral reasoning.

A resource of reason is always also a resource of skepticism. It is, I would maintain, also a resource of a true toleration, one that can indeed be found in all of the monotheistic religious traditions. The Islamic *kalam* (theology) no less than the Jewish *halacha* (a system of religious law that regulates the life and practice of the religiously observant Jew) present us with a method of reasoning and legal interpretation based on what John Clayton has termed "localized" or "group reasoning."[18] That is, processes of moral reasoning which while recognizing sacred authority also recognize the limits of human reason and hence the inherent abyss between general principles and their instantiation in the orders of the world. A *phronesis* of casuistry, and for that matter of Jewish halachic thought, can thus be seen as a basis for toleration from within a recognized authority rather than from a world defined solely by power, where tolerance can never be more than a contingent balance of forces.

This position of skepticism, or what, with our interlocutors, we shall call an epistemological modesty or humility, is a critical tool in the toolbox of religion to provide sources of tolerance. The modern world, defined by the Enlightenment dictum of Immanuel Kant "*sapere aude*" of those who, according to Kierkegaard, seek to go beyond faith and beyond the tensions of the particular, universal, and absolute defined by faith, has much to gain from such a perspective.[18] It may in fact prove to be a critical corrective to our relationships (both individual and collective) to the other.

Religion, with its contradictory injunctions to the universal and the particular, as well as to nominalist and realist (or essentialist) definitions of its own categories, exists in tension.[19] Indeed to some extent it can be said to exist only so far as it exists in these tensions. Modernity and secularism are attempts to overcome these tensions in one direction. Religious fundamentalism, which interprets religious categories almost exclusively in realist terms, is an attempt to overcome these tensions in another direction, in response to the challenge of modernity. Neither modernity/secularism nor religious fundamentalism provides resources for tolerance. The first, as we shall explore below, seeks to elide the whole problem of the other, and the second, to negate the very existence of the other. But in fact, only by re-engaging with the tension of religion and transcendent otherness can sources of tolerance be found.

This then is the challenge facing us all. If the progress of secularization has indeed proved much more questionable than it seemed a generation ago and if the further progress of modernity—and perhaps even postmodernity—is not to be automatically accompanied by the further spread of a secular consciousness, but (as it seems in many places) by a return of some sort to religious orientation—a return that is almost mandated by the human need for self-expression, by the need for at least certain aspects of the self to be seen as constituted and not simply autonomous, constituted by a heteronomous authority—then how can a principled position of toleration be maintained?[20] People are returning to positions of principled belief, and that in itself opens the historical possibility of returning to either some of the most horrendous authoritarian terrors of the past, or, what is preferable, to resurrecting a language of toleration based perhaps on a skepticism towards one's own principled held beliefs. To do this we must enlist the help of precisely those beliefs (among which are beliefs in revealed truth, including, for better or worse, those of the three revealed monotheistic religions). The following dialogues and analyses hope to offer a modest contribution in this direction.

CHAPTER ONE

The First Dialogue

*On Pluralism, Religious Liberty,
and Definitions of Community*

This first set of dialogues begins with the problem of tolerance and pluralism in the Jewish tradition. The discussion, which evolves around the presentation by Suzanne Last Stone, stresses tolerant (and intolerant) attitudes towards both "insiders" and "outsiders" in the different religious traditions. Central to understanding these attitudes becomes an understanding of the boundaries and nature of the normative community and the limits of individual freedom within that community. Claire Wolfteich's analysis of John Courtney Murray and the dynamics of change in Vatican II is an important example of how a particular normative community—that of twentieth-century Catholicism—sought to maintain the boundaries of community but also to accommodate change and transformation. As is made clear in the ensuing discussion, the challenges faced by the Catholic Church in navigating these contradictory desiderata are those faced by other religions as well. And it is in this context that Shlomo Fischer's presentation of different existing strategies for tolerance as they present themselves today in Orthodox Jewish circles in Israel brings the two prior discussions together. The problem of maintaining the boundaries of the normative community and the need to develop concrete, empirically workable resources for tolerance within Orthodox Judaism become the crux of these different strategies, whose strengths and weaknesses Fischer explicates most cogently.

Suzanne Last Stone's Presentation
(Cardozo Law School, Yeshiva University)

Jewish Particularism and the Terms of Tolerance

Let me first place myself. Since I am speaking about the Jewish tradition I think it is important to note that I am speaking from the American and not the Israeli context. Because the American context is the one in which I developed my thought, what interests me most is the question of how groups get along, particularly the questions of intercultural exchange, of the possibilities of some kind of collaboration between groups. This is of course a very American interest—the search for some form of common collaboration that will cross religious boundaries, engaging not just dialogue, but social action. This is the perspective that I have brought to bear on the problem of tolerance in terms of trying to analyze sources within Judaism that are conducive to creating an environment in which intercultural exchange can take place.

With that said, I look at two particular forms of tolerance within the Jewish tradition. The first is what I call pluralism. Now pluralism is not quite tolerance because pluralism does not assume that you are in fact making a concession to something with which you disagree. Rather, one is positing that there are multiple and also mutually exclusive ways of accessing some form of truth, meaningful way of life, or divine plan. Pluralism, we must acknowledge, is as equally difficult a position to uphold as is the position of tolerance. It is a difficult position because one is constantly questioning what one's own position in life is. One constantly must have the other in view if one is not rejecting the other. That kind of traveling along with the other is, I think, just as much a form of tolerance as the conventional, liberal versions of tolerance. I also think it is important to put pluralism as a major form of tolerance on the table, because the modern, liberal language of tolerance is already fading from view. If we speak, for example, of the new multiculturalist perspective, which is based on value pluralism, tolerance in the old liberal sense has already become something of a dinosaur, and the question of how to get along with plural, multiple, mutually exclusive ways of life in the public domain is the main question.

The second form of tolerance I am concerned with is what I call interpersonal tolerance. By this I mean a situation where there is no actual decision to continue relations with a person whose actions and beliefs one in fact finds intolerable, and yet, either because tolerance is seen as a virtue or for other reasons I will come to (such as collective needs) one agrees to keep the other person "within one's sights," within one's horizon, and continue relations with them. Here then, we are not dealing with any kind of restraint of judgment or actions or of opinions. We are rather dealing with a model much closer to the religious structure of forgiveness. I think that both forgiveness and tolerance can be viewed as supererogatory and that they are structurally related in that both of them proceed from some notion that it is possible to understand the other, to understand another person, to understand why they have done something that is otherwise intolerable, and to create an interpersonal connection and relation with that person while not condoning the act at all. These are the two models I want to address from within the religious tradition I am looking at.

Let me begin with pluralism. It seems to me that pluralism, as a feature of Jewish thought, arises from the simple fact that the Jewish tradition is structured so that it is limited to one religion or nation. This very limitation of religion to one nation, what we would call the particularism of Judaism, opens up a space for the other. It is possible, of course, to have a religion that is particular to one nation and to view the rest of the world as consigned to purgatory or hell, a religion where there is only one position of truth resting in one very particular religion and falsehood in all the rest. It is possible to see this attitude in at least one strand of Biblical Judaism. But we find as well a different strand of thought in Rabbinic Judaism, in which difference is not viewed as bad. There is a structure of thought within the Jewish tradition that values diversity, difference, and distinction. The value of diversity and distinction I think goes back to valuing it as a feature of creation: created order is one of difference, distinction, and diversity. A monolithic universal human order is something that is described even in biblical terms as a horror. Think of the Tower of Babel, for example, as a unification of humanity around one idea, which is viewed as essentially dangerous, and the division of nations into different languages and different laws as a corrective to the evil of a universal human order.

The particularism of Judaism combined with a mental structure that is oriented towards the valuation of some diversity as part of created order leads to a different model than the idea that truth can be found only in one place and nowhere else. This is what I see and others have described as a tendency to mediate between Judaism and what is seen as the "truth for non-Jews." You can find this already in the early talmudic period in the Noachide commandments.[1] The Noachides are those who abide by a minimal set of moral principles (including refraining from murder, robbery, incest, blasphemy, and idol worship) and who are granted, in talmudic thought, what may be called the prime marker of tolerance from within a religious tradition—access to the world-to-come. One might say that access to the world-to-come is a kind of ultimate good for a religious tradition and the extension of the notion of salvation, of justification, to others must be seen as a very important step in a positive valuation of other forms of life.

In talmudic thought there is not yet a full development of this concept, though it is primarily used in one very important way: in terms of the plurality of groups that may reside in the Jewish polity. Hence the principle of application of the notion of the Noachides to those who believe in a form of universal moral order and who therefore are granted a positive evaluation is applied in talmudic thought to resident aliens. The resident alien is equated with the biblical stranger, who must be loved as one loves oneself. He or she is one who formally accepts the Noachide laws and therefore may live in a Jewish polity without assimilating. This is not an assimilationist model of the other, but an accepting of their national identity. The idea is that the resident alien ought to adhere to his and her ancestral customs so long as there is a common and shared allegiance to a minimal set of moral principles.

In medieval times this notion was taken one step further, primarily in the view of Menachem Ha'meiri, the thirteenth-century philosopher who extended the concept of Noachides as morally abiding people to entire nations and not just individuals. This again, I see as a very important step because he speaks of a distinction between the nations of old and the nations who are "enlightened-by-the-way-of religion." The nations who are thus enlightened are for him a category that is in-between Judaism and paganism. They are those who were formally identified as resident aliens or Noachides. An investigation into Ha'meiri's work I think illustrates that it is not just an idea of a nation or a people being constrained by religious values in matters of opinion. But it is rather an idea of religion that is not private, but public. This is significant, for public religion means practical religion, and practical religion for medieval thinkers meant government—the ability to create laws for a nation. So what is really included in Ha'meiri's categories is the notion of systems of justice, an evaluation of different, non-Jewish systems of justice which are affecting God's plan by bringing some form of moral order into the world, some form of justice. This is a very important concept. The notion that governments and communities and national communities that establish systems of government are, in fact, doing God's plan, that they are engaged in the project of what we call *tikkun olam* ["repairing the world"], of establishing social order, is a tremendous concept and allows the basis for social collaboration between Jews and others.[2]

Now this project of historical collaboration has, for many reasons, been quite minimized. It has been minimized in part because of the particular history of Judaism which has, as an exilic community, not been in a position to collaborate socially in a meaningful way with other communities. In the eighteenth and nineteenth centuries Judaism began for the first time to enter the marketplace of world religions in a positive way. This was disrupted by the Holocaust, which created a despair of all forms of social and cultural collaboration. But I see in America, even among the extreme religious right, a move towards reclaiming this heritage, a move towards a form of understanding that there is an obligation to participate with others who are advancing precisely the aims that Judaism believes they should advance. I think that this tradition is something that will be drawn upon increasingly and will emerge as something of tremendous value and importance.

The second part of my remarks touches on the question of intellectual pluralism. The notion of the particularism of Judaism and the fact that there may be multiple, mutually exclusive ways of life that are all avenues of salvation is a pattern of thought that is reinforced by the ability to view truth as something that is multifaceted, partial, and sustainable through the notion that there are a multiplicity of viewpoints, each of which may be legitimate, though any individual can follow only one of them. To be sure, Judaism has an equally strong view about following only one of those opinions as it has of the very basis of multiplicity of opinions, so that when we speak about a kind of epistemological uncertainty or skepticism, we do have to bear in mind two factors. One is that we are speaking about a certain kind of respect for multiple viewpoints that exists *only* within the normative community. That is, the extension of a kind of legitimacy to the other person's position is one that we find only within the rabbinical community of decisors to "legitimate" others. It is not a pattern of thought that can be taken too far given the fact that it is, I think, quite constrained by the normative community. That is one aspect.

The second aspect is that there is a tension between skepticism and order in Jewish thought. It is as equally important to canonize one position as it is to grant legitimacy to the other position. When we speak about intellectual pluralism we have to understand that it is in the realm of ideas, and not in practice. That, too, is an important limitation that we have to come to grips with. This leads me to a third issue, which is structurally similar to forgiveness, and that is tolerance among, or between, group members as opposed to tolerance of one religion to another religion.

Precisely because intellectual pluralism does not extend to practice and is really limited to the realm of the theory of ideas, there is tremendous impulse to punish and to ostracize those who practice differently. Practicing differently from within the Jewish tradition is viewed as an ultimate breach of loyalty to the community. One of the questions from within the tradition is how does one keep within the community those who have breached, in public, the basic principles of the religion itself. There has been a long tradition of thought which has viewed this not as a question of condoning acts, because one is required to hate the sin, even to hate the sinner, but rather as coming to understand the position of the person who has committed these kinds of breaches.[3] To understand that the person who has sinned—while we don't condone either the acts or opinions—has done so because of outside excuses, outside pressures, is very similar in the criminal law to the whole field of excuses, or diminished responsibility. The person is, in fact, not fully responsible for his or her acts because, for example, of the modern conditions of skepticism, secular upbringing, and so on (*tinok s'nishba*, i.e., captured child.) Although this is very different from pluralism in the sense that it is not a legitimization in any way, shape, or form of another form of life, what it does accomplish is a kind of "bearing of the heretic" within the community. Yet the bearing of the heretic within the community means that the community itself will inevitably become pluralized. It will become a more diverse place than it was, because the community, instead of becoming narrower and narrower in excluding all those who are different, sustains itself in some way to accommodate diversity without legitimating it. This too is a form of tolerance.

Discussion

Menachem Fisch
(Department of the Philosophy of Science, Tel Aviv University):
If I may, I would like to highlight a couple of ideas from Suzanne's presentation. First of all, the problem of tolerance: Although I agree with

all that Suzanne has said about Judaism acknowledging a plurality and diversity of positions, you have to admit that the problem of tolerance doesn't arise with regard to someone who is different, or who is regarded as legitimately different. A gentile who, from the point of Judaism, is a proper gentile is not someone whom you need to tolerate. I am talking from the point of view of religious thought, and so I think it is best to concentrate on those who are regarded as sinners and heretics from the point of view of the religion.

Now drawing the line between pluralism and tolerance is extremely important. The pluralist values the other. The person who is tolerant merely undertakes to suffer the other's presence. Pluralism is what we are looking for, because pluralism, as opposed to tolerance, gives reason for forming a society, for maintaining a society, for wanting to live with others, not merely tolerating the other's presence. If there is value and worth in having people you disagree with around you, that is a reason for forming a multicultural society, not merely tolerating the fact that it exists.

Peter Berger
(Institute for the Study of Economic Culture, Boston University):
I would want to make two points: one minor and terminological. "Pluralism" can be used to describe a fact as well as a value. When I talk about pluralism, I talk about it as a social reality, all these other people who are around us with whom we have to deal. We may regard this as good or bad—it's a fact. The way which Menachem just used the word "pluralist" is as a value, which is fine, but let's make the distinction clear.

The second point has to do with the idea of epistemic or methodological modesty. It seems to me there are two very distinct problems here which cut across the categories that you are making, Suzanne. There are these epistemological, modest people, or skeptics, in every tradition. I belong to them, and it's an interesting question, theologically and philosophically interesting, how we epistemological and modest types deal with our own traditions and with other traditions. I find that of great theological and philosophical importance. It is, however, politically insignificant because we are not going to kill each other anyway. Probably most of us are more or less in this category, and therefore can talk to each other around the table with mineral water and so forth. The politically more important question, however, certainly in places like Bosnia, but unfortunately in other places as well, is how to deal with the people I call the "certainty-wallahs." In other words, those who are not coming to terms with the loss of taken-for-grantedness that leads to epistemological modesty, who want to retain or, as is more likely, violently restore the taken-for-grantedness of a particular tradition within a particular community. What arguments can one use with them?

Fisch
The only way to convince such a community that is traditionalist, a community of "certainty-wallahs" as you call them, of an antitraditionalist option is to show that there is a tradition of antitraditionalism. That's the one way I can think of convincing the "certainty-wallahs" that there's a tradition of uncertainty within the tradition that they are obligated by.

Stone
I want to underscore what Menachem has said. I think it is important to understand that when we speak about this kind of epistemological modesty, or intellectual pluralism, we are not talking about the skeptics around the table. The test of such a position is not to speak to those who are liberals or reformers, but to speak to the perspective of the most religiously engaged community. So I think we have to take our remarks as pertaining to the center of the tradition, the center of the normative textual community—but with all the constraints that are involved in locating this intellectual pluralism within that normative community. For the normative community does assume a certain community, and there is an identification of who is a member of that community and who is not. I think, moreover, that any kind of easy distinction between the skeptics and the "certainty-wallahs" is not actually applicable to the tradition that we are talking about.

Shlomo Fischer
(Yesodot Center for Torah and Democracy, Jerusalem):
The central question thus becomes, to what extent is pluralism able to break through the grounds of normative community. I will say that in Israel, that is one of the issues that is currently being contested. In other words, to the extent that non-Orthodox people are engaged in the study of sacred texts, (and there is a small movement like that, between five thousand and ten thousand people), the question arises if the principle that "these and these are the words of the living God," is to be extended to people who are nonnormative in their practice yet claim membership within the bounds of legitimate interpretation and pluralist discussion.[4]

Nasr Abu Zayd
(University of Leiden):
I would like to comment on the notion of pluralism from an Islamic perspective because according to Islamic history, pluralism exists and can be recognized though not always accepted. For example, in the Arab world today, in the political sphere, there is pluralism, but there is no democracy, which means pluralism is recognized, but is not functioning. Pluralism can be found in every religion, in the history of every religion, but it did not always develop into tolerance.

Claire Wolfteich
(School of Theology, Boston University):
This is precisely why it is important to distinguish between pluralism, toleration, and liberty. These are the three terms that we have out on the table now, and it seems to me that the basis for toleration—as epistemological modesty—seems actually to fit with pluralism or liberty, but I don't know that it fits with toleration. It seems that toleration implies a judgment that a certain belief is in error. Epistemological modesty steps back from that judgment. So it seems that there might be a contradiction there. Affirming a position of epistemological modesty means that one is skeptical or at least hesitant about one's own beliefs, and yet toleration requires that one make a judgment that the other's position is in error.

Adam Seligman
(Institute for the Study of Economic Culture, Boston University):
One has to make judgments, and cannot shy away from making judgments, but must nevertheless realize that judgments could be mistaken, and hence one is hesitant about the judgments made. And that is precisely this great weight that it demands, that Suzanne referred to, and this is why it might be, as Peter says, a negligent political option because you can't school people to live in cognitive dissonance.

Stone
Peter has also put on the table the difference between the fact of pluralism and the value of pluralism. What we are speaking of here is the value of pluralism, but we are speaking about it, I think, from two different perspectives. One aspect is the recognition of plurality rather than tolerance based on indifference. In actual fact there exists a moral obligation towards what is different. Religion creates a moral obligation of some kind of aid and assistance, but—especially in a religion that is so particularistic and

therefore also separate—it also creates a breach in that notion of separateness. The existence of an other deemed legitimate implies that there is no longer a community that one is supposed to be entirely separate from, but rather one which you can engage in some kind of interaction with. How far, how extensively, that engagement can be taken, however, is a whole other subject.

The other aspect of value pluralism may be deeper because it is theological and you find its most intense expression actually in mystical strains of thought. Pluralism as a value comes from the fact that divinity is in some way plural, so that understanding the plural nature of creation as having value and significance is a refraction of divine pluralism. That may seem like an esoteric factor. But it is in fact extraordinarily significant, and I think that in point of fact, as one traces certain aspects of halachic development, one sees that the most free and normative interpretations come from the mystical strands in halachic thought because that freedom correlates a little bit with the notion of truth and existence as deeply plural and as an instantiation of divine pluralism in the world.

Abu Zayd
The question of the existence and of the legitimate existence of the other brings us to the question of identity. If identity includes the other, then the pluralists may be accommodated. If identity is exclusive, this would not lead to such inclusion. Again, if identity is limited to religion, then there is no way for tolerance to develop. This is an important question, the relationship between pluralism and identity and the relationship between identity and religion, most especially in the contemporary Islamic world. In Islam, moreover, the plurality of divinity as leading to a form of epistemological modesty can only be found in Sufism, in mysticism. This is the only discipline where we find truth not limited to one expression, not limited to one experience.

Berger
In these terms of identity, I was struck by the concept of resident alien and the idea that the non-Jew is not a problem. He is outside the community, and as long as he obeys certain Noachide moral principles he is not a problem. The problem is the person within the community who doesn't perform as he should, not so much believes, but practices as he should. It struck me, and I'm asking in terms of the Jewish tradition, could one say that what Menachem is after and what you seem to be after, Adam, is to enlarge the concept of resident alien to include Jews?

Stone

Of course the real impetus for including the deviant Jews is for national reasons. That is, you have a community that is defined not just theologically, but also nationally—the sort of plural sources of identity that Nasr just alluded to. The wish is to keep that historic community going, and so it has to become more inclusive.

Fisch

The question is how can this be accomplished, given the reigning theological assumptions? Now the simple model of these assumptions, which very many people accept, is that God has a view. It is related to us via the text and we submit to it. Talmudic Judaism, however, has three other models, one more surprising than the other. They provide interesting models or potentialities for developing that type of tolerance we are discussing. The first is that God has a view, but we don't know it. In other words, the act of interpretation is fallible and open—this is where religious epistemic modesty kicks in for the first time. The second notion is that God doesn't have a view. In other words, he wrote a text, gave it to us, and there is no divine sanctioned interpretation to it and all God knows is that this rabbi thinks it means so and so and the other such and such. An even more startling view, which I think lies at the very heart of the Jewish idea of the covenant, is that God does have a view and we know what it is and we must wrestle with it. Now this is a very, very different notion of man up against it, as it were, wrestling with the angel. It's Abraham standing on his hind legs [arguing with God over the destruction of Sodom], if you'll excuse the expression, saying, "How can you do such a thing?" and God changing his mind as a result of that confrontation. This is an even more startling notion of wrestling with the text, wrestling with tradition, interpretation as an act of getting away from what you know the text means but you won't allow it to mean what it means, which is even more startling. A request of mine would be to hear more about the mystical connection because everything I know about epistemic modesty is rational; it's the reasonable, halachic, down-to-earth, a cool-headed notion of halachic dispute, legal dispute, rather than mystical, so I'd like to hear more about where this can lead.

Stone

All I mean is how halachic decision making and the justification for halachic decision making is linked to models of revelation. There are mystical models of revelation that differ from the rational mode, which is much more linked to this notion of human fallibility or a kind of arbitrariness to decision making, which in fact dovetails with your last remarks, Menachem.

CLAIRE WOLFTEICH'S PRESENTATION

John Courtney Murray and Religious Liberty

I would like to consider the American Catholic experience and, in particular, one major thinker who emerged out of that context, and that is John Courtney Murray. He was a Jesuit who lived from 1904 to 1967 and was very important in trying to reconcile two identities which people thought couldn't be reconciled: American and Catholic. He set out to defend the American proposition, or the American experiment as he called it, which entailed the separation of church and state, limited government, and religious freedom. In so doing he also critiqued some of the basic liberal assumptions which usually had been used to defend that system. Some of those liberal assumptions included freedom without responsibility, an emphasis on individualism and individual rights severed from community, and a solution to the "problem of pluralism" as the privatization of religion. He resisted all of those, and yet, at the same time, tried to defend and reconcile and to give a theological and philosophical support to the American system. There were several strains of his argument.

One of them was what he called the Gelasian principle. Here he said that the system of limited government actually is not just a product of liberalism, but rather is the product of a central Christian insight, which is the distinction between the sacred and the secular. He calls it the Gelasian principle because it goes back to a statement made by Pope Gelasius in 494: "Two there are." There is not one, not the classical understanding of a state which is also merged with a theological vision, but rather there are two. There is a sacred and there is a secular realm, and we need to preserve a sacred sphere which will not be trespassed by government.

At the same time, we need to respect a State power which has its own distinct function in society, which is not co-extensive with society, but plays a limited role in it. This, said Murray, was a crucial insight of the

Christian tradition that was carried forward by the Christian tradition, although he notes that, of course, there were aberrations—the Crusades and the rise of nation-states which subsume the church were such aberrations. Yet, according to Murray, the American system recovered some of this fundamental insight in its principle of limited government. He defends the freedom of the church. He insists that the church retain its own autonomy, that it have freedom, and for Murray religious liberty is primarily liberty from government coercion. It is primarily a political right. That is one of his major arguments, predicated on the Christian insight into the distinction between sacred and secular spheres.

Another major argument is based on human dignity. Here he says that religious freedom is essential because human dignity requires freedom, it requires the search for truth, the free and responsible embrace of truth that cannot be coerced. Any act of faith must be free. His major arguments are political and philosophical. He did not extend them as far as they might have been developed in the area of theological arguments, and he noted that himself. He died prematurely in 1967 just as he was starting to think about the connections between the Pauline notion of freedom and this understanding of religious liberty that he was developing, so he really didn't carry it forward.

John Courtney Murray was a major shaper of the Vatican II Declaration on Religious Liberty. This declaration in 1965 was a reversal, pretty much, of the nineteenth-century Catholic position, which was articulated in the Syllabus of Errors in 1864 and summarized by its statement "Error has no rights." In the Vatican II document, error does have rights. In fact, human dignity and the development of human consciousness demands religious liberty. This was acknowledged in the Vatican II document as a development in doctrine, and it was controversial partly for that reason, because it ran the risk of undermining Church authority. The Vatican II document was largely shaped by Murray, and it adapted many of his ideas which included this progressive understanding of the Church. The Church is not static, but it is a historical entity which, as we pay attention to the new insights of the human consciousness, develops its doctrine in light of that consciousness. This was Murray's thinking.

I would raise three points for further discussion. One is that Murray explicitly changed the terms of the debate from religious toleration to religious liberty. That goes back to what we were talking about earlier. The Catholic experience was that toleration implied condescension. In the nineteenth-century context, toleration was a pragmatic concession to a situation which was not the ideal. The ideal was still the vision of the

Church as a perfect society, and that would include the Church as very influential in the State. As that was not possible, toleration became the working hypothesis until the ideal could be reached. This was the nineteenth-century system. What the declaration did, and what Murray pushed for, was to move out of that framework of thinking about toleration, and to talk not about toleration, but about religious freedom. This is one point that I think is very important. I would argue, perhaps, that toleration is a term which may have appealed to the "certainty-wallahs," to communities of certainty, because I think that it does imply a judgment—a judgment that another position is in error—and that may have a certain appeal to communities of certainty.

Religious liberty, I think, makes the argument based on certain presuppositions about the human person and human dignity. The Vatican II document, however, was very clear that in its assertion of religious freedom, it did not endorse the privatization of religion. In fact, the freedom of the Church entailed the freedom to exercise belief, to practice belief, in the public sphere. For Murray, religious liberty meant that one could not be forced to act against one's conscience, but also that one could not be impeded from acting, even in the public sphere, according to one's beliefs, except as it went against public order.

One thing that I think is very important for Catholics, in particular, and perhaps especially for American Catholics in Murray's social and political context, was the idea of the role of the laity. I would ask whether there are parallels in other traditions which might be useful here. The idea was that the layperson—and there is the distinction between clerical and lay—that the layperson has a calling. That calling is not to exercise ministry within the Church, but to exercise ministry in the secular sphere, in the public place. That too renews an emphasis on the layperson and the lay vocation. It uses the term "leaven in the world." It says that the layperson is like leaven in the world, scattered throughout the public sphere, perhaps invisible, and yet through the exercise of faith it causes the whole loaf, in a sense, to rise. That is an image that I think can be very powerful to empower religious action in public life while also asserting the value of pluralism and religious freedom.

Finally, we must confront the implications of Murray's arguments for religious liberty, toleration, the religious communities themselves, and, specifically, religious authority. Murray was an obedient Jesuit. He was ordered by his superiors to stop writing on the topic. He did so for about six or seven years, and yet, I think, the implications of his arguments cannot be ignored. If he asserts freedom of religion, because of the demands of human dignity, one has to ask whether, at some point then, people within the religious community would also need freedom to search out truth on their own. Note a developing and strange tension here between freedom of the Church and freedom in the Church. Murray was writing at the time, the 1950s and 1960s, when there was a huge furor over birth control. (The Vatican II document appeared in 1965.) The Church's declaration on birth control appeared just around the time of Murray's death. The papal birth control commission report was leaked to the press in the United States (by the National Catholic Reporter), and it raised quite a bit of dissension when people expected birth control to be endorsed and a year later the Pope came out with *Humane Vitae* and said he would not accept artificial birth control and made his argument largely on the basis of papal precedent and authority. We find a very strange combination of events, where in 1965 Vatican II is pushing arguments about freedom and accepting the idea of a development in doctrine and three years later, *Humanae Vitae* comes out, which closes the question of dissent, based on papal authority.

Discussion

Sohail Hashmi
(Department of International Relations, Mt. Holyoke College):
In terms of principle how did Vatican II reverse centuries of papal fiat? How did Vatican II rationalize this major turn-around?

Wolfteich
They did say that they acknowledged that it was a development in doctrine, but the way that they justified their action was to claim that they simply brought new things out of the old. Actually there was some precedent. John XXIII in *Pacem in Terris* had entertained some of these thoughts as well, but Vatican II adopted an understanding and an ecclesiology which was progressive rather than classical, and that was crucial, I think. The idea that the Church was growing in its own sanctification was one theme within Vatican II thought, and in Murray's as well—that the Church was sanctified and yet was still being sanctified. I think there are actually implications here for the whole notion of epistemological modesty as well—that the Church, that the community itself, might recognize its own limitations of knowledge and its own inadequacy of prac-

tice. That was one thing that Murray talked about: the unbelief of the Christian. That the Christian, and the Christian community in fact, contributed to unbelief through its own practice in ways in which, perhaps, shielded knowledge of God rather than opening it up, that in some way the Church could become an obstacle to people's glimpsing a vision of God.

Joan Estruch
(Center for the Study of Sociology and Religion,
Autonomous University, Barcelona):
I'd like to join you in your answer to this last question. You see, I think that in the Catholic Church, the introduction of change always follows the same path, more or less, and it traces, I would say, three steps. In the first period, the Church says, "This thing, this new thing, this novel thing must be condemned." In the second period, the Church says, "It must, perhaps, not be condemned, but it is anyway very dangerous." In the third period, the Church says, "The Church has proclaimed it forever." This was the case in the matter of religious freedom. I still remember some Jesuits trying to explain to lay people in Barcelona how there was no contradiction between the Church service and the declaration of religious freedom. But those Catholics in the 1960s were already able to read, they were literate, and so the contradiction was evident. In fact, I think this ability to present changes, which were absolutely against tradition, as something which is to be incorporated into the tradition is one of the charms of the Catholic Church.

One further point: No doubt the American Catholic Church played a very important role in the declaration of religious freedom. In fact, American bishops practically organized a lobby of the Vatican during the council in order to advance the discussion of this declaration. Nevertheless, the American bishops were not the only ones. The French Catholic Church also played a role, as did the Dutch Catholic Church and the German and even the Austrian Catholic Churches. The Archbishop of Vienna played a very, very important role at the Vatican council and precisely on those kinds of questions.

Fisch
Listening to you I realize that in some sense we may say that Judaism has a head start on pluralism. All we have to do is recall Hobbes's nightmare of a religious community of free agents reading the Bible differently, and therefore needing the Leviathan to dictate the religiously proper reading

of it. Now the rabbis would have laughed out loud at that worry. The very idea of biblical exegesis is a multiplicity of voices, as long as it's not laying down the law. When it comes to theology, however, and as opposed to other religions, Judaism has no dogma and so lives comfortably with a multiplicity, even encourages a multiplicity, of interpretations.

Having said that, we have to realize, and I'm talking now from within the Jewish community, that the temptation of certainty, the temptation of dogma, the temptation of having something to lean on which you don't have to doubt and question, is enormous. We can discuss this easily around the table, but it lays a lot of responsibility on the religious leaders to account for their fallibility, to rethink, to take responsibility for change where they have a sense of sacred text they can lean on easily, and the vast majority does exactly that.

The ways of negotiating innovation are interesting, too, and the taxonomy of these that Joan has pointed out is revealing. Within Orthodox Judaism it often happens that rather than say that the halacha was wrong, a novelty is described as a lacuna, as something no one has thought about. Reinterpretation is done that way. You reinterpret and make believe that this is what the text really meant. There is a whole set of strategies of shrugging off the responsibility, of living with change without acknowledging it. I think the challenge of modernity, and the challenge of the multiculturalism we are living in, is to take this epistemic modesty out of the closet and for religious people to talk openly about it and talk about human error. That's very, very difficult even within the religion I come from, where a plurality of voices is welcome.

Stone

Let me respond first to Menachem, and then I want to ask two other questions. I think, Menachem, what you are describing is the casuistic method, which I think has been a neglected topic here. What the casuistic method accomplished was the notion of not thinking globally, not thinking in terms of principles, but thinking, instead, in terms of cases, test cases, small, each step at a time. I think, first of all, it is important to understand that is what we are talking about.

Second, I wonder whether you are right, that it would be better to take this notion of epistemic modesty out of the closet and put it on the table and say, yes, we are innovating; we are innovating out of a position of doubt and uncertainty as opposed to approaching things through the casuistic method. I actually think the casuistic method is a very remarkable and flexible tool for mediating between tradition and modernity. That's what it does, and it does so in most forms of legal practice, not just in Judaism. It is, in fact, a method of the common law as much as it is a method of Judaism, and it allows the common law to be a kind of live tradition as opposed to establishing a new constitution every ten years. I think that is something we have to keep in mind and can come back to later.

I'd like to add a comment to Claire, who invoked not just the Gelasian principle, but also the notion of human dignity as being the second major source in developing Murray's thought, and I guess that I want to put on the table a comment on how little weight the notion of human dignity, despite its being a major theological principle of Judaism, really bears this notion of being created in the image of God. I think that, actually, this is very appealing. It doesn't bear a tremendous amount of halachic weight, at least in the normative community.

Fisch
Except for forms of execution.

Stone
I think it might be interesting to understand why that is, why is the concept of human dignity, in some ways, attenuated?

Fischer
This isn't so much a question; it's more a comment of interest to you, Adam. I'm just curious whether this is accidental or not, or is this session the "American session"? I think there is an analytical point here because your whole assumption of the conference is that you want to go outside the Protestant tradition and look at other traditions which don't share Protestant notions of privatized religion and so on. The point is that John Courtney Murray and the American bishops in Vatican II were from a society, or a civilization, which is organized, for better or for worse, along Protestant principles. This seems to have been critical to their politics, or at least such an argument can be made. In America, speaking broadly, everybody fits in—Catholics fit in, Jews fit in, the Muslims, who now are becoming a group of noticeable numbers, I imagine will fit in. These people then go out and they influence other communities all over the world. In other words, you have Vatican II, so the American bishops come, Murray comes, and they produce this document. I can tell you that a lot of people working on toleration in Israel in the Orthodox

community are of Anglo-Saxon origin. It is no accident that Menachem speaks the way he does and I speak the way I do [with Anglo-American accents]. No doubt the impact of American Orthodox Jews in Israel has gone in all kinds of directions. Kahane was also American, for sure. Yet do we not have to recognize that through the back door, Protestantism and liberalism comes in and influences the various traditions? Here I would connect up with Suzanne's remarks about casuistry. In other words, what we are doing is mediating, and we are doing it specifically through casuistry. Perhaps each tradition in its own way is producing this mediation between modernity, Protestantism, Americanism, etc., and their own traditions.

Seligman
I think that is very helpful, though as Suzanne indicated earlier, there are limits to this shared civilizational undertaking—certainly from the Jewish perspective.

Friedrich Wilhelm Graf
(Department of Systematic Theology and Ethics, University of Munich): I would like to take up Menachem's point. In a certain way Claire presented a very conventional reading of the Second Vatican. In all modern Catholic Church histories you have the same picture. There were the dark Middle Ages, which we call nineteenth-century Catholicism, and then somehow, in the 1960s, the world changed and it all became better and we accepted certain principles. I doubt it. There was a lot of continuity between the first Vatican and the second Vatican, so one has to look at the strategies. How did they really do it? How did they change theologies? My point would be that in a certain way they maintained an enormous amount of continuity. They were speaking of religious liberty, but they did not accept Protestants as really being churches. So what changed and what remained the same?

Berger
What changed?! Think of the role of the Catholic Church in the Spanish Civil War. It would be unthinkable today. If you think of Samuel Huntington's book *The Third Wave of Democracy*, a major factor in democratic transition in Latin America, and in the Philippines, was the role of the Church. Change has been enormous, and yes, of course, Murray was still a Catholic, but that's not really the point.

I would like to make a further observation from what can be called a sociology-of-knowledge perspective. Suzanne and Menachem and Shlomo each made the point in different ways that in Judaism it doesn't matter so much what you believe, but whether you accept certain behavior. I've heard this before. You hear, for example, that Hindus can believe anything as long as you keep caste and the dharma that goes with caste. Therefore pluralism is not as difficult for them as it is for Christians, who insist on these dogmas. Frankly, I think it is an illusion, and the sociology-of-knowledge point I want to make is, if I may put it in somewhat sociological terms, every behavioral norm has cognitive presuppositions. If the cognitive presuppositions are no longer taken for granted, then behavioral norms become increasingly implausible. Sure there is a difference between saying that in order to be a good Catholic or a good Christian you have to believe in all the fine points of the Nicene Creed, as against saying you can't eat ham sandwiches. Admitted, there is a difference, but unless the presuppositions, which are cognitive, of the ham sandwich business are taken for granted, then why shouldn't I eat ham sandwiches? So I think that this difference between praxis and dogma should not be exaggerated.

Fisch
But that makes the point all the more valid because here you have a move which is declared rhetorically as wild and liberal but at rock bottom is far more conservative than it may seem to be. All moves in Orthodox Judaism will be declared to be conservative but in fact will be more radical than they declared themselves to be. Emmanuel Rackman of New York is saying that he hasn't changed one letter of the *Shulchan Aruch* [a compendium of law and daily obligations that guide the life of the observant Jew] and yet he is making massive changes and speaking as though he hasn't.[5] Again the tactics of change are very, very interesting.

Wolfteich
I just want to clarify what I meant to say. I don't think that either Murray or Vatican II presented itself as a major, radical move. I think they both tried to find continuity and that is one reason why Murray argued that the American experiment was in fact a continuation of this basic Christian Gelasian principle. They were Catholic in the sense that the tradition was very important and that they tried to establish their continuity with it. They might be perceived as more radical than they themselves proposed themselves to be.

Shlomo Fischer's Presentation

Strategies of Tolerance in Contemporary Israel

Several preliminary remarks. When Adam started to talk to me about this, I said to myself one can interpret traditions as elastically as one wants. Everything has been and can be read into any religious tradition. Therefore, I wanted to enter my remarks in a specific context and not so much to argue what could be said or what could be interpreted about a religious tradition, because I think, as I say, that's something that is fairly elastic. So I want to anchor myself in a specific historical, sociological context. The context which is natural to me is the Israeli context, and I'm interested in what strategies are actually employed, not what strategies could be employed, because I think anything could be, and has been, employed to justify practically anything. I was interested specifically in what contemporary writers and decisors (to use a term I learned from Suzanne) have been doing. I do try to relate to certain cognitive structures that characterize Judaism, that characterize the notion of a covenant, and that have become actualized in the thought of rabbinical authorities, for the most part, in the twentieth century. None of the most significant of these decisors, neither Rabbi Israeli nor Rabbi Kook nor Rabbi Yeshayahu Karlitz or any of the people concerned, are skeptics that one would find sitting around in a university cafeteria.[6] That should be clear.

I'd like to address Rabbi Kook's strategy of tolerance based on pro-nationalist sentiment, because this is the strategy that became institutionalized. I'd also like to address several remarks to the strategy of what I call "Revelation is not available." I would put this issue in terms of the time context, in other words that the Jewish tradition has a notion of time that is bracketed time, which is the time in which the covenant cannot be fulfilled. Following Suzanne's remarks, I'd like to put that in a slightly more general context. Generally, the more that a religion like Judaism encloses itself within itself, and does not become capable of realization, or universalization, then, paradoxically, the more it becomes tolerant. That was Suzanne's point that to the degree that Judaism is particular—one may also say to the degree that is particularistic—other people are not a problem. This was in part the Chazon Ish's strategy.

The Chazon Ish represents the inspiration, in many ways, for ultra-Orthodox Judaism in Israel today. The entire ultra-Orthodox edifice, which is about 7 percent of the population at this point, had been inspired directly by him. I refer to the *haredim*, the group of Orthodox Jews that effectively constitutes an alternative society to mainstream Israeli society, mainly through the mechanism of not going to the army and hence not joining the work force. This is a community that to a large extent exists through the Israeli welfare state and special arrangements; they are supported, in large part, by the country as a whole, and, at least theoretically, the adult males engage in Torah study the entire day. This is a very rough, a very general characterization. There are, of course, many people who consider themselves to be *haredim* who do work, particularly after the age of thirty-five, but as a general characterization the above holds.

The Chazon Ish represents a very deep theological sensibility for these people. I think that the theological, sociological issue of the exile is a central issue, has been a central issue, in Jewish history. Most movements of Jewish modernization understood modernization as an end to the exile. The end to the exile meant the end to the marginalization of the Jewish people which characterized the Jews from the sixth century to the middle of the eighteenth century, or the beginning of the nineteenth century, and the end of the exile meant the ability to join the mainstream of society whether through citizenship, through cultural interaction, through nationalism, or through a host of other things.

Now Orthodoxy, as Jacob Katz has pointed out, is a modern phenomenon, and it is a modern phenomenon precisely because its world-view can no longer be taken for granted. In other words, the traditional world has been seriously undermined, and Orthodoxy consists of a systematic attempt to maintain a "constructed" social reality within whose boundaries, the cognitive structures that enable Orthodoxy, its cognitive underpinnings if you will, can be sustained and maintained. What seems to have happened within modern Jewish history is that the Orthodox way of life has been associated with socioeconomic and cultural marginalization.

Hence, movements of modernization which wish to exit marginalization have a social-revolutionary, antitraditional character, as was often the case in Catholic societies. Either because of the nature of the Catholic Church itself or because Catholic regimes went (since the seventeenth century) together with autocratic, organicist types of regimes in

Spain, in the Hapsburg countries, France, etc., they developed strong, antitraditionalist, antireligious revolutionary energy for change, which went in a strong secularist direction. Similarly, in Central Europe and in Eastern Europe, movements of Jewish modernization went in a strong antitraditionalist direction. In Germany and in Hungary, there was, it is true, a veneer of religious reform. Yet I don't think that as a phenomenology it is comparable to the Protestant Reformation. It was a veneer of religious reform only, which, as described in Jacob Katz's last book, saw the war of Neology and Orthodoxy in Hungary, where there developed two counter-communities at war with each other.[7] To a certain extent that pattern has continued in the Jewish settlement in Palestine and now in the State of Israel. Other social conflicts, including political and class conflicts, have become linked to that central conflict. What emerged was a revolutionary elite founding the State of Israel, who erected a secular monopoly. Interestingly, common parlance among religious people in Israel and among traditional people and Middle Eastern immigrants is that the Labor Party and the elites affiliated with it are collectively *Habolshivikim* [i.e., the Bolsheviks]. They, the Labor Party, are referred to and thought of as "Bolsheviks" who imposed their vision on all of society.

This is the second point I want to note. I believe that this historical development has conditioned all discussions of tolerance and all behavior vis-à-vis tolerance. There exists in Israel a very defensive, very conservative religious community which is used to being at war with revolutionary Zionist elements. That's on the one hand. Now, ultra-Orthodoxy in its original form rejected the program of modernization and has rejected the program of fulfillment, that is, the fulfillment of the covenant through Zionism. The Chazon Ish's stance was that since the covenant (that is, the fundamental relationship between God and Israel) cannot be fulfilled, we are cut off from all the sources of revelation, hence we have no authority to enforce our way of life (and that's where the epistemological modesty comes in). We have no authority to put heretics to death even though that is the law. We have no authority because we are cut off from the sources of revelation. If we had revelation in our hands, if we had a continuous chain to revelation, then the situation would be different, but the classical Orthodox position is that God is hidden and that we are Jews because and despite the fact that God is hidden.

Now, I would grant on the other hand, that the modern religious Zionist sensibility is opposed to that of the ultra-Orthodox, *haredi* stance. The religious Zionist sensibility is that the covenant and revelation are in the process of being fulfilled, and can be fulfilled now. I will give you an example: A friend of mine came to my door the other day. He is collecting money for a kindergarten, and he asked me if I wanted to buy some videotapes about bringing of first fruits to the Temple in Jerusalem. So I supported the guy, I supported the kindergarten, and I bought the tapes and I played them for my seven-and-a-half-year-old daughter and the tapes were amazing, they simply took current Israeli social reality with its contemporary slang and conventions and superimposed them on the ancient rite of bringing the first fruits to the Temple in Jerusalem. There was a total conflation of contemporary Israeli reality with the bringing of the first fruits to the Temple. This is the type of consciousness that led to the Jewish terrorist attempt to blow up the Mosque of Omar and restore the Temple. In this context the ultra-Orthodox position becomes somewhat attractive as a source of tolerance. Since we are cut off from the sources of revelation we can't create the society that we want, we don't have the authority nor the means or divine guidance to try to hasten the fulfillment of the Covenant, and therefore what we do is wait.

At present, I must admit that even in ultra-Orthodox circles this idea is being eroded. That sensibility which is so pristinely expressed by the Chazon Ish in the 1930s is being eroded, and even ultra-Orthodox people in Israel are divided into two camps: ultra-Orthodox, who do not identify, or supposedly do not identify, with the Zionist enterprise and religious Zionists who see it as fulfillment of the covenant. This erosion is due to political developments since 1977 in which the ultra-Orthodox have received such massive political power and such massive support and state resources that this notion of lack of identification is becoming somewhat of a sham.

I would just like to make some allusions to new strategies of tolerance which are now being thought about, discussed, and pursued, and I would like to elaborate some of them. Here I would like to mention the uses of religious romanticism. Religious Zionism is a romantic movement. It is romantic in a nineteenth-century sense, and hence it shares good things and bad things with romanticism (it is, for example, entirely nationalistic). On the one hand, it believes in many genetic properties that the Jews supposedly have; on the other hand, it is characterized by a quest for spontaneity, authenticity, especially religious authenticity and spontaneity. This can go in many different directions. One of the directions it has been going in, or some people have been taking it, has been the direction of trying to build a religious order upon—this is going to sound Catholic, but I don't think it really is—the notion of natural morality. This is a notion that is found in Hebrew, *musar tivi*, rational morality, or natural morality, and it is something that is, again, found in the classical texts of religious thought. Yehuda HaLevi [a twelfth-century Jewish-Andalusian poet and philosopher, author of *The Defense of a Despised Faith* (*The Book of the Kuzari*)] is one of the prime exponents of the importance of natural morality, as the first foundation upon which religious life can be built.

Nobody, it is true, defines what natural morality is. People seem to see it in terms of natural law. In discussions of politics, people see it as a natural state built upon natural morality, and they always give the example that the gentiles have natural morality and we can learn natural morality from the gentiles, in a sense referring us back to what Suzanne had spoken of this morning. This was very strong in Yehuda HaLevi and strong in Nachmanides [Spanish Talmudist and biblical commentator, 1194–1270] and other medieval authorities and has been revived in romantic, religious, Zionist circles, specifically in Rabbi Kook and in the Natziv of Voloshin—Rabbi Tzvi Yehuda Berlin, who was the Rabbi of Voloshin. On this basis, people are trying to reconstruct a notion of natural rights in relation to the dignity of man. Such thinkers take the verse "Thou shall love thy neighbor as thyself" and they give it a Kantian reading. They talk about natural morality in a Kantian context. The next move taken by some is of giving social contract theory a Rawlesian twist. The social contract becomes based on Kantian morality, in other words that you wouldn't want your own rights infringed upon and hence you can't infringe upon the rights of other people. If you claim that natural morality is, in fact, a religious necessity and claim that without some form of natural morality which recognizes the natural dignity of man (that man is an end and not a means), then you have no choice but to construct a political order based on social contract theory and upon the mutual recognition and universalization of human rights. Hence, religious freedom becomes a part of human rights. As I say, some try to hatch this whole structure out of a Jewish version of natural rights theory and of social contract. One of the people who did this was the former chief rabbi of Tel Aviv, R. Haim David Halevy, who published some years ago the notion that the attitude towards non-Jews has nothing to do with all the laws on idolatry, which doesn't apply to Christians or Muslims (which was the traditional claim), but rather placed the discussion on the basis of Kantian or Lockean principles. The last lecture he gave before he passed away was one on the fundamental centrality of Kantian and natural morality for the rights of non-Jews in the state of Israel, where he affirmed an ongoing decision that had been given over and over again that non-Jews are entitled to have the same civil and human rights as everybody else. This is the most labile of the strategies that are being employed today.

Discussion

Fisch

The resources in Judaism for tolerance are immense, and you have added a whole bag full of them that I wasn't aware of. Yet we have to bear in mind what I call the problem of sovereignty, which is the problem of Orthodox Jews committed to halacha who find themselves around not a skeptical table like this, but a government table in Israel. Now we have, for example, a minister of interior, minister of education, minister of finance who are religiously, halachically committed Jews. Their job however, is not simply to tolerate and turn a blind eye to idolatry, to single-sex marriages, to knowing violation of the Sabbath—they have to write the checks that ensure that all these violations are performed effectively. We have a minister of education with a yarmulke on his head, who is religiously, halachically obligated, yet whose job is to improve the desecration of the Sabbath by the Jewish, nonreligious youth movements who go on the festivals and the holy days on their field trips, and he has to study what they did last year and render it all the more effective and worthwhile and better run the next year. This is a whole new kettle of fish. And what we want from people like this is not to give up their notion of Sabbath or to rethink what sin is, but to develop a two-tier system by which, within the community, they preserve their sense of right and wrong, but as governmental officials in a multicultural environment, they are able to see value in the sinner and a worthwhileness of heresy and sin that merits financing them actively.

Fischer

In the meantime, the minister of interior, Shlomo Yishai, has been closing businesses on the Sabbath illegally and has been reprimanded by the courts for that because, far from writing checks, he has been actively infringing upon people's liberty to run businesses as they see fit. I think that the reality of Israel is that a minimalist policy of tolerance on the first level is important because at the very least you want to stop the illegal closing businesses through illegal police action.

Berger
If I may ask a question here, the two examples that you gave, it seems to me, raise very different issues. You gave desecrating the Sabbath and same-sex marriages.

Fisch
Add idolatry to that.

Berger
Yes, but I just want to stick with those two, and in terms of what Shlomo said before, I mean the desecrating of the Sabbath, I could see the rationale that is being suggested here. Within the Orthodox community you stick to your belief, but these other people can do as they see fit. But with same-sex marriages, it seems to me, you run right into the question of what is natural law. I can very well see that even within the strategy that you are recommending, we would say, "No, this I have to forbid." An analogy would be a Catholic magistrate or politician who has to deal with abortion. That's not a matter of being Catholic; it is a matter of, supposedly (for them), homicide.

Stone
Menachem has put on the table a problem that occurs whenever somebody religious is in a situation of authority. It is a traditional question of what to do with a Supreme Court judge who is religious in the United States. What are their obligations and what happens to the sort of natural morality and violating of one's own precepts of conscience? I think there is also, mixed into this, the whole modern question of splitting of selves in which people see themselves as occupying different places at different times and operating from within different systems.

Fisch
Can one do that halachically? That is the challenge. The phenomenon is there; there have been religious people who have thought this through.

Stone
I think that there is a tradition of a kind of two-tiered system of thought in traditional Judaism, and that is the notion reminiscent of a kind of ideal Torah and a pragmatic Torah. There is already, even within the tradition itself, a way of conceptualizing two levels of behavior in a two-tier system.

Wolfteich

Suzanne, I think this relates to the question of how to distinguish between sacred and secular and yet still assert a vocation of the layperson. We may think of JFK. There was a major debate about whether he could hold office as a Catholic and what would his faith have to do with a public role. His solution to that was to compartmentalize his faith and say, no, it's private, it doesn't have to do with my role as President. I think one of the challenges for us is to say that one can exercise, in some way, a public role, though I'm not sure what alternative we have when doing so other than privatizing religion.

Fischer

The same issue came up in Israel: the question of pension rights in same-sex marriages and other benefits. For purpose of pension rights and other social benefits, the Supreme Court recognized same-sex marriage (though the explanation for this may be that they were "Bolsheviks" and not religious pluralists). I would however like to come back to Menachem's point and the limits of the types of things that Menachem has been advocating. In the past, religious ministers of education had been funding everybody; that included vanguard dance groups and nonreligious youth movements, provocative theater, etc. This was done most probably out of a pluralist perspective. For there is a persistent tradition within certain strains of Israeli Orthodox religiosity (following the writings of Rabbi Kook) that liberalism, secularism, socialism, etc. are all movements which have to be learned from and which have to be dialectically engaged with and applied in the achievement of a synthesis between conservative Orthodox defensive religiosity on the one hand and Jewish emancipatory ideologies and practices on the other. Rabbi Kook argued that the emancipatory ideologies of modernity have something to contribute to a synthesis between tradition and emancipation. Hence, as long as the emancipatory ideologies were very nationalist, as long as they were social democratic in orientation and contributed to communal solidarity and to a sense of justice and nationalism, that was all fine. Such events could be secular and that was fine because it was seen as complementing and completing the religious message. They weren't seen as contradictory. However, when the case of same-sex marriage came up, at that point certain people, Hanan Porat [one the leading figures of the Gush Emunim settlement movement in the West Bank; right-wing religious Member of Knesset from 1984 to 1999] and other people, said: This is no longer within our pluralist universe. This does not complement our religious orientation. This is not an emancipatory philosophy that complements Judaism as we understand it. The point which worries me about pluralist approaches is that generally they are substantive. If they are substantive, then there is generally a boundary, a limit beyond which they will not go. There is an attitude that assumes such and such I can subsume as complementing my religious orientation, but beyond that (whatever "beyond that" is; if it is same sex-marriage, polygamy, abortion) is something that I can't countenance within my pluralist universe. I would prefer a rights-based approach, which can mean, by the way, that you are in error, that you are an idiot and it's your perfect right to be such and I will defend it to the death and so on. I can say that you are in error, and every human being has the right to make whatever decisions they want, it is part of the inherent dignity of man. This is similar to the position of John Courtney Murray.

Wolfteich
I think that you can say that a particular view is in error, but that the error could have a right to exist.

Fischer
Right, that the error has a right to exist, that people have the right to make errors. That is perfectly clear. Whether I accept something as within my circle of what is acceptable or not will not depend on whether it fits my notion of what complements religion, whether it is a secular ideology or some other one. A rights-based approach will countenance anything as long as it does not harm other people.

Berger
I do not see how that gets you out of the need to draw boundaries.

Fischer
The question is what is the nature of the boundaries? The nature of the boundaries on a rights spectrum would be more approximate to liberal boundaries.

Berger
Claire and I were discussing Governor Cuomo the other day. He was the first of a long line of Catholics who personally opposed abortion but took the position that as public servants they were duty-bound to enforce the law. Well, I believe, this is crazy. If one accepts the official Catholic posi-

tion on abortion, which I do not, that it is murder, how can you say, you oppose it personally but will support it because it is the law.

Fischer
Unless you have a realpolitik approach which says that the law must be enforced as a higher good even if it is amoral. You could argue that the law has to be enforced because the alternative is anarchy, and the alternative to anarchy is a social evil which overrides the individual case of murder.

Berger
I first heard this argument when I taught in the South at the very beginning of the Civil Rights movement and I was appalled by segregation. It was new to me and it was awful. What Shlomo said is exactly the argument I heard from white Southerners—we personally disapprove of this, but we don't like these disruptive tactics by the Civil Rights movement and the law is more important than a particular evil. Therefore, while we will try to change the segregation laws we must uphold the law

Fischer
That's a very good point, but it also highlights the fact that you need intermediate steps of protest. In Israel this is constantly raised in terms of a peace settlement. Those people who believe that returning or relinquishing portions of the land of Israel is religiously forbidden have an issue of conscience with the peace process, and that was one of the immediate causes of the assassination of the prime minister. Israel does not have a tradition of civil disobedience, which means that if you disagree then you open fire. Israel does not have a graded tradition of institutionalized protest, rather it has a hundred-year-old, or two-hundred-year-old, tradition of two warring camps using all means available to them, so conflict immediately moves into violent tactics. One of the things that people have been trying to do in Israel today is try to institutionalize a graded tradition of civil disobedience and protest which is within some sort of civility, some sort of boundaries of civility, and not necessarily open civil war, which is what it would tend to do naturally.

CHAPTER TWO

The Second Dialogue

On the Boundaries and Meanings of Revelation

The second set of dialogues moves from the boundaries of the community to the boundaries of revelation. The three presenters, Sohail Hashmi, Dorothee von Tippelskirch, and Menachem Fisch, devote their remarks to explicating just what potentialities for tolerance appear in the revealed traditions of the three religions under consideration. Sohail Hashmi analyzes three different readings of tolerance which can be found in the Qur'an and with which most non-Islamic scholars and citizens are not familiar. Dorothee von Tippelskirch weaves together insights from Sigmund Freud and Emmanuel Lévinas to develop an understanding of biblical tolerance rooted in the very idea of the stranger, the neighbor, and the injunctions of love. Inevitably, discussion of this piece turns around the issues of love (and forgiveness) and justice as well as a delineation of the neighbor and stranger. Just how the other—and which other— stands at the boundary of the self (and of the normative community) and in what set of relations he or she stands becomes a critical factor in discussion. Any discussion of love—especially via Freud and Lévinas—of necessity leads to discussions of sameness and difference, as these are understood in different traditions. This discussion both harks back to the earlier presentation of Qur'anic moves of tolerance and forward to Menachem Fisch's presentation. Fisch centers his remarks on the meta-legal logic of Jewish law (halacha) and the resources this provides for a politics of tolerance predicated on Jewish legal reasoning. Juxtaposing traditionalist and antitraditionalist readings of Jewish texts, Fisch argues for an internally pluralist moment within the Jewish legal tradition—one with singular implications for the definition of life with the stranger and the other.

Sohail Hashmi's Presentation

Modalities of Islamic Tolerance

I will confine my discussion to just one expression of Islamic ethics within the Qur'an, focusing on one particular verse which I consider to be the summation of what the Qur'an is trying to get at when it speaks of toleration. In other words, this verse encapsulates the normative thrust of the entire Qur'anic revelation, in my opinion, on this topic. However, before I turn to the Qur'an let me quickly run through my argument. As I see it, toleration, or tolerance, evokes at least four sets of meanings. We can begin with the minimalist reading of the word "tolerance," which is simply putting up with something or someone one disagrees with or even finds repugnant. Then if we continue on the spectrum, we would come somewhere in the middle of the spectrum, a median position which would be a sort of benign neglect. It's born out of the conviction that one's position is superior but remains neutral, or perhaps completely unaffected by contending positions, and therefore would just leave them alone.

A more robust form of tolerance would be respect for different positions and, perhaps, even a willingness to engage with them, but reserving to oneself the conviction of one's own superiority or possession of the truth. Finally, at the end of the spectrum, we would come to a maximalist position which expands upon the respect that is found in the previous definition, but with this added difference: in this maximalist position, the respect is born out of acknowledgment that one has only a limited knowledge of the truth and that, in fact, other contending views may carry equal validity, and, in fact, may have equal claims to the truth.

When we turn to look at the Qur'an—and of course, the Qur'an has been analyzed for centuries on this topic by various commentators, Muslim as well as non-Muslim—we can find, in the text of the Qur'an itself, verses to justify each of these four positions along the spectrum. The traditional view that has been put forth, primarily by Orientalists in the nineteenth and early twentieth centuries, was that the Qur'an evolved in a certain direction.[1] The Qur'an has, as all the Qur'an commentators acknowledge, two distinct sets of verses, one belonging to the early Meccan period, which lasted for roughly thirteen years and the second, the Medinan period, lasting for roughly ten years. The traditional argument of the Orientalists has been that the Meccan verses are the ones that carry the most expansive understandings of tolerance, and that the Qur'an progressively evolves in the Medinan chapters into a more exclusivist, more intolerant, position. The reason that is advanced to explain this evolution is that the tolerance in the Meccan chapters was not based on principle, but on a pragmatic tolerance because in Mecca, the Prophet Muhammad and the earliest Muslim followers of the Prophet were militarily weak. They were, in fact, disenfranchised, dispossessed, and therefore they could not do anything but be tolerant. In Medina, once Islam had been converted into a state, into a political community with military power that began to be demonstrated in a number of engagements, the Qur'an evolves to reflect the changed historical social circumstances to one of increasing exclusivity. Therefore, the Medinan chapters, the Medinan verses, moved towards the minimalist interpretations of tolerance.

This is a view that you will find expressed in the work of prominent Orientalists, and I don't want to belabor the point. I do, however, wish to reject it. Based upon both an analysis of the chronology of the Qur'anic revelation and the content of this revelation, I think it is a false view. If we look, even superficially, at the chronology we realize that this argument of the progressive evolution of the Qur'an's intolerance cannot be borne out because, in fact, some of the most important verses dealing with tolerance are revealed in the Medinan period. They are revealed in the context of the Muslim community's clearly recognized military prowess and clearly recognized political domination in a large part of the Arabian Peninsula. The most important verse is that which Muslims always cite in gatherings such as this, "Let there be no compulsion in religion." I don't know of anything that can be more explicit than that on the topic of religious toleration. This verse was revealed in the Medinan period, and it was revealed in the context of ongoing polemics between the Muslims and the Jews, the Jewish tribes of Medina, as well as Christians who lived in other parts of the Arabian Peninsula.

Let me turn now to what I consider the much more important task, which is to analyze the content of the Qur'anic message. If there wasn't an evolution, then are the verses simply contradictory? Are they mutually incompatible? How can we reconcile, on the one hand, verses which say, "Fight the unbelievers," or the famous verse of the sword, "Slay the polytheists wherever you find them," with other, tolerant verses? This is a problem that has long exercised Muslim exegetes, and it continues to do so today. Suzanne, I think, captures it best when she says that religious law evolves through casuistry. Religious law, of course, is not unique to this idea of casuistry. Yet religious, scriptural interpretation is also very much based on casuistry, and we can find many casuistical readings of the Qur'an. But the most convenient device that the medieval commentators employed to try to reconcile these seemingly incompatible verses is the sledgehammer approach. The sledgehammer is the notion of abrogation. The Qur'an, in fact, according to these commentators did evolve. The Meccan chapters were replaced by the Medinan chapters; the Medinan chapters overruled, in fact repealed or abrogated, much of the revelations that had come before.

This is a basic problem because what these commentators are saying is that roughly two-thirds of the Qur'an has been abrogated by one-third. One commentator analyzed all of the repealed verses and one verse, the verse of the sword which I quote in the paper, is claimed to have repealed 114 verses by some commentators' readings, by others, 124, which are spread through 56 chapters. If you employ this method, what you are doing is saying that the Qur'an itself doesn't carry any moral weight, just as these commentators argue that earlier scripture, also, does not carry moral weight because they have been superseded or they have been replaced by the Qur'anic revelation. That is obviously a problem for modern Muslim interpreters of the Qur'an who are unwilling to abrogate the vast majority of the Qur'anic revelation.

Let me now try to advance a reading which argues that there are no irreconcilable verses in the Qur'an and that, in fact, if you read the entire Qur'an as a totality, and place the verses in context, what you come up with is a rather clear message on this topic. Let's go through the four positions on tolerance that I had outlined earlier. We can find each of these positions outlined in the Qur'an. The minimalist, or exclusivist, position is represented by the medieval jurists, who argue that the sword verse, the normative verse when it came to jihad in particular, overruled all other verses on toleration. Basically what they were arguing was that the Qur'an commands Muslims to wage an incessant battle not necessarily for conversion, although there were some jurists who advanced the position that jihad was a war of conversion—they were the minority. The

majority preferred to say that jihad was a war of conquest with the ultimate goal, somewhere down the road of course, of making it possible for
non-Muslims to convert to Islam. This is, again, a huge topic, but let me
just mention one very prominent difficulty that immediately arises with
this interpretation, and this in the very first verse that sanctioned jihad.
For the verse sanctioned jihad as a way of preserving not just Islam, but
as a way of preserving Judaism and Christianity as well. The verse reads,
"Had not God repelled some people by means of others, that is in allowing force to be used for the first time, then cloisters, churches, syna-
gogues and mosques all places where in the name of God as mentioned
would be razed to the ground." Of course this verse indicates to me very
clearly that jihad's purpose was not a war of religious conquest or religious conversion.

The more tolerant position, if we continue to move down the spectrum, the median position would be, of course, acceptance of other religious communities but with the goal of circumscribing their adherence
until they are ultimately eliminated. Of course this is a very popular view
among medieval jurists as well. This reading of tolerance in the Qur'an
led to the rise of the *dimmi* system in which Jews, Christians, other peoples of the book, as well as eventually Hindus, Zoroastrians, in fact just
about anyone that had any kind of organized religious community were
incorporated as a *dimmi* community, that is as a protected community.
But again, the notion of *dimmi* status was hardly one of equality with the
Muslims, and we can find many examples of intolerance based upon the
ultimate goal of converting the *dimmi* into Islam. There is a more tolerant
reading of the *dimmi* status, which I would say then moves us farther
down, and this is based upon the idea that, in fact, Jews and Christians
are recipients of a revelation which has validity because it comes from the
same source, but that they have a sort of corrupted revelation and therefore, Islam is the more perfect example, or more perfect manifestation of
this same revelation. It doesn't necessarily argue for the ultimate elimination of other interpretations of the divine message, but it certainly
holds Islam to be the truth. Again, the *dimmi* status is preserved in this
interpretation.

Now finally, we come to what I claim is the maximalist ethic encap-
sulated in verse 5:48. This verse is quite different from the *dimmi* verses
(by the way, the notion of *dimmi* is not contained within the Qur'an itself;
it was a construct of the Muslim generations that interpreted the Qur'an).
The maximalist position is captured in verse 5:48. I will just read the

very end because to me it has always been the beginning and the end of Qur'anic interpretations, or Qur'anic views on this issue. "If God had so willed, he would have made you a single people, but his plan is to test you in what he has given you, so strive as in a race in all the virtues. The goal of you all is to God. It is he that will show you the truth of the matters in which you differ." I call this the maximalist position because here religious diversity and pluralism is not simply a manifestation or aspect of human life that one has to tolerate, in fact, it is something that is celebrated. Why is it celebrated? Because just as human beings urge each other on towards evil actions all the time, so according to this verse, religious diversity can also lead to human beings urging each other on to the good. The metaphor here is one of a race in which there is competition, competition to do what every religious community considers, in common, to be virtuous acts.

Discussion

Rusmir Mahmutćehajić
(President, International Forum Bosnia):
I think that it is important to understand what was said in this speech. One of the most frequent interpretations of the Qur'an is that it was revealed to Muslims. The Qur'an itself claims that it is a revelation for mankind, and in the original meaning of the word, Muslim and Islam, there is little of what we understand today with these words. Muslim is derived from the word Islam, meaning submission, and if you were to pass through the Qur'an you will see that Islam, as submission, is the word used for every religion. We could say that submission to God is essential for all religions. But the institutionalization of this word in historical form over the course of historical development darkened its essence. To submit yourself to God is a rational choice. You can choose it. But to be a believer, which is essential, cannot be chosen. You can wait; you can work in this direction, and have it as God's grace. This is an essential Islamic teaching of the Qur'an.

Abu Zayd
According to the Qur'an or according to a comprehensive reading of the Qur'an in its totality, Islam is the religion of God. Islam has so many

manifestations; Abraham and Isaac's religion was Islam, the religion of Jesus was Islam. So Islam is the comprehensive religion manifested in other religions, including Judaism, Christianity, even Magism (Zoroastrianism), which are specifically mentioned in the Qur'an. Some modern scholars would say that anyone who believes in God and the afterlife is a Muslim. Then we can derive a distinction between a Muslim-Christian, a Muslim-Jew, and a Muslim believer who believes in Mohammed as the Prophet. This is the modern explanation and interpretation of Islam and Muslim and Mohammed. A Muslim in the terminological sense is like a Jew, like a Christian, but he believes in Mohammed.

We have to bear in mind the fact mentioned in Sohail's presentation about the history of the Qur'an, that it was revealed in fragmented verses over more than twenty-three years. There are two kinds of arrangements, the chronological arrangement of the Qur'an, which is very essential to any scholar, to interpretation, and the present arrangement in the Qur'an, which is absolutely different. I don't know of any Islamic scholarship that tries to discover, or at least to explain, why the chronological arrangement was diverted to the present arrangement. This is something that should be carried out. I agree absolutely with Sohail about the use of abrogation as a political tool. Thus a particular jurist would abrogate what did not agree with his interpretation in the Qur'an. Abrogation was used as a human tool in the history of Islamic law, and this also is true of this one verse, pushing Muslims to kill the infidel. It has abrogated more than one hundred verses that speak about tolerance.

Stone
I'm going to get us back to a different topic, but I was very struck by Sohail's explanation of one strand of the tradition, which understands Islam as a kind of perfection of both Christianity and Judaism. I do think the question of how one views the progression of history is a very key issue for all the traditions. Of course, from the perspective of the Jewish tradition, which views itself as primary, the problem of the progression of history is just that: that it is claiming, in fact, to have all the truths of history, right from the beginning, so that the old is intended to criticize the new as opposed to the new becoming a kind of perfection of the old. I'm wondering what happens in Islam with regard to that, because if one aspect of the tradition is that there is a progression of human history to a greater truth, does that in fact get carried over beyond and past the revelation of Mohammed?

Hashmi

It doesn't. It doesn't according to mainstream Islamic views, and all you have to do is ask the Bahais and the Ahmadiyya (known also as Qadianis) on this issue and they will say that Islam is just as troubled on this issue as any other religion that believes it is the perfection and culmination of revelation.[2] This is, again, an interpretation, and this is not grounded in the Qur'an. I've cited a verse here which speaks of most of the Old Testament prophets as well as Jesus as being bearers of the Islamic message. One thing I want to say in response to what Rusmir was saying earlier, on the Qur'anic references to the word *al-Islam*. It is by no means clear that it is talking about *al-Islam* with a capital *I*, so what he is saying is absolutely correct that it could refer to the message that Christians and Jews also subscribe to.

Fisch

I'm very curious and baffled about the epistemological aspects of all this. Now submission to the will of God cuts across all three religions, but I'd like to know the epistemic status of what we make of as the will of God in each of the three religions. The position of epistemic humility, where we do our best to figure out God's will, but we can't ever be sure because after giving us the text, revelation has stopped, coupled to the idea that God is perfect and good and therefore could not have ordered us to do something which is morally wrong in our eyes—that has great corrective force. What happens, again, in Jewish Orthodoxy is that there is a tendency not to take that responsibility seriously because we are less an ideological religion and more of a halachic religion; the law we do have, the legal text, which obligates, and the choice always is, do we stick to the text despite the fact that it rubs against our moral sensibilities, or do we correct it surreptitiously or not?

A colleague of ours whom Shlomo and Suzanne know, Noam Zohar, gave a very controversial talk at my synagogue. It was "Does halacha discriminate against women?" Noam was very smart. He said, "Listen, before we get into it, before we actually raise the question, let's imagine that you are convinced by my arguments that halacha does discriminate against women—what will your reactions be?" He let people answer from the floor, and he got three types of answers straight away. One answer was that if it turns out that according to what we think, halacha discriminates against women, that means that our notions of morality are wrong. Another was not to ask questions like that because of what is written in the book and we have to do what the book says, this is religion. There is not even a self-correction of what we regard to be moral; the question of morality and law is not raised. The third option was that in case of disagreement we would change the law. Our duty, our religious duty, is to keep religion as moral as possible.

What Noam Zohar did then was to give sources for each of those three meta-halachic positions so that everyone had a handle to hang on-to and then proceed to prove that halacha discriminates heavily against women, but everyone was happy because they had a meta-halachic reaction in their pocket to start with. So just what submission to the will of God means is open to interpretation and open in consequences. Religious people are zealots by definition, but where is that zealotry to be applied? Is it applied to changing the law, rethinking and redescribing after a religious moral mission, or is it applied to resisting the moral impulse, as Yeshayahu Leibovich claimed religious people are obliged to do? Resisting the impulse to bring our morality to bear and do what we are told according to what we understand the text to be telling us.

Nilüfer Göle
(Department of Sociology, Bogazici University, Turkey):
We see in Sohail's paper a different image of Islam than we usually find, one that seeks to rescue Islam from the Islamicists.

Hashmi
I would like to reformulate Nilüfer's contention. It's not that we have to rescue Islam from the Islamicists, it's that we have to rescue Islam from the apathetic; I'm very happy to engage with people who challenge my reading because at least they are thinking about the Qur'an. What I am concerned about is apathetic people who don't even bother to try to find out what the Qur'an is actually saying.

Dorothee von Tippelskirch's Presentation
(Lutheran pastor, psychoanalyst)

Tolerance and the Other

I would like to begin with the way Calvin and Luther explained the sixth commandment, "Thou shall not murder." I think especially Calvin is very interesting. He cites two legal bases for this commandment. On the one hand, the human being is in the image of God, and on the other if the image of God is to remain intact, other human beings have to be sacred and inviolable for us.

The creation of mankind in the image of God is interpreted as the sanctity and inviolability of other human beings. At least in the Reform interpretation of scripture, tolerance means that God's commandment is observed. His image remains intact on condition that the "disturbing" other is not subject to my desire to eliminate him. I must bear and suffer. I must accept my responsibility for the other, for his freedom, his life, his well-being, as long as I uphold, or honor, or just "carry" him. This is a question of biblical anthropology. It is precisely what Moses, the transmitter of the Torah, did for the people of Israel. I don't know whether you remember the verses where Moses complains to God and says, "Lord, wherefore hast thou afflicted thy servant?" and "Wherefore have I not found favor at thy side, that thou lay the burden of all these people upon me. Have I conceived all these people? Have I begotten them that you should say unto me 'carry them in thine bosom as a nursing father, bear with the sucking child unto the land which . . . unto thy fathers.'" Carrying the one to whom I neither gave birth nor engendered, like Moses who carried Israel through the desert, like God himself who carried Israel on eagle's wings to Mt. Sinai, is in a sense reminiscent of the argument in your paper, Suzanne.

Tied to this is the question of *t'shueva, metanoia* (repentance), which I understand as turning back after failure to keep the commandment of tolerance, the commandment to "Love one's neighbor." I find in this verse an exegesis on the unpronounceable name of God. When we try to understand our enormous failure to obey this biblical lesson I think it will be helpful to speak of another commandment, which, in a way, is the other side of the sixth commandment, the one which says, "Thou shall not murder." This is from Leviticus, the third book in the nineteenth chapter. I quote two verses: "Thou shalt not avenge nor bear any grudge against the children of thy people. Thou shalt love thy neighbor as thyself. I am the Lord." And just a little further, nearly with the same words, there is the reference to the non-Jew in Israel, the stranger: "That the stranger that dwelleth with you shall be unto you as one born among you and Thou shalt love him as thyself for you were strangers within the land of Egypt. I am the Lord, your God." This *I* is always the tetragrammaton, the unpronounceable name of God. This is the name, according to rabbinical tradition, of the merciful God, though there is another one,

Elohim, for the God of justice. So the name of the merciful God, which we do not know how to pronounce, is interpreted through love towards the other human being, towards the other who is close and familiar, as well as the other who is strange, uncanny.

In this context I'd like to present two observations of Emmanuel Lévinas. First, he made the connection between the Hebrew word for mercy, *rachamim*, and *rechem*, which means the womb. According to Lévinas, God the merciful is God defined by motherhood. At another place in his writings, he has spoken about motherhood in terms of the merciful God, the one who carries and supports the human being with patience. It is the tolerant God who chose for himself, and for human beings, the relationship of the covenant, which is to be observed by the partners of the covenant. This name of the merciful, of the tolerant, God is above all interpreted by the commandment to love one's neighbor.

At this point I would like to refer to Sigmund Freud. I don't know whether you remember, but he spoke of the commandment "To love one's neighbor" as one of the essential ideal demands of all civilized society. He did so in his text *Civilization and its Discontents*, in the context of what he termed the "narcissism of the small difference." He claimed that the advantage of the smaller cultural area consists in directing the aggressive inclination towards outsiders. I'd like to quote Freud: "It is always possible to bind a greater group of people in love if only other people remain for the expression of aggression. The apostle Paul, having made the general love of humanity the foundation of his Christian community, the extreme intolerance of Christianity towards those who remain outside became an inevitable consequence."[3] The question of the narcissism of the small difference is that it is especially the ones who are close who are conceived of as critics of our own position. Their very closeness questions our own position and is seen as a threat to it. The nearby-stranger is understood as a dangerous one for narcissism, which means the love not for an object, in Freudian terminology, but for the subject himself—narcissism.

Some elements necessary to understand the sense of the commandment "To love the other" and its failure in the Christian West are first the narcissistic attitude of Christians who understood the Jews religiously and socially as strange neighbors or close strangers. The taxing commandment "To love" left no space for ambivalent feelings, including aggressive inclinations, within one's own community. There was a need for outsiders, to provide an outlet for aggression. I think this critique of

Freud strikes to the core of theology because as we have seen this commandment affects the name of God in a unique way. In the biblical tradition it is quite clear that it is not easier to love the one who is close than to love the one who is not close (who is a stranger) because the two are not really separated.

Two final points. First the question of "thy neighbor *as* thyself," the Hebrew word *kamocha*. From this I find the idea of a subject, a human subject. The other point pertains to the point of difference. What is the meaning of *kamocha*? Is it in the object of love? Is it a self-love, which begins with a love of self and only then looks to the other, to see whether the other is a worthy object of your self-love? Lévinas has spoken of the priority of the other relative to myself. He said, "There exists always a priority of the other relative to myself. This is the biblical contribution as a whole." Then he comes to our verse "Love your neighbor, you yourself are all this." "You are this work, you are this love." *Kamocha* doesn't refer to "your neighbor," but to all the words which precede it. The Bible is the priority of the other relative to me. "No line," he continues, "of what I have written is valid if this doesn't exist, and that is the vulnerability. Only a vulnerable subject can love his neighbor."[4] These are important words. It is no longer the narcissistic subject who does not endure the critic and the questioning with which the other confronts him. But it is the subject who exposes himself to the other and to the law, which obligates and subjects him. I thought of this in the morning when we were talking of submission in Islam. With this form of submission and relation to the other, we find the genesis of the subject. The subject is the one who undergoes this process. Of course the priority of the other is very hard and very difficult to live with, as we can see from the biblical stories of the pairs of brothers and their struggles. The priority of the other is thus grounded not in any difference between us empirically, but it cannot be defined or negotiated in relationship to our situation, but only in our different positions *quram Deo*.

This refers to the invisibility of God. Lévinas says somewhere that only an invisible God would be capable of giving ethical commandments. He talks about the invisibility, and he develops this from the quite famous verse when Moses asks God to let him see his face and he receives the answer, which is at the same time an answer and a nonanswer, you cannot see my face for no man shall see me and live. Then what he sees is God's back or behind. This seems to be the appropriate way to see God, for the other then is the one who is positioned in front of God. The commandment to "Love the other" is thus not concerned with the other who is as I am, or with whom I can make a comparison, but the other who, because of his different position in front of God, is completely different. This is a difference that is eternal.

Discussion

Wolfteich
I very much appreciate your remarks and the image of God patiently tolerating us, and the profound respect that you showed for the other. However, I can't help but question the equation of love and tolerance if I understand you correctly. I think that I am very sympathetic with the whole idea of epistemological modesty for myself, but I'm putting myself, say, in the shoes of an Evangelical Christian and I think that I could be an Evangelical Christian and love the other and respect the other and therefore want to draw that person to a taste of the truth, of salvation, of grace, and of the freedom that I have experienced in my religion. In that case, love would not necessarily mean tolerance of another's alternate position, but rather an attempt to change their position or convert them. I'm very hesitant about equating tolerance with care of another person, because I think that one can show care for a person and not necessarily be tolerant of their beliefs or positions.

Berger
To concretize this, think of the Southern Baptists who about half a year ago issued one of their missionary statements, "Go out and convert the Jews," whereupon a number of American Jewish organizations protested this as anti-Semitic. Yet, the Southern Baptist response was logical within their own scheme of things, and it was: We would be anti-Semitic if we didn't do so because otherwise we would be excluding Jews from salvation.

Fischer
Yes, but this goes back to what we said this morning about the particularism of Judaism as leading to tolerance.

Wolfteich
Or indifference.

Stone
Unless you feel you have an obligation to help other people to achieve their ends. If it is part of the divine plan.

Wolfteich
Going back to Suzanne's paper, I think I would also question the equation of forgiveness and tolerance for a similar reason, perhaps, because I think that one could show care and concern for a person, but also that forgiveness generally might imply some sort of repentance on the part of the person to renounce that position. I think that toleration does not require that, it lets the otherness stand even as it may withhold judgment.

Stone
Meaning that it allows the person to continue holding their own views and practices.

Wolfteich
Right, I think that forgiveness generally implies that the person would be self-critical as well and perhaps would try to turn, in some way, away from their wrong.

Stone
I think that is an interesting point as to whether forgiveness requires that or not, especially in the Judaic tradition, which often views forgiveness as requiring some act of repentance. I actually only meant to imply that they are structurally similar, not that they are the same.

Fisch
If we are going back to the Bible, to the bare text of the Bible, for a relationship with God, I'd like to go in a very different direction. Think of the Patriarch Abraham. The Bible tells us next to nothing about Abraham. There are two half verses basically. The words used in the Hebrew are precisely the same words used about Noah. You ask yourself, why was Abraham chosen? Now, what happens two chapters later is you get that wonderful verse where God is talking to himself and the Lord said [and it does not say to whom]:

> Shall I hide from Abraham what I am about to do, since Abraham is to become a great and populous nation and all the nations of the earth are to bless themselves by him. For I have singled him out, that

he may instruct his children and his posterity to keep the way of the Lord by doing what is just and right, in order that the Lord may bring about for Abraham what He has promised him. (Genesis 18:17–19)

One way to understand the verse is as saying, well I'm going to let Abraham in on my plans because I know he will be an obedient soldier, and will not argue at all. Then what happens is that Abraham is anything but an obedient soldier because the minute he hears about this plan, fully acknowledging the abyss between him and the Lord, Abraham says, "Will you sweep away the innocent with the guilty?" (18:23) What Abraham demands is personal justice. How can you kill the just with the wicked? God answers back with some kind of divine arithmetic of merits and demerits, in other words, if there are fifty, I'll save the city, but that is not what Abraham asks for. He asked for personal justice for the just and the wicked, and so then Abraham sort of questions God: what happens if there are forty? Will the forty perish? Where is the critical mass of righteousness below which only the wicked perish, and they stop at ten, and that is a very, very disturbing moment because you come away with the feeling that if there are only eight then they have had it, which is against the very notion of personal justice.

What God does of course is go down to Sodom and rescue four. In other words, there is a sense in which Abraham could be said to have challenged and wrestled with God and taught God a lesson in personal ethics, or brought the idea across. If you go back to that initial verse where God decides not to hide his plan from Abraham because he knows that Abraham will keep the Lord's path so that the *Lord* will do justice and righteousness—and the Hebrew tolerates that reading. If we go along with that reading (which I admit is a very radical reinterpretation), here is man standing and confronting God, wrestling with God in a way in which both learn from the process. Now if this is tolerant, if this is the way you confront the other, confront the other in a process of learning and a process of moral outrage and a process of engagement under the assumptions of belief that this is God, but not under the assumptions of blind submission. This is what I am trying to drive at. This is at the heart of the covenant of Abraham. This is a very, very different reading from most, I admit. And just as a footnote, this is precisely where Noah fails completely. No moral fury. He is told that the world is to perish and he says "Okay, you are the boss, you know what you are doing, you ask for an ark, fine, how long, how wide . . ."—that is all Noah is interested in.

This is not a joke. Read those chapters again (Genesis 6:7), that is exactly what Noah lacks, that moral fury in confronting the Lord himself, and it doesn't matter now if God was right or wrong in the debate—it is the confrontation itself. Now if that plays into toleration, facing the other, God representing the other, then it feeds into the epistemic humility learning from the other. This is the type of pluralism that I'm aiming at. I think there is a way of reading the Bible in that way.

von Tippelskirch
I have always thought that the idea of modesty came from this discussion because, if I'm not wrong and mistaken, it is the moment when Abraham says, "Although I am dust and ashes."

Hashmi
I want to follow up on what Menachem was saying because there is a very similar role given to Abraham in the Qur'an. Not that he is wrestling in the same story that you have been discussing, but he is wrestling with his own heart because he still has doubt. The story is that even after he has been chosen by God as a prophet, and even after he has been promised so many rewards to himself and his prodigy if they maintain their Islamic faith, even then Abraham says, "I still don't believe. I don't believe, God, that you can raise people from the dead." It is very interesting. God says, "You don't believe even now?" Then Abraham says, "No, I do believe, I do believe, but please tell me one more time so that I can quiet my heart, so that I can give reassurance to my heart." So it is obvious that even in this Qur'anic story he is an example of a man who has complete submission but can also harbor doubt and must grapple with it.

Stone
I love the image of divine patience and I want to juxtapose it to divine vengeance and divine justice because the issue of boundaries, especially the boundaries of tolerance, is an unavoidable subject. One of the comments that is frequently made about Jewish thought is that it is what is called the "coincidence of opposites." That there are these pairs of opposites that are in tension with one another, and they are never really resolved. When we talk of tolerance, we tend to stress one part of it and avoid the other part, and this point has been made around the table. This is wonderfully useful in providing exactly the image of that sort of coexistence of opposites, of divine mercy versus divine justice and the question of boundaries, because the two are so inextricably linked in biblical

and later in rabbinical thought. When is one supposed to be merciful? When is one supposed to be just? That is the critical moment, and it relates to the moment of actually creating a judgment and acting upon the judgment. In fact, it relates very much to the verses that you cite about "Love the stranger" because, of course, the process is to constantly narrow down and try to understand who exactly is the stranger. It cannot mean the whole world; if it means the whole world, it means that you are not exercising critical judgment. There must be something out there that is a mark of he who is not yet human, who is morally corrupt and not able to achieve a posture of civilization, of whom it is forbidden to be tolerant. So that the stranger is the other, but yet not everyone; it is another who is in some position of instantiating a level of morality that actually does trigger that commandment.

Seligman
I'd like to read a quote from R. H. Tawney, the English historian, from his *Commonplace Book*. It is one of my favorites:

> What is wrong with the modern world is that having ceased to believe in the greatness of God, and therefore the infinite smallness [or greatness, the same thing] of man, it had to invent, or emphasize, distinctions between men. It does not say, I have said ye are Gods, nor does it say all flesh is grass. It can either rise to the heights or descend to the depths. Those meet in a spiritual exultation which may be called either optimism or pessimism. What it does say is that *some* men are gods and that some flesh is grass and that the former should live on the latter combined with potatoes, *fois gras* and champagne. This is false. For what elevates or depresses, what makes man regarded from one point of view as an angel and from another an ape is not something peculiar to individuals, but characteristic of the species. Something which cannot distinguish between man, precisely because it is inherent in man.[5]

My question has to do with the Freudian notion of the narcissism of small difference, which I think is a very useful concept. My question, clearly relating to the quote, is what does the existence or nonexistence of transcendence within consciousness have to do with the narcissism of small difference and hence with the other to which Suzanne was alluding? I just read Tawney's answer. I don't know if it is the only answer or the right answer, but that is my question to you. Does the existence of God, the consciousness of God, emphasize or de-emphasize the narcissism of small difference among men and the question of the stranger?

Berger
Let me ask you, how would you go about answering that question? I don't want to be a crude empiricist, but it seems to me you could start making body counts. I'm not sure how it would come out in all of history. In this century, I think the godless have a slight moral edge, but if you take all of history, I'm not so sure.

Fischer
These issues are all related to Claire's question, and I think that the difficulty of Lévinas is in trying to redefine love. Lévinas is such a difficult thinker because he is counterintuitive in these matters. He uses metaphors that are very difficult to understand, like "fracture"—you know, that transcendence "fractures reality"—or when he talks about the priority of ethics over epistemology, over knowledge, which can be seen as a wholesale attack upon Western philosophy. In other words, the assumption that if I love you, you must become the same as I, seems to be based on a Greek idea of what being is and that we have to move towards this being and you must become as I am in the movement. In this sense I recall the epitaph with which my friend Daniel Boyarin once opened up an article. The quote is in Yiddish, but in English it reads that "Paul was the first Bolshevik," in the sense of the idea of making everybody like me. Lévinas was trying to formulate a different ideal of love, where the other can remain other and he would yet command me and remain other and that would be the genuine love and that would fracture reality, and that is where the transcendence comes in because only through a radical transcendence can we achieve such things. Now I have no idea if in reality anybody can live this ideal of Lévinas. It could be that the structures of our mind are more Greek. That is what makes Lévinas's a very radical, religious position, and if you take the Bible as saying that, then the Bible becomes a radically religious book.

von Tippelskirch
One would hope.

Seligman
This is a great surprise to some of us.

Göle

We seem to have two images of tolerance: tolerance through confronting the other, wrestling with him and so on, and the image of tolerance on the contrary, of caring, holding, and suffering. I think these are very different images. It is very different to speak of confronting the other and of wrestling with him, which is after all very conflictual, and perhaps very male-oriented. Yet in Dorothee's paper, this image of motherhood also comes up. This suffering and taking into one's arms. Suzanne has also used concepts that are very close to suffering in the idea of forgiveness, and there is something in that definition—more a kind of criticism of the modern world, of the modern personality I would say, in the definition of this baring of the soul and holding—as a strong definition of tolerance.

That is why it is very interesting that this image of wrestling and confrontation is an image of tolerance which holds very much in the modern world: distancing yourself from authority through conflict. The other image is the one that is counterintuitive and antimodern. That is why, perhaps, it is also disturbing. I was in fact astonished at Dorothee's remarks and said to myself, well here is something which tells me that religion has something to do with tolerance. Not only that there are seeds of tolerance, but almost that there is no way of being tolerant if we are not to go back to religious origins. In this sense, what you present is very contemporary. It raises very contemporary issues. Whereas imagining it only in terms of wrestling, although it seems to be stronger as a statement, it is also very modern in feeling—wrestling with authority. Dorothee's remarks are not apologetic towards modernity. They tell us to carry, to bear, to suffer together. Why should I love someone with whom I don't feel any affinity? Why should I carry you as a burden? This is a burden of religion in both senses.

Berger

I think what you, Dorothee, did was to present a Christian version of the Muslim notion of the people of the book. You said you don't want to convert Jews—fine. I presume you would say the same thing about Muslims; you might extend this to a number of other traditions. What about cannibals? What about people who practice human sacrifice? Are you still going to say you cannot go out and tell them to become like you?

Fisch

May I help? I think that the secret lies in the small differences. First of all there is an antagonist, there is a great difference between loving out of compassion and viewing the other as valuable because of the criticism and challenge he or she represents. Forget the wrestling, we are not talking antagonism, we are talking critique. People are bad critics of themselves. They are too intimately involved. For someone to be a good critic, he needs to be near and yet distant. If tolerance and comradeship and pluralism and social cohesion are to turn on epistemic humility in the sense of being able to learn from the other, the challenge has to be meaningful. The challenge will be meaningful if we share common ground. Therefore, cannibalism, Nazism, the vastly distant positions are just mere antagonisms and there is nothing to learn from them, and therefore the boundary, the epistemic boundary, will have to do with nearness in that sense.

Fischer

How can you be sure that what you engage in is criticism and not narcissism?

Fisch

There is no absolute answer to that question. If you are dogmatic, the small difference will be an embarrassment, and we know people who are dogmatic. They stand fast to their views. If just one thing is wrong, if someone is just like them but does one little thing differently, he is the real enemy, he is the real threat.

Berger

Now Menachem, that doesn't help me, because the whole small difference thing doesn't help me much. In terms of religious traditions, I would argue that from the perspective of the three Abrahamic faiths, there is nothing more distant than Buddhism. I would be enormously tolerant of Buddhism, willing to learn, certainly not interested in converting Buddhists to Christianity. There are moral crimes which are much closer to me in terms of my culture, where I would be absolutely intolerant. I think, frankly—I am sticking my neck out—I think one can be epistemologically modest and be extremely arrogant morally. That I think is the solution, not the argument from small difference.

Fisch

When I talk of epistemic humility, I'm talking of humility about one's own moral system. About our sense of the good and the bad and what God wants of us and what is proper and what is improper.

Fischer

Would you apply this epistemic humility to Nazism?

Fisch

No, because it is not near. It is too diametrically opposed. It is blatant.

Stone

What about idolatry?

Fisch

The *Meiri* showed the way with idolatry. Idolatry gets redefined. I don't think Nazism can get redefined into comradeship the same as *gedurim bedarchei hadat* ("enlightened by the ways of religion").

Estruch

I can quite understand and I agree one can, and perhaps ought, to be morally arrogant. But I think one should not be morally arrogant in the name of the gospel or in the name of the Qur'an.

Fisch

Are you then suggesting using morality as a critique of the gospel or Qur'an?

Estruch

That is perhaps too strong a statement, yet it is not because of anything in the gospel that I am against cannibalism.

Berger

I am tempted to tell a story on moral relativism recounted by James Morris: When General Napier conquered the Singh, which is now part of Pakistan, he did what the British usually did in India. The British let the natives do whatever they wanted to do except certain things which they found intolerable. One of these was *sutee*, widow burning. The story Morris tells is that when Napier promulgated this ruling, forbidding the burning of widows, a company of Brahmins came to see him and said that he could not forbid *sutee* and he said yes I can and I have. They replied, no you can't do this; it is an ancient tradition of our people. Whereupon, Napier appeared completely unfazed and said it is an ancient tradition of my people that when people burn a woman alive we hang them. Let us all follow our traditions. This is what I mean by moral arrogance. I like it. He didn't try to convert at all, he just didn't let them burn widows.

Fisch

I read some letters written by Jesuits back to the Vatican from New Guinea. They are full of epistemic humility, frantically asking for arguments to convince the natives that ritual cannibalism was bad and that the proper way to treat the dead was to let them rot in the earth rather than for all the sons to drink his blood and the widow to eat his heart and keep it in the family.

MENACHEM FISCH'S PRESENTATION

Jewish Sovereignty and Problems of Pluralism

My presentation has two parts. The first part outlines a position that is not inherently religious. This needs to be put on the table. One does not have to be particularly religious to value a plurality of conflicting positions for the way they challenge and enrich one's own. This was a position that was put forth originally by Sir Karl Popper, in the *Open Society and Its Enemies*, in 1945. It is an idea that I like very much.

It is a position I argue for its own sake, claiming that it is one that halachic Judaism is capable, in my view, of developing out of its own texts. The argument runs, very briefly, as follows. Minimal tolerance, in the sense of undertaking silently to put up with objectionable norms of conduct, is easily accommodated by Judaism, and I suspect it is easily accommodated by most religions. I also caution that tolerance, minimal tolerance per se, does not promise much. It promises little more than to ensure that communities that disagree with each other don't shoot at each other over the fences. It breeds disinterest. No dignity is involved; no worth is ascribed to the other. It is a sullen, silent, inactive, de facto acceptance of someone who happens to be, unfortunately, there. It gives no incentive for forming a society, for seeking out other people, for wanting a plurality. It is a position that is incapable of grounding a sense of solidarity. Moreover, it will not suffice for religious people who find themselves in positions of power, and that is actually my prime concern.

Earlier I tried to make a case for the idea that governmental executives cannot get away with merely turning a blind eye on the objectionable. The role of the sovereign in Western democracies, which is the form of society most welcome for the religious as member communities, is to take active responsibility for the safety, the well-being, and the flourishing of all legitimate forms of conduct, including those held as blatantly sinful from the perspective of your own private religious point of view. So here, mere toleration of the other is not enough; he needs to be valued. The question is, how can genuinely religious people value and actively seek to assist and promote what they consider sin and heresy? I think that's the $64,000 question for the group.

I would argue that halacha, Jewish law, as it is perceived today by the vast majority of its practitioners, not including Shlomo Fischer, is incapable of doing so. I think that the example of the chief rabbi, Bakshi Doron, proves that. I think his halachic reasoning is impeccable, and just imagine the nightmare of the person asking him about whether one is allowed as a travel agent to cater to the idolater. I think this brings out the basic problematic. There is a paradox here, certainly for Jews, that the form of government that is most desirable for us as member communities is precisely the form of government which is most awkward for us to run. Since halachic Judaism in the State of Israel is in the business of thinking through problems of sovereignty and running the lives of others, these problems are very, very real, certainly for me.

The Popperian position has not primarily to do with the moral duty to defend individual autonomy or with the moral obligation to keep out of one's neighbor's hair. Popperian tolerance, if I may call it so, entails such liberal visions of autonomy, but ultimately rests upon epistemological rather than moral or metaphysical arguments. The belief systems and lifestyles of all communities are tolerated by members of the open society not merely out of a moral or legal obligation, but out of a realization that the environment of a plurality of engaging, especially conflicting, voices is the setting in which one's own voice is best and most effectively articulated and developed. Now the obvious advantage of grounding ideas of tolerance in this way is that the arguments for them involve far less by way of ontological, ideological, psychological, moral, and metaphysical assumptions about the dignity of man, the rights of people, their image, and so on and so forth. It allows you to get around a lot of religious problematic in that sense. Most importantly, in my opinion, it sidesteps the entire issue of fundamental rights, an idea (and I may have to retract this after studying Shlomo Fischer's work, because what you said yesterday was an eye-opener to me and I need to read more about it), that halachic Judaism has great difficulty accommodating as a given. Shlomo claims differently with the notion of natural law, and I am very excited by that notion.

In any event, the acknowledgement of humankind's profound fallibalism, especially in the public sphere, of the fundamental time-boundedness and context-dependent nature of all social planning, coupled with the almost built-in instability of those very contexts, permits little more than that life, especially social and political life, is exceedingly complex and unpredictable and that the chances of us making a mess of things are enormous. With this view even religious people would agree. The upshot is an epistemic hesitance, a modesty, an openness and awareness that we are poor critics of our own plans and strategies, and things are best done piecemeal. That dovetails nicely with what Suzanne said yesterday—that other viewpoints are not merely to be tolerated, but to be highly valued not for their own intrinsic worth but for their capacity to challenge our own by highlighting the flaws and shortcomings of our own positions. Though this position has real advantages for the religious person, it can only work for such religions for which that kind of epistemic modesty, hesitancy, and self-doubt are a real option, and here, as I said, I can only speak for halachic Judaism.

In my work on the formative texts of halachic Judaism, I have argued for the existence of a fundamental disagreement between two halachic schools of thought which I have dubbed, for want of better terms, traditionalist and antitraditionalist. Briefly, the two schools differ gravely with regard to the limits of legislative discretion granted to the halachic authority of each generation. The halachic authority of each generation has both judiciary and legislative powers. Traditionalists view all former rulings as absolutely binding and limit halachic discretion to answering new and formerly unanswered questions. In other words, the halachic system is viewed, strongly viewed, as a cumulative body of law which develops, at most, where lacuna exists. There is no rethinking, no self-correcting element except for troubleshooting for holes.

Now antitraditionalists view all former rulings as binding too; that should not be questioned. But the Parliament, the legislative, halachic authority, is not merely permitted or has the power, but is encouraged and its job is, to view the halachic legacy as an object of serious reflection, but not to limit halachic discretion in the same way as the antitraditionalist. It is motivated by a religiously, theologically grounded, and perpetual self-doubting that the will and the word of God are deeper than any one generation can fathom. Circumstances change in ways that no one can think of, our ideas and moral understanding change, the world is shifting and being created by us and what God wants from us is to do our best. Therefore, this type of self-doubting is further deepened in the context of religion. This is what is nice about it. It is fueled and motivated by the sense of the great distance between God's will and knowledge and the meaning of the text and our ability to fathom all of this. Therefore, the halachic authority is permitted and encouraged, actually, to view its own halachic legacies as the object of keen criticism. I cannot and shall not burden you with the sort of in-house debate as to the reading of the texts themselves. This work is under review at the moment—two of the reviewers are actually sitting around the table—there has been lots of disagreement, there has been lots of agreement, and this is a controversial position. I am not a "certainty-wallah" about the uncertainty mechanism. This is a thesis I am still willing to defend strongly and deeply and truly and as a religious person, not merely as a commentator on the text.

The antitraditionalist, talmudic position provides two very valuable resources for the issue at hand. First of all, if I am right in analyzing the halachic position at the moment with sinners such as idolaters and secular Jews, in order for a halachically committed Jew to sit at the government table and partake in the running of a Western, multicultural democracy, the order of the day has to be halachic change; something here, the attitude to sin, needs to be rethought. The antitraditionalist position allows for rethinking halacha. That is the first resource, which is very, very important. It allows for rethinking halacha not in a concealed way of making believe that the text that we used to read differently really means something else, but to look the text in the eye and say, "We understand that this is exactly what it meant, and it has to be changed." I think this voice is present and out there in the open at the very foundational *tannaitic* level of the talmudic text.[6]

The other resource that the antitraditionalist option offers is the methodology, the sort of learning environment, the discursive environment, in which the antitraditionalist finds himself. There are some very striking talmudic passages to do with the idea of the antitraditionalist who enters halachic polemics not for the sake of defeating the enemy or showing the strength of his own position, but for the sake of genuinely learning something and in the end agreeing to change his own position. A person like that seeks out opponents who disagree with him. He surrounds himself with a plurality of conflicting voices. There is a resource of pluralism, at least in principle of pluralism, and a resource for halachic change, both of which should be the order of the day in Israel today.

I'll use these last two minutes for two points Suzanne raised yesterday which I think are very important. First of all, she acknowledges the fact that there is a plurality of voices, but she claims it's an in-house pluralism. There is, she claims, no disagreement beyond the limits of the community, and therefore, if you are talking about granting value and worth to sinners and heretics, it's a different order of a plurality.

The second point she made is that skepticism and self-doubt go hand in hand with disorder and therefore it is okay at the theoretical level (certainly those familiar with halachic texts know that disagreement is encouraged and so forth), but you are supposed to cease all dispute the minute a ruling is made. When it comes to halacha, a practical halacha, what one is supposed to do once it's ruled is to line up behind the decision and abide by it. If that is not the case, disorder kicks in. Now I'd like to contest that last point. I think disorder kicks in—and the talmudic texts are aware of it—precisely when no self-doubt is around. The one place in the Talmud where a disagreement is supposed to fragment the Torah in two is precisely the most antitraditionalist text, where, of course, since no one is a perfect transmitter, no one is a perfect receiver of tradition, there are always partings of ways and some people end up committing to a tradition which is different from others. Precisely because the traditionalist cannot self-correct what he has, and he has no procedures for shelving a tradition, fragmentation occurs. I would argue exactly the opposite, that the traditionalist's rigid obligation to the tradition is the recipe for disorder and chaos and fragmentation precisely because it is not self-correcting. There is more unity in the world of modern physics (which is a prime example of antitraditionalism and plurality of opinion) than in Orthodox Judaism, which is fragmented into any number of sub-communities who won't talk to each other.

The other point is the limits of in-house debate. Beith Shammai and Beith Hillel, I won't burden you with those, but the two sparring schools of thought were paradigmatic of halachic controversy at the *tannaitic* level, and disagreed on very fundamental points of halachic conduct, to the point that they are not allowed, or rather the question was raised whether they were allowed, to marry each other or not.[7] The limits of these debates are pretty wide in the talmudic text themselves, although they are bona fide.

Orthodox Judaism wouldn't enter into dialogue with and value Roman Catholics, for example, in order to rethink how to shake the *lulav* [the palm branch used ritually during the Feast of Tabernacles] or how many times to wrap the phylacteries around the arm. Those won't be the questions we can learn from them. However on questions to do with the public sphere, on the questions to do with the quality of life, there is much to learn.

Discussion

Berger

As Menachem knows, I was enormously impressed with what he said in Berlin last year. I have been thinking about it ever since, and I am enormously in sympathy with the sort of spirit he represents. I want to make some comments directly on this and then expand on something briefly which I said yesterday. What I like so much is this whole notion of epistemic modesty. To what extent this is halachic Judaism, I'm not of course in a position to judge—I will take his word for it. What I find interesting is there are some very interesting parallels here, it seems to me, to Protestantism. What Paul Tillich calls the Protestant Principle is, I think, coming from a very different corner yet going in the same direction. My own understanding of the Protestant notion of justification by faith alone goes in the same direction, and whether old Martin Luther would have liked this interpretation or not, again, is another question. I think there are in the Protestant tradition very interesting parallels to Menachem's approach, which would be useful to pursue.

But even though I find this very promising, I want to come back to something I said yesterday. I want to enlarge on it slightly because it troubles me, not in terms of Menachem's presentation, but in the general issue of epistemic modesty, and that is the issue of moral judgment. Actually, it is a fairly recent insight of mine, which came about a year and a half ago, and it surprised me. I was sort of in a state of neo-infantilism, asking myself again, "What do I really know?" when you get away from direct sense experiences—I mean when I have a toothache, I know with absolute certainty that I have a toothache, but that's not very interesting philosophically. Beyond that, I have long known, and certainly Popper fits into that beautifully, that anything that has to do with what I think I know as a social scientist is probabilistic. There is no certainty in science. This has long been clear to me. When it comes to religious affirmations, I believe there is no certainty, which is precisely why one talks about faith and not about knowledge. The only thing, other than the toothache, that I am absolutely certain of is moral judgments. Absolutely certain. We only have to read the newspaper these days, it seems to me, to verify that principle. There is nothing in the world, no argument could be made to me, which would make me approve of what Milosevic's troops are doing in Kosovo. I am absolutely certain that this is evil. Now you can then make arguments as a social scientist that this is time-bound, that I am a Western-educated person with a bourgeois mentality and so on, that all of this is historically and socially relative—I would say I don't give a damn. I know that this is so. My problem with Menachem's argument, which again, I very much like, is how does one relate epistemic modesty or epistemic uncertainty or skepticism, with what I think is very important, which is moral certainties. I thought I should put that on the table because I think it should trouble all of us.

Seligman
Why are these moral certitudes so certain to us? Because, I would argue, they are us. Our identity is tied up to them. We cannot be otherwise. If we did not have them, we would not be who we are. This is an important element and brings us to an aspect of religion which we haven't touched on at all, that religion is intimately bound up with our identity, with our place in the world. And so when you said that an epistemological foundation for tolerance gives us something that moral or philosophical foundations don't, that is true, but it is also weaker in a very different way because the moral and philosophical foundations are bound up with precisely that aspect of self in the world. What makes moral certitudes so certain to us is that we cannot be otherwise. That is precisely the certitude of it.

Fisch
I would acknowledge everything you and Peter say. One thing about modern man, and this is a modern development and a modern challenge, is that we are wary about our identities and we are wary about our certitudes and we as historians look back on our development and morality and see changes despite the certitude we feel. Our concepts of man, our concepts of the good and the bad, our concepts of solidarity do shift and change. The way the Popperian goes about understanding this is to organize a nonviolent forum for the violent exchange of ideas in which we sit around the table and all we agree to is to the principle of tolerance. That is the way parliaments operate.

Stone

I would like to add to Peter and Adam's remarks. I do think that this is the critical question because it is the question of the capacity of religion to criticize modernity rather than the opposite, and we don't want to lose that capacity because then you don't add anything to the discussion. We might as well collapse tradition into modernity. The second question that I think is the one that Adam is raising is not only the capacity of religion to criticize modernity, but the capacity of the tradition to stay as its own tradition and not leap into someone else's tradition. To an extent, tolerance has the capacity, if you really extend epistemic humility to voices past the normative community and then even past that to the large community of the universe—you risk going from one tradition to another tradition. That, I think, is something that we have seen happen before. Allegory was the way to get from one tradition to another tradition in the past. Law and certain kinds of ways of interpreting a text are actually the constraints that keep one from moving from one tradition to another. The notion of precedent, for example, is one way of not moving from one tradition to another, as opposed to the allegorical method which allows one to make certain kinds of leaps. It's that notion of discovering something in the text, even if in fact one has invented it, that creates and maintains the traditional view of constraints of some kind and of staying within them. The traditional versus the antitraditional argument that you are speaking about could also be recast in some way as one in which there is the mentality or veneration of early masters. That is, in some way, what the debate is, and I'm wondering whether you are pushing it into something more than dwarfs on the shoulders of giants, in which case you are risking going past the discourse.

Fisch

What I think we should bear in mind is Adam's very touching quote [see p. 149], describing Sarajevo with a public sphere and each retaining his and her identity going back to a traditional community with its rituals, with its beliefs, with its texts, with its canon, and yet meeting in the public sphere. Managing their lives, acknowledging the presence, disagreeing with the theological foundations of the other, and yet acknowledging their presence because there is more to gain from living side by side, certain of your own roots, with a rich communal life and yet open, not insulated. Insulation has other dangers. To be dwarfs on the shoulders of giants is one form of epistemic humility, but one must also not be dwarfed by the tradition and afraid to take a stand. As you know we get to a situation such as that facing Jewish family law where the religious person feels bound on the altar of halacha, powerless to do what they feel in their heart of hearts is morally and religiously right. You stand before God saying, you are the boss so I can't exercise my identity. The idea I'm talking about is a way of exercising our moral identities within religion. Merely acknowledging the fact that we change, that the world changes, and new challenges arise, new understandings of old challenges arise, is the living force of religion. I'm not preaching a new kind of religion to anyone but my own co-religionists, but I think this voice, with which I am passionately aligned, is a voice alive in the tradition, though there are other voices there as well. The beauty of the talmudic text, which speaks of its pluralism, is that it is polyphonic even with regard to the understanding of its own project. This is a meta-halachic, not a halachic, a meta-halachic disagreement.

Fischer
I'd like to move this on to a slightly different issue. I think that what Menachem is arguing is that epistemic modesty is part of the identity of Talmudic Judaism. That is part of the ethos of it and it is part of the identity. This is a persistent strain in modern Jewish thought. You get it in Mendelssohn's *Jerusalem*, where he argues that, because Judaism is a *Gesetz Religion*, because it is a religion of laws, you can therefore think whatever you want, and this then tends to identify traditional Judaism with the openness of modern society because of its epistemic modesty. I would say that many, many people, many talmudists, many traditional talmudists, would say that Menachem has put his finger on a very real moment in the tradition. Is it the only moment? No.

Moreover, if you go to any religious leader in Israel or in America and you say, "You have two choices. In the face of modernity, in the face of modernization" (and I think modernization here is a crucial issue because modernization puts Judaism, and it seems to me other religious traditions, on the defensive), "you have a choice, you can either have a new, improved, constantly improving Judaism with the risk that exposure to new ideas, to secular ideas, will undermine the foundations of the younger generation of the faith, and weaken the community. Or you can have mediocre, second-class religion *but* it includes everybody. Everybody, because they have these blinders on, and so remain within the religion and accept it and go to heaven, etc." Most people would say, "Well, it is very interesting what you have to say, Menachem," but everybody, I can't imagine anybody from Bakshi Doron to anybody, everyone would say: "Well, it is very interesting what you have to say, Menachem, but no thank you. We would prefer our mediocre religion, where we make sure that everybody stays inside. In this way we protect the boundaries and we protect the tradition." In other words, putting this in respect to Sarajevo, you know needless to say—I think that is what Rusmir indicated—that the Sarajevo that Adam quoted doesn't exist anymore. It seems to have had very specific premodern conditions that enabled it to exist. Modernity, which creates nation-states, nationalism, markets, also created new fears. People are afraid, in the face of nationalism and markets, in the face of science, and so in consequence religious communities close in on themselves. I think that halacha is self-correcting but that self-correction is concealed. Yet what is the advantage of rendering explicit the self-correcting mechanism over and above the casuistic method which conceals the self-correction?

Fisch

I'll start with the second question. The advantage is that it grounds pluralism. It grounds epistemic modesty as an explicit driving force. With a surreptitious antitraditionalism disguised as traditionalism, you will not be able to acknowledge the other in the very same way. What the antitraditionalist, meta-halachic position offers is precisely what we need as sovereigns, not as member communities. In the mediocre religion, everyone goes to heaven and nobody asks too many questions, a very comfortable, very easy, a deep sense of religious obligation precisely because we are forced to do what we do. It is fine for a member community, and exilic Judaism has survived perfectly for two thousand years precisely because of that. The Zionist revolution changed that. There is a decisive moment now, over and above the academic fascination in finding this very modern epistemology in the texts of late antiquity, but the relevance to this conference and to Israel today is precisely the problem of sovereignty, which doesn't get solved with that type of blanket religion. Therefore, I perfectly agree that no halachic authority will take this as an option, and that is why you and I and others are talking to headmasters and yeshiva directors and we have to get this position sneaked in surreptitiously in order for it to come to the surface. I am being very devious now using it.

CHAPTER THREE

The Third Dialogue

On Power and Historical Contexts

The final dialogues deal, in different ways, with the historical contexts in which all religious interpretations (including those bearing on tolerance) are structured. This theme is opened by Rusmir Mahmutćehajić's presentation of religion in the Balkans, which becomes almost a metaphor for religion in the modern world. In Bosnia (and Croatia and Serbia and other Balkan societies) religion came, in his assessment, to serve ethno-nationalist and secular ideologies and as such lost its traditional religious dimensions. This, claims Mahmutćehajić, is the fate of religion in modernity in general, where religion becomes but a sentimental prop for very different modes of mobilizing identities. In this move, he notes, the traditional tolerant aspects of religion, rooted in their transcendent orientation, are lost.

To great extent, both Nasr Abu Zayd and Nilüfer Göle's presentations follow this line of thought within different Islamic contexts. Abu Zayd stresses again and again how the specific internal Islamic power relations and historical conjunctures always influenced the process of textual interpretation and hermeneutics. He notes how impossible it is to develop an understanding of any one tradition's attitudes towards tolerance and towards the other without historicizing the contexts of interpretation.

Göle's account of Islam in contemporary Turkey can be taken as a case study of these more general remarks, where the historical context of a strong secular state and Western-looking elites provides a very particular arena for the growth of an Islamic ideology as a form of protest based on lifestyle demands. It is this demand which, she shows, is itself transforming the public sphere of a classic secular polity and with it, the terms of tolerance and pluralism in society.

Joan Estruch's intervention and F. W. Graf's presentation both continue to focus our concern on the intersection of religion and modernity and on the problem of sameness and difference and how they are constructed in modernity and within religious discourse. Estruch is most concerned with the sameness of monotheistic traditions and perhaps therefore their need for tolerance (as we again encounter Sigmund Freud's "narcissism of the small difference"). Discussion of this thesis and disagreement with its assumptions provides the segue into Graf's understanding of Protestant theology as a resource for tolerance, by stressing the extremely circumscribed possibilities for human knowledge or goodness. Focusing as well on what he terms the "structural ambivalence" of the nineteenth- and twentieth-century Protestant tradition in Germany, he too argues for how broader historical contexts structure different and emergent interpretive paths. The dialogues end with a discussion of these points, especially as they pertain to other religious traditions (Judaism and Islam in their ambivalent relation to modernity for example). The more analytic summation of these insights and the attempt to bring them into a more unitary understanding of tolerance and tradition is left for the following chapters.

Rusmir Mahmutćehajić's Presentation

Modern Ideology and Religious Tolerance

You know that the war against Bosnia began in 1992. At that time, I was engaged in almost all important discussions dealing with the situation in Bosnia during the years just before the war. In 1991, it was impossible for any to foresee the possibility of war, even though we could see artillery placed around Sarajevo. Maybe this is comparable with the German intellectuals before the Holocaust, I do not know. What we cannot understand, we should experience. Only a year later, after many discussions of this kind, all these intellectuals could witness the beginning of what was the forty-four months of the siege of Sarajevo and the killing of 250,000 men in Bosnia, and the expulsion of two million people. It was the Bosnian experience. But through almost a thousand years we could witness quite a different situation in Bosnia. Bosnia was a community of communities, a community of different sacred communities. It survived for almost two thousand years, but it could not survive the last decade of the twentieth century. This enigma is, from my point of view, of basic importance. It is paradigmatic for understanding what we are discussing here.

How was this possible? The situation in Kosovo that Professor Berger mentioned is unavoidable, but who could believe a year ago that this is what we would witness now? It is worse than you know. Yet there is no level of rational discourse, or explanation, for what took place. In the past one could witness, in the reality of the Bosnian villages, Bosnian towns, and history that Muslims, Christians, and Jews could live together. They could tolerate each other, but how was it possible? What was the reason? While I have no clear answer, I would like to bring to your attention one Bosnian word that I would like to introduce, and though I myself have investigated the history of the word, I couldn't find its translation or its explanation. The word is *gehuta*, often translated as "wrong," but this is an approximate translation. All Bosnian children from the traditional schools learn this word. The etymological origin is the same as "sin," but it is quite different. "Sin" is, in this understanding, something that is determined, but *gehuta* is the permanent presence of a possibility to violate our connections with all that is in and about us. On this basis we can say that in Bosnia you will find that putting garbage in the river is *gehuta*, but to say a harsh word to anybody else is also *gehuta*. *Gehuta* was emphasized also in the case of members of other traditions. We, as children, learned that not being respectful toward those of other religions is *gehuta*. For us, it was the deepest content of our being. It touched on the deepest content of particular communities and the predominant content of each Bosnian inhabitant.

In the Qur'an you will find the following sign: "Our God and your God are one and the same." On this basis, Jews are on the path toward the same God, Muslims are on a different path toward the same God. Bosnia had its own Christian church rejecting the authority of the Pope and of Constantinople. This Christian Church was connected with many Gnostic elements, and Bosnian history will show that the Church included heretics; even Muslim Gnostics were included from the earliest period. Through all this period—from the eleventh century on—we can see that different Christian denominations were present in Bosnia: Catholics, Orthodox, and Bosnian Christians (they used this name and only later were they called Bogomiles). In the thousand years since, this religious understanding presented that core or essence of internal pluralism. Yet, by the beginning of the nineteenth century, especially in the second part of the century, ethno-national ideologies began to emerge in this region. These ethno-national ideologies were in conflict with this essential presence of deep religiosity in this region, in Bosnia. And especially two ethno-national ideas of nation-states, of Serbia and Croatia, become the two poles of development in the nineteenth and twentieth centuries. In all these ideologies, religion was incorporated as a subordinated component. In this way, the religious communities, step by step, came to doubt their central religious content. They became instruments of ethno-national ideology, and the Bosnian religious pluraformity became a most ugly thing in the eyes of their ethno-national ideologies. We are now in a situation where this old tradition of pluraformity in Bosnia cannot survive. Only on the basis of the third-party enforcer can it be kept, maybe, for some time if we will not find a chance for a new breath of understanding of tradition; it will be a factor of destabilization and further sufferings of the people there.

Discussion

Berger

You began with a question, "How can one imagine certain horrors?" and that is a question that keeps repeating itself whether one discusses the Holocaust or one discusses other monstrous events in history, and I'd like to reverse the question. How is it possible that occasionally such horrors do *not* happen? This is an anthropological issue. Here again, I'm afraid that I am rather Protestant. I believe in original sin—as one friend of mine said, original sin is the only Christian doctrine which doesn't require faith; it is empirically observable. So I think the question is why are the murderous passions which human beings naturally have sometimes kept under control? I think maybe in the case of Bosnia, I don't know its history in the earlier period, but say from the middle of the nineteenth century and on until now, Bosnia was ruled by four regimes, each of which had an interest in suppressing nationalism. The Ottomans, the Hapsburgs, the Royal Yugoslav regime which had just created a fiction of Yugoslavia, and Tito—each one had an interest in suppressing nationalism. When that was no longer the case, then various gangsters in Serbia and Croatia had an interest in exploiting it. It was not all that difficult to mobilize the murderous passions which are always there. That is how I would answer the question "How is it possible?"

Abu Zayd
I think suppression is the key word, or the key concept here. Suppression means not allowing different aspects of identity to express themselves in a free way. So you should be either a Serbian or a Croat or a Kosovar or an Albanian as if there is contradiction between the ethnical aspect of identity and the religious aspect of identity. This channeling of identity into one dimension, by suppression, I think can explain much.

Hashmi
I actually have a couple of things to say; one directly relates to what Nasr just said. As I was listening to Rusmir's presentation, it reminded me of my own background from the Indian subcontinent, where there was a very similar situation in 1947. People were confronted with the necessity of taking on constructed identities, and especially in the Punjab, where we had three, at least three major, religious communities—Sikhs, Muslims, Hindus—living side by side for centuries. Partition forced individuals to all of a sudden become, sometimes, what they didn't feel.

My second point: As a political scientist I go to conferences attended by political scientists who are trying to keep religion out of their discussion as much as possible, but it is interesting that religion keeps creeping in over and over again, especially in the realm of political philosophy or political ethics, and one interesting area in which Islam has been mentioned over and over again recently, as a result of what happened in the Balkans, is with regard to containing ethnic pluralism within one state. All of a sudden I hear the *millet system* being brought up again as a model. I find this remarkable as someone who has worked on humanitarian intervention, because the notion of humanitarian intervention evolved in the late nineteenth century precisely in opposition to the millet system. The millet system was supposed to be inherently oppressive, and inherently incapable of protecting the rights of minorities. And yet now, there is a wistful longing for the days when people could actually live together as distinct communities but within the sort of overarching sovereign framework. Rusmir, I would be interested just to hear your thoughts about the validity of that system. Do you see any merits to it or do you see that it is the basis of all the current evils in the Balkans?

Mahmutćehajić

In some ways this is another story, a new lecture. I would not like to say that Bosnian history was the history of paradise, but the different communities did survive and maintain their differences. What, from my point of view, is one of the worst problems we are facing now is that religious communities have lost their strong connection with their center. We now have religious organizations without God. This is the predominant situation. Religious organizations are now—you can see this especially in this region—the first instrument in the hands of ideology, they cannot resist ethno-national, ideological programs. You will see a great need all over this region, especially now, a great show of religious symbols, but almost empty of any essential religious content. Religion has become an appendix of these ethno-national programs. Religion is not formally suppressed, thank God now, but large and developing religious organizations have lost their essential content. They become a kind of political structure, or ideological structure. Sacredness is multiplicity. What we have now is large religious organizations without this sacred content.

Göle

Rusmir's paper was the strongest defense of the premodern tie to the concept of sacred as the very foundation of multiplicity that we have yet heard. It is not the millet system that Rusmir is defending, but he is really defending very strongly this need, this precondition, for multiplicity as a premodern tie to sacredness. I think this is something we see in terms of the aims of this project—how religion can be a source of criticism of modernity and a source of the public good. This is a very strong argument, both historically and intellectually. It is not the millet system. I think that is the wrong question here. Although it is a good question in the sense that we go back also to the idea of empires in order to resist nationalism, to go beyond nationalist positions. In his paper, also, the criticism of nationalism, although it is not so intrinsic to the paper, appears almost as a consequence. It is really a kind of metaphor for the premodern period. It is a very strong criticism of modernity, as the collapse of religious multiplicity is related to the rise of nationalism. What I would like to know is why this model couldn't resist, why it couldn't perpetuate itself. Is it really only a problem coming from Western or other strategies, or was there something more intrinsic? I think if we know more about the Bosnian case, maybe we will understand more the evils that are intrinsic to our modernity.

Seligman
As usual, I can do no more than repeat other people's comments, but I would like to start in response to Peter's comment on original sin. Twenty-five years ago I was one of Shlomo's *Bolsheviki*, as a member of the kibbutz, and I remember vividly a discussion at five-thirty in the morning in the garage before going out to work, about what we are doing in the kibbutz. Are we trying to invent a new man? Are we trying to suppress all evil in man? Or are we trying to provide institutional frameworks that will limit the ability to express the evil that is there (not that we used these terms)? I thought of that when I was thinking of Peter's general intervention, of Nasr's intervention, and of what Nilüfer is saying now, because all these comments really try to isolate sociologically those social conditions that permitted the existence of this pluraformity or plurality within unity. The answer, so far, seems to have to do with the suppression of these evil impulses.

What Nilüfer has done is to remind us that in modernity religion becomes defensive, and when religion becomes defensive, something happens that connects the sacred, negatively, to certain aspects of modernity. In other words, there might be something in the way religion rethinks the sacred when it defends itself against modernity that is already pulling apart or making it more and more difficult to supply whatever those more specific preconditions that allowed the pluraformity before.

Mahmutćehajić
When we are speaking about religion in modernity, or in the post-Renaissance age, it is quite obvious that religion has been reduced to morality and sentimentality. This is characteristic of almost all traditions. But in this way, for example, the real situation in Bosnia of plurality in confrontation with modernity didn't have the possible level of intellectual discourse to explain and to defend itself. This is the predominant problem with religion in the world today. Religion is predominantly the doubt corresponding to the intellectual response to modernity. This is my feeling.

Fischer
Okay, you know, I live in Israel which also used to be, since 1517, part of the Ottoman Empire. Hence I think, not a little bit, about successor states (Israel, Palestine, Lebanon) of the Ottoman Empire. It seems to me that toleration seems to work in multinational empires. I also think

of Spain, where there was a very clear Erasmanian option in the sixteenth century in Spanish Catholicism which was not taken, and it went someplace else and Spanish Catholicism went in an opposite direction. There was an argument in the Court and in Spanish Catholicism for a tolerant Catholicism, for an open Catholicism, and that wasn't taken, and Spain became a nation-state instead of a multinational empire.

Now it seems to me that the problem with multinational empires is that they are not democratic. I think there is an inherent connection between nationalism and democracy. There is a tragic connection, but it is an inherent connection. The connection is that in multinational empires, ultimate order, ultimate cosmic and hence political order, is not tied to the immanent aspects of people's existence. What happens in modernity is people demand that those immanent aspects become tied to ultimate order. The easiest way to do that is through nationalism. Of course, that is the most primordial aspect, you know; your color, your hair, the way you look, your nose, your language, your customs, your mother's milk, all that becomes tied to ultimate political order and the like. By contrast, the Ottoman Empire and other multinational empires can be compared to a Las Vegas casino. The metaphor is that everybody is playing poker and shooting dice, and the casino (the empire) provides the table, the drinks, the waiters, the mineral water, and they take the 20 percent off the top, and that is how the empire works. Everybody plays the game, and everybody—Jews, Christians, Muslims, whatever—is playing the game and the empire takes its cut off the top. When you have a concept that ultimate order is in the social order and not in your inner life, it is easier for religion to be an absolute, to be ultimate. If we return to what Dorothee said yesterday about the Levinasian moment of the transcendent, we realize too that there are certain sociological conditions which encourage the absolute or the transcendent and don't permit religion to become ideology. The modern period encourages religion to become ideology because of the connection to nationalism and democracy and the consequent loss of the transcendent.

Fisch

I'd like to throw out another notion on the table, for there is something else about religion which needs to be said, which needs to be understood properly. Where I think the religious have an advantage over the irreligious is in the messianic moment. We have to tread carefully. The idea of the messianic moment, or the messianic tension, is not in the messiah arriving, that is when it collapses. The messianic tension, as long as it is alive, sees the genuine religious person living or existing under the cloud of life and society, and the existing realm is basically flawed. There is a fallibility built into that tension on both levels. There is a fallibility as to what we imagine to be the perfect state of affairs to which we strive, and there is also the obvious fallibility of knowing that the way we live is probably not the best possible and therefore given to questioning. This is a resource religions have which can fuel again, and I come back to the same point all the time, rethinking.

NASR ABU ZAYD'S PRESENTATION

Hermeneutics and Power

I would like to make some general comments because I feel that though we are able to see the world in the eyes of modernity, we are unable to see it religiously. It seems that modernity has been presented as an evil, a monster that came out and pushed religion to be defensive. Religion had to surrender itself. Are we really discussing such a dichotomy of the devil and angel? Are we not also able to find the devil in our own religious traditions? As I am Muslim, not even a liberal or enlightened Muslim, just traditional Muslim, a very Orthodox Muslim, I can easily quote and memorize very important verses of the Qur'an and of the Prophet which emphasize tolerance, human rights, women's rights, equality between male and female—it is not hard to do. One of the God's names in Islam is "Tolerant," *Al-halil*. In this case, however, I have concealed, or at least not brought to your attention the other names of God, the names of "Mighty," the "Torturer," the "Destroyer." If I would like to show you the bright image of Islam, I would do this very easily without any problem. More than that, I would go to the anthropology of Islam to show you how Islam from the very earliest moment recognized Christianity and recognized Judaism. When the Prophet Mohammed had his first vision, his first experience with the angel who came to him, he had the suspicion that it was false, that this was the devil and that he was possessed by the devil, and he retreated back to his wife, trembling and afraid, and she tried to calm him down. But look to the story—I am reading here a very classical Islamic authority—and his wife took him to one of her cousins, and this cousin was a Christian priest. They wanted to consult the Christian priest about what kind of vision this was. Was it the devil? Was it evil? Was it an angel? And the story goes, in Islamic tradition, this man, who was able to read the gospel in Arabic and in Hebrew, when he listened to the story of Mohammed said, "Well, this is the same angel who came to Moses."

Similarly, the first Muslim migration movement, before all Muslims migrated from Mecca to Medina, was to Abyssinia. Here we have the Islamic authority saying, the Prophet Mohammed saying, why don't you go to Abyssinia? There is a very just Christian king; you will be protected there. And that is exactly what happened. Which means there was in reality a relationship, a good relationship, and good terms, between Islam and Christianity. Of course, we know that the direction of prayer for Muslims, while they were in Mecca, was toward Jerusalem. There is a whole chapter in the Qur'an on the name of Israel, the sons of Israel. The second chapter in the Qur'an, the whole chapter is a discussion with Jewish history, with the Jewish people.

The second point concerns the autonomy of tradition. Here I come as scholar of the theory of hermeneutics and of the Qur'an itself, as a text which can be discussed intertextually; not only from the perspective of the gospel or from the Bible, but from pre-Islamic history and tradition as well. If I apply an intertextual approach to the Qur'an, I see a text that is from God, but a God that spoke in history and spoke through language (of course this is not the view that would be accepted by many Muslims). Hence we must look to history. And if we look to the Islamic tradition and speak of the first century, the heart of the first century of Islam, during the civil wars, Muslims fought each other, and this was a political war of the tribal system trying to combat the new system created by Islam. But when the Islamic state, the first Islamic state, was established and moved to Damascus, we witness the actualization of the basic Islamic teaching and the Christian teaching: Islam, acting then in history. So too the rational theologians in Islamic history who raised the issue of predestination or free choice raised it in a political context in order to fight against the *Umyyad* political regime because of how the *Umyyad* legitimized their rise to power as an act of predestination. To fight against this the Mu'tazilites brought up the issue of free will, and that is why they were severely excluded and ultimately repressed.

We can go on, to the history of philosophy, to al-Farabi, the Muslim philosopher, who called himself the second master, because Aristotle was the first master, and he recognized Aristotle as a master without any feeling of contradiction or even inferiority. We come to Averroes, for whom the truth was not limited to any faith, or to any group, and who believed that people have to live with each other because truth has no specific place or specific faith. In accepting all these traditions, or parts of traditions, whether Greek or Indian or Persian traditions, of course Muslims had always to reinterpret the Qur'an in order to divulge its meaning to accept these parts of other traditions. Islam, as I say, always only exists within the specificity of a larger context. That is why the interpretation of the Qur'an is a very, very essential topic. To give just one example, most of the schools of interpretation have agreed on some principles, but they differ on applying these specific principles. For example there is a verse in chapter three, verse number seven, that talks about how the Qur'an was revealed to Mohammed and which includes clear verses and ambiguous verses. The ambiguous verses should be understood in reference to the clear verses. As if to say, the text has its own self-reference. Of course, all Muslims have agreed on this, on this ambiguity in the Qur'an, there are some ambiguous verses and some clear verses. Yet when we come to the matter of religious obligation, to the practical application of this verse or that, Muslims differ on what part is ambiguous and what part is clear.

I could continue and produce examples of pluralism in jurisprudence or philosophy, but that would not bring us closer to issues of tolerance or human rights, not in and of itself. There was, for example, in the seventeenth and the eighteenth centuries a self-correction, a self-revision, of the tradition trying to find a new path from within. This was disrupted by the intrusion of Western modernity, which brought a crisis of identity, and to solve this problem, the reformists in the late nineteenth and the beginning of the twentieth centuries, in the Arab world and in India, tried again to alter the text, to include modern values. They rejected the past as a misunderstanding of Islam. You will find this in Mahmud Khan and Mohammed Ali Emir in India, and Mohammed Abdul in Egypt and others in North Africa. The notion was that Muslims, through all history, have misunderstood Islam, and only now are able to understand it. In this new dichotomy they tried to accept modern institutions and modern concepts and even the philosophical concepts of modernity. Even if we take the example of Turkey, modernism and secularism was imposed, literally, and that is why the caliphate was abolished in 1924. Yet, this in turn created a reaction, a very strong reaction, against modernity, against the West, and at that time fundamentalism emerged, in Egypt, in 1928, as the Muslim brotherhood was created. My point is that we must never forget the role of the historical context in the development of religious theories.

And, finally, tolerance involves a choice, an idea of individual choice, not always acceptable to Muslims. The most important thing in Islam, after all, is not the individual, it is the consensus. An individual is allowed to do as much thinking as he would like, on the condition that he does not contradict the consensus. Consensus is a religious term, but it was used by the nationalist state to talk about the good of the nation. Changing, shifting the language from religious language to political language to limit individual thought is unfortunately one of the characteristics of contemporary Muslim societies.

Discussion

Fisch

I think you touched a very important point. I'd like to connect it up, if you'll excuse me, with the casino model Shlomo left us with earlier. I think that multicultural, liberal democracy is the new empire. It is just like the casino, replacing the emperor with a democratic, representative governing body. The idea of this casino-cum-multicultural-empire is precisely what you are warning us about. It doesn't allow ethnicity and religion to define nationhood. The modern nation is the collective of communities. The challenge to us around this table is not to describe and bask in the advantages of this model, but is how to make the multicultural casino empire a meaningful society religiously. In other words, how can we, from the resources of our religions, make this type of empire the religiously meaningful state of affairs we'd actively like to strive for. I think the pluralism I've been talking about does that. My question to the others around the table is, are there resources, texts, positions within your religion that would, in a religiously meaningful way, push you as a Muslim, as a dedicated Muslim, away from the association of your religion with nationhood? This is where we enter modernity by taking advantage of what the multicultural casino of modernity offers, but also to reshape that religiously.

I'm addressing a question which is the gravest question for Israel at the moment. That is to drive a wedge between the idea of the Jewish people and the idea of the Israeli nation, which I would love to see far more along Turkish lines than the way Israel is defining itself at the moment.

Berger

I'd like to step back for a moment to ask where we are. Everyone has established that from his religious tradition it is possible to devise ways to justify tolerance and pluralism, which is great. But politically speaking, so what? Politically speaking. The perhaps uncomfortable analogy occurred to me that while the Soviet Union was still in existence, all sorts of Western Marxists were developing concepts of a Marxist humanism with enormous intellectual sophistication, from Gramsci on, and it didn't have the slightest effect on the Stalinists. One can develop the most magnificent intellectual visions which lead nowhere. The question is then, again, what are the political implications of all this. Politically, I'm quite convinced that the only way you deal with fanatics is through violence.

Wolfteich

This doesn't directly respond to Peter's comment but I do think that it is important that we clarify what, exactly, we are tolerating. This goes back, in a way, to the comment about epistemological modesty versus moral certainty and builds on the whole discussion of original sin. I think that there is definitely a link between one's views about toleration and one's anthropological assumptions. I saw this in my studies of American Catholicism. Initially you have people like John Carroll, the bishop of Baltimore, who were very supportive of religious freedom. They had a very positive understanding of the human person. That shifted in the nineteenth century, and what developed was a much more negative anthropology, which corresponded to a much more intolerant position on the part of Catholics. I think we can go several ways. If we are talking about tolerating belief, if we are talking about an epistemological kind of toleration, then we have the question which Nasr, I think, raised, about what is the state of human reason and can human reason ascertain truth, or to what extent can it ascertain at least a limited truth in addition to the truth which might be gained through revelation. If one has a vision that reason has fallen, then on the one hand there is more reason to be skeptical about one's own position, but also to be wary of anyone else's and perhaps intolerant of the ways in which people might be misled and see truth which is not truth, to see falsehood and proclaim it. That seems to be one aspect of toleration and the question of reason.

The other aspect, I think, is the moral aspect. Here we are not talking about reason but about the will. Again, we have an anthropological question of how strong the will is, or to what degree is the will corrupt, misled, likely to embrace and act out falsehood, or weak? Then we have another set of possibilities, which is if we see the will as weak, corrupted, etc., there is all the more reason for intolerance because there is more reason to suspect that there will be these very damaging, harmful, dangerous positions, which one would want to destroy.

Hashmi
Are you equating reason with tolerance then? Are you saying that the more one becomes rational the more one is open to tolerance?

Wolfteich
No, I'm saying that if one has a view that human reason has a fair capacity to seek and find truth, then one might be more respectful of each person's path to that truth, or each person's ability to find truth. If one feels that reason is fallen, that we don't have that capacity and we depend wholly on revelations or nothing, then one might be on the one hand more skeptical about one's own positions, more modest, and yet also more modest about anyone else's proclaimed truth as well.

Fisch
If reason goes, there is total relativism. The only way to resolve a disagreement is by force.

Fischer
I'd like to thank Nasr for putting on the table something which hasn't been mentioned until now, and that is the connection between tolerance and power. He put this on the table, I think, very much in the Islamic experience that the confrontation has been a confrontation in the context of imperialism, in the context of colonialism, and in the context of brute force being exercised in what we call, here in Vienna, third-world countries. I think that Nasr has taken a similar line to mine and said that yes, religious Islam has enormous resources for tolerance and they can be used, but the question is do we have the necessary geopolitical constellation? Do we have, in this case, an international constellation that allows these forces to be put into play? The question then becomes, how are the power relations in the world, you know the north-south power relations, altered in the world. Then it becomes more than just an educational program, or just an educational program about tolerance, something very forward and very engaging, but it becomes a much larger economic and geopolitical problem. I'll leave it at that.

Estruch
May I add just one line to Shlomo's direction? I was reading last week an essay by, I think it is a professor from Lebanon, Emir Maluf, who wrote that you may study thirty volumes on the history of Islam, and you still will not understand a word of what is happening in Algeria now. Read thirty good pages on the colonization and decolonization process and you will start to understand immediately what is happening in Algeria.

Wolfteich
I would just caution, too, that a minority can be quite intolerant.

Fischer
People who are on the receiving end of the power relation, who believe themselves to be, as I say, exploited, are people who develop, perhaps, the intolerant side of their tradition because of the power relation.

Stone
But also because it has fewer consequences that you have to confront when you are not in power. You are not actually doing something violent. You don't have to confront evil in the same way.

Graf
Just one additional remark to this point. It is important to talk about the anthropological assumptions Claire noted, but the way she described it has something to do with the old internal Christian conflict between Protestantism and Catholicism. Her position was classically Catholic; I could argue the other way around. You are talking about the good man, and reason being capable of doing what truth claims, realizing God, developing dutiful theories, speculation, metaphysics, and things like this, but you can also talk about sin, original sin, and things like that, and you arrive at the skeptical view, both towards yourself as on the others.

Abu Zayd
In this funny game of adding sentences, may I suggest one more? On the subject of tolerance and power, yesterday we saw that in Judaism, everything is "open" except the halacha. In Islam, everyone is free provided they do not go against the consensus. In Christianity, or rather Catholicism, one could say the same, everyone has freedom provided it doesn't go against the official church point of view.

Seligman
This relates directly to Sohail's story of the Punjab and that when identities are threatened for whatever reasons, the consensus of the community becomes all-important.

Abu Zayd
But that is, again, a power question. Who has the power to define what consensus is? Who has the power to impose official definitions of reality? So we are in the middle of a question of power.

Seligman
Certainly one can find good and bad verses; that is no problem. You can find anything in a tradition. However Nasr's original point was much more subtle than that, for he added that the very verses that will be found depend on power structures. And he said more, for "mining" a tradition for certain verses is not enough. Like Menachem, he said we have to go to cognitive modes of a tradition. And the cognitive modes themselves are dependent on our geopolitical constellations. Not just the simple matter of which verses are taken to justify a tradition in the light of modernity, but the cognitive modes themselves are dependent on power relations, and that is a very interesting twist to the argument.

Because the challenges thrown out to human existence are universal, we are all dealing with the same questions. Yet we are all giving different answers. The different answers do have similarities. There are similar moves within each tradition and there is some overlap. However, it would seem, in terms of tolerance and in terms of working towards tolerance at an intellectual level, certain possible responses seem hard-wired within certain traditions and not others. And so, for instance, whereas skepticism, a skeptical epistemological modesty, exists in all traditions, my sense of it is that as a way into toleration, it is hard-wired in Judaism. I have noted Castellio's arguments with Calvin, so I am the last to say that it doesn't exist in Christianity, but I think it exists with a certain valence and a certain saliency in Judaism that is not found in other traditions [see introduction]. I agree with Suzanne and with Shlomo that a notion of individual autonomy and rights can exist in Judaism. I think however that it may well be hard-wired in Christianity. It is rooted in the Passion and the structures of belief which crystallized around that event. It exists in all faiths but perhaps it is hard-wired in Christianity, in a unique manner. It plays itself out in Christianity in a different way. Mysticism, as we know, is an element to be found in all faiths. Yet, in Islam, as a resource for toleration, it might well be hard-wired. Now I am just throwing this out as a hypothesis, I think it is an interesting thing to think about.

Nilüfer Göle's Presentation

Islam as Ideology

I'm happy to come after Nasr because I will continue the problematic of Muslim self-identity. Once on French television a journalist asked me a very simple question: "Are you a Muslim?" I was being interviewed on my books and so it was a very appropriate, relevant question, but I was terribly embarrassed and angry with him because I didn't know how to answer. There is a simple answer, "I am Muslim" or just "Yes." But it was very difficult for me and then I tried to understand why I was so embarrassed and could not answer simply. For one, secularism had taken away from me my identification as a Muslim. We are Turks, modern, and maybe only at some third level do we start saying of ourselves that we are Muslim, although this is very difficult to say for a person born after the Republic.

Moreover and with an eye to the current trends termed fundamentalist, if you are a Muslim, you are expected to be in conformity with the newly refined requirements of Muslim identity, to put on the veil, to behave in this way, to choose such-and-such a lifestyle, and so on. I must also admit that I was embarrassed as well in relation to the person who asked the question, the Western journalist, who had all sorts of prejudices and images of Muslim identity. Yes, there is a problem of Muslim identity. When we speak of, as Nasr put it, the identity crisis, I think we should understand that being a Muslim is not a simple, natural definition of identity. It is problematic in our day. What annoys us is what helps us to define ourselves. Without upsets, there is no identity question. In this sense, my presentation is related to this problematic identity of Muslims. It is not a question only of religion, but of how contemporary Islamist movements (and I am choosing my words carefully)—not only religions, but movements—are a response to this very problematic identity of being a Muslim in the contemporary world. The modern world changes, or pushes Muslim actors to change, their languages of religion, to change their ways of appropriating religion. How is Islam reappropriated by Muslim actors today? On the one hand, they are trying to define themselves in relation to modernity or modes of secularization within their own contexts. On the other hand, they are giving a nontraditional response. There is almost a rupture with the traditional definitions of Islamic religion because they are criticizing the self-definitions of Muslims given by traditions, and so they empower themselves through this ideologization of religion. All this, we shall see, bears on the issue of tolerance.

Some of this can be seen in the term "Islamist" itself. It is not just being Muslim, but Islamist. There is a sort of exacerbation of identity at work here, as expressed in issues of women and feminism. I would say, really the correlation is very close because instead of being assimilated to modernity, they are trying to redefine their identity in a nonassimilative way and say "Islam is beautiful" like "Black is beautiful" or "Women are beautiful"—it echoes this nonassimilative trend in our cultures. I think we must understand how, from the contemporary prism, the question of identity of Muslims is today a question dealt with by a range of social actors, including contemporary Islamist movements who themselves change the religious language. There are new languages. That is why I think that going to sources, or interpretations of Islam, as Nasr also put it, is not independent of the social practice in which all these factors are involved.

Because these movements are nonapologetic of their Islamic identity, there is also a kind of wrestling, to take the vocabulary of this workshop, with modernity and with religion. There is a critical relation between religion and modernity, and the question for us is if there can be some alternative sources of tolerance, alternatives to the Western, liberal definitions?

Can such be found without religion being totally collapsed into modernity (as in the Turkish case)? It is very interesting to observe this phenomenon of inclusion of Islamist and religious practices in the liberal market and in its pluralistic political system. Religions lose their specificity. They don't bring anything new, they just collapse. This is one possibility. The second is that they attempt to annihilate modernity, as with the Iranian revolution. In Iran there is much of this affirmation of identity and of maintaining community boundaries by authoritarian politics, and the result is antimodern. There is then an affirmation of identity, but an annihilation of modernity as its concomitant.

In contrast, the secularized public sphere in Turkey suffers from an excess of secularism. When we think of a Muslim country we have the tendency always to think that there is less secularism than in Western Europe. I am always confronted by this image. You can't be as secular as we are, my French colleagues are always saying. Yet to my astonishment I discovered that I am much more secular than the majority of my friends, who keep asking me to come to the baptism of their children and so on. I started to understand that there was a kind of secularism we in Turkey idealized. The Turks took it so seriously, as they are taking nationalism so seriously today. So this is something I want to push, a methodological shift; that we need not only to posit a difference from the Western, liberal, secular model and introduce religion, but also to think about other experiences in terms of these asymmetrical trajectories, which don't lead, always, to something very different and authentic, but sometimes to ways of appropriating modernity, secularism, and the exclusion of religion, in an excessive way.

One example I would start with, is the secularized public space, because without that we cannot really understand the return to religion today in the public arena. There is in Turkey the Jacobin model of secularism, which involves the forced secularization of the public sphere which went hand in hand with Westernization of lifestyle. This is very important. It illustrates (among other things) that secularism was not the precondition for a more pluralistic society as it has been in the Indian case, for instance. In the Turkish case, it was a transmitter, in a way, a vector of modernity which went almost equally with the Westernization of lifestyles. That is why there is a total repression of any symbols or organizations of faith, in general, in the public sphere. It is not the autonomy of religion which is looked for, and this is an irony of history because today it is the Islamists who are looking for perfect secularism—for a perfect separation of church and state—because of their need for autonomy. They search for complete autonomy from the state because religious schools today are under the control of the state.

Today we see how the public sphere was really under the tutorship of state, which through authoritarian means imposed a secular way of life. When I say imposed, it was not only militarily, rather through a whole gamut of civil society associations, of women's associations, youth organizations, and so on. Secularism has thus become part of social imageries, of civil societal movements. In the Turkish case, modernity is not some strange outside alien, but it is in the social actors' imagination.

What we see since the 1980s is the emergence of new social actors, Muslim actors, in urban environs, trying to introduce religiosity or sense of belonging to the Islamic religion through the symbol of the head scarf (banned in the universities, I might add) and other symbols as well. What we see is this Islamic idiom as part of the public debate for the first time. The public debate is, in some ways, becoming "Islamicized." There are also new spokespersons, not *ulema* (especially in the Turkish case where there is no religious authority, as it was totally destroyed by secularism). What emerges is almost a democratization of religious knowledge. Everyone can come up with a religious interpretation, so the new spokespersons are not religious leaders, but those who have two forms of social capital, both secular education capital and also religious capital. New actors and a new idiom emerge with them, and there is also a new public space. These new Islamic actors are carving a new space in the public life. To give you an entertaining example, new hotels are being constructed for the vacation of the newly enriched Muslim middle classes, who can take vacations on the beaches, but with separate beaches for men and women. I note this because of what I have read on the Jewish tradition and how the question of lifestyles is a major issue in politics. I think this is another common point, and I think we should put more emphasis on it because lifestyle is not a trivial issue. There are actually three beaches, it is very pluralistic—you can choose your beach: men, women, and family. The secularist elite felt terrible hurt by that.

Discussion

Fisch
On the religious kibbutz it is even better. There are different hours in the swimming pool for men, women, and families.

Göle
It is of course not an issue of physical space. Islamism brings pluralism, or may I say, a fragmentation of the public sphere, and there is no common arena where people can learn from each other, but it is more like a ghettoization and the introduction of new ways of redesigning borders between private and public. Can we find something in these practices, something which can generate, as you would put it, learning and enriching?

I would respond in two ways to this question. Two tests, two important tests. One is, I would say, the question of tolerance in this context is tolerance of Muslims of their own other self, the modern Muslim, because they are encountering modernity and living with that experience all the time. The majority of the texts today deal with this. How do they cope with this affirmation of identity as something totally different from the traditional Islamic way of life? Everyday life—film festivals and so on—at every level of life exemplify this. Even my students don't know if they are going to embrace Islam or become sociologists. This is the problem of "modern and Muslim" or "modern and/or Muslim." Can they be modern Muslims without annihilating one or the other? It is a big issue. The question of tolerance is very much a question of the inner-self, I would say.

Second is the question of women. In Muslim experiences of modernity, women were at the forefront because the emancipation of women and progress of the nation were almost synonymous. The question of women is the marker of much else because they are the most important actors in the new Islamist movements.

Veiling, for example, is a self-limiting of one's presence in the public sphere. This can go in two directions. If you limit your presence in the public sphere, it might correspond to the shrinking of the boundaries of the public sphere. In that sense, it might mean more communitarian control through women's bodies and authoritarianism. On the other hand, it can be a criticism of modern life and an urging of people to contest the modernist exposure of the self. In the religious criticism of modernity, I find a new self-definition of women, a self-limitation through this concept of modesty, and it is not epistemic modesty here, but a very physical modesty, a self-modesty. In a very interesting way, this can be seen as a resistance to the transparencies of modernity, to the tendency to disparage, to confess, to expose yourself in the public life, which is the definition of modern individual.

Fisch
This withdrawal, this modest withdrawal out of the public sphere—what does this do to acknowledging the other? What does this do to the public sphere, does it leave it to liberal modernity or does it leave it changed religiously in the way you indicated in the beginning? I'd like you to come full circle.

Göle

A good point that I am not sure I can answer. Note, however, that the veil itself is another statement of the self and of redesigning borders between private and public. For veiled women, acting in the public arena is a very different social form from the traditional seclusion of women in the home. Now, however, women are entering public life. Hence on the one hand they are obliged to criticize Islamic precepts as these are interpreted by today's Islamic fundamentalists. On the other hand, they are obliged to make criticisms of traditional texts and sometimes go back to the traditional sources to find the justification and legitimization they need to justify their presence in the public life. The question is, are they going to take off their veil? This would be dilution into modernity. Or are they going to design (which is already happening) new self-definitions. I think the question of pluralism is not independent of this redesignation of borders between public and private.

Fisch

Still, I'd like to press you on the content. What is in this redefinition and economy of spaces to enrich, morally enrich, the notion of society and acceptance of the other? That is what I am still lacking. It is a brilliant sociological analysis of the way these boundaries are negotiated and the way they are going today, but convince us that they are going in the right direction.

Göle

That is an open-ended question. It is not withdrawal, physically or professionally, from the public sphere, but a resistance to the modernist urge to define individuality through the exposure of self. This self-limitation I find interesting, even in bodily terms.

Fisch

Shlomo was pushing me, saying that any religious leader listening to me will say, "You know, it is all very interesting, but we don't want any part of that because it is a threat to religion." The answer back to these religious people is that religion can enrich the public sphere and gain a lot from it. This is what I am still lacking in your description. I'm sure it is there.

Hashmi

I just wanted to add one quick sentence. The others that are being asserted here are the Muslims themselves. They are the other.

Göle

Hence recognition of women's difference within and among Muslims, recognizing women's voices is the most important test, or marker, of this pluralism developing within. This all-encompassing tendency of Muslim religion is very interesting. Always taking in, and not recognizing individual voices in this sense, as Nasr has said.

Berger

Well, a number of times the phrase "religious critique of modernity" has come up, and now very interestingly in Nilüfer's paper. Which is fine with me. I think there should be a critique of modernity; religion is helpful for it. I don't believe in progress, I don't believe in modern utopianism, this is all fine. But I think that critique has to be discriminating. For there is one element of modernity which I would absolutely want to come out of that critique unscathed, and that is the autonomy and the liberty of the individual, which I think is the great discovery of the modern age. Now we can say that is great, but it has some very uncomfortable implications for religion.

A couple of things were said here which I thought were interesting. I think it was Menachem who first used the phrase "everything is up for grabs, except for halacha"; Nasr said, "everything is up for grabs except the consensus." Suzanne said something very interesting: she said that there is a "danger of falling out of the discourse completely." I think I am quoting you correctly. Now, the history of Protestant theology is a very interesting example of bargaining with modernity. We are going to give up this, but not that. In other words, everything is up for grabs except "X" or "Y," and I think at the end of this road, nothing is left which is not up for grabs. I don't think that is bad, unlike Suzanne, who used the term "danger." In other words, it seems to me that if one really accepts the liberty of the individual, religions become a matter of personal choice, and nothing can be taken for granted. This means rather than a danger that one falls out of the discourse, it is a challenge to the discourse. You may risk falling out of the discourse; you may also reconstruct the discourse on much more positive and defensible grounds.

A final observation, I think I mentioned it to Nilüfer. The French sociologist of religion Danièle Hervieu-Léger has just written a new book, *Le Pèlerin et le converti*, based on pilgrims and converted people. She uses mostly French empirical materials, but you can certainly find the same kind of material all over Europe and North America and elsewhere I think. She shows how traditional religion, in the sense of taken for granted, in the sense that certain things are not up for grabs (she doesn't use that phrase, but one could), is declining everywhere and will continue to decline. There are two religious types that are emerging. The pilgrim, who is the one who begins to construct his religious edifice as best as he can, negotiating with tradition, and the converted one, by which she means what most people mean by fundamentalism. The self-enclosure reaction, vis-à-vis the challenge of modernity. To me there is no question as to which is the way to go, but if one goes the pilgrim route, you have to accept the fact (and you are kidding yourself if you do not) that however you define the discourse, the whole thing is up for grabs in the sense that its plausibility cannot be taken for granted. That is what I mean by it is up for grabs.

Graf

I would like to make a few remarks. The first point you were speaking of was the Turkish way of secularism. I do not think that Kemalism could be described as a type of secularization. Rather, the public space and the public sphere were filled with specific modern religious elements. You created something like a new religious hero, but of a specific type. It came with a religious image and a religious approach.

Abu Zayd

This is a Muslim experience with secularism, with worshipping of pharaoh.

Graf

It is not a type of modernity that has a lot to do with tolerance. It is very authoritarian, very state-centered. And so my point is that Islamic reaction is not a reaction to a process of secularization. It is, in a certain way, a very modern reaction to an experience they could not mediate between Muslim tradition and the civil religion of Turkey.

Fischer

I'd like to see if I have understood correctly. You have a sort of Kemalist steamroller of secularization, which comes out in a very authoritarian way and flattens everything. Then you get a movement from below based on lifestyle changes and an affirmation of an Islamist identity based on lifestyle and composed of negotiation with forms of modernity. Maybe I didn't hear correctly where that is coming from, or why it is emerging after sixty years of Turkish secularism. I am interested in this because it could be that this is another way of getting at that particular Israeli religious, political enigma known as Shas. Shas, for those who don't know, is the movement of ultra-Orthodox Jews of Oriental or Middle Eastern or North African origin. It has been one of the fastest-growing forces in Israeli politics. In the past I have used a number of models to try to understand what Shas is. So far the academic and political discourse of Israel has been largely based on European models, so models taken from the Middle East and North Africa are hard to come to terms with. Earlier, I wrote a paper in which I used the Catholic Church as a model for Shas, as an all-inclusive model instead of a sectarian model. What Nilüfer says interests me because as Israeli secularization had Kemalist attributes, there emerged a form of resistance in this fashion; not a sectarian fundamentalist resistance, but rather a much more modulated response. So, yet another point of intersection between Middle Eastern realities—not just segregated beaches.

JOAN ESTRUCH'S PRESENTATION

Monotheism and Intolerance

I have been thinking of Sartre's sentence *"L'enfer c'est les autres"* ("Hell is the others"). And to me the opposite also holds, which is that there is no considerable heaven without them. Now, my question after all these hours of discussion would be, I wonder if the difficulties we have with a real acceptation of pluralism are not, above all, difficulties which arise around the internal plurality in our own traditions. We seem to have less problems in interreligious dialogue, and sometimes real difficulties with our own co-religionists.

To say, perhaps, the same but more seriously, let's imagine that the young man sitting there behind the tape recorder is not what he appears to be. He is, in fact, someone invited by the Institute. He comes from one of those specific islands studied by Malinowski some decades ago. He is here disguised with handicaps because he has to translate into his own language what we are saying. Tomorrow he will be interrogated here at the Institute about his observations of what has been going on. The Institute is going to ask him, "Why do you think those people gathered together in order to discuss tolerance?" What will he answer? "They were here because they are so different that they had to discuss tolerance because they are different." I don't think so; he will, however, say, "They were here because they are the same. They belong to the same family. I have difficulties, after two days, to discover any real differences between them besides small nuances. They all say one group, one revelation, one God, and they pretend to be different. Well, no, they belong to the same family and this is why they discuss tolerance. They would not discuss tolerance with me, who comes from the Apua Island. They discuss tolerance because they belong to the same family, because they are so similar."

True, we say—and it is probably correct—that particularism in Judaism leads more to indifference. Perhaps the conquistador spirit of Catholicism leads to a surplus of intolerance. Yes, all right, but not for him, the outside observer. It is for us who are able to distinguish these kinds of slight differences. But then his conclusion, I think, would be not only that all these people are the same, but that they belong to the same group, the same family. I think that his conclusion would be, at the same time, that it is probably their monotheism which makes them so intolerant, which obliges them to discuss the issue of tolerance. It is because they are all monotheists, and historically, in effect, we have been intolerant. Empirically there seems to be a real connection, or an elective affinity, between monotheism and intolerance.

If this is all true, there are then three possibilities: (1) We may keep on being intolerant; (2) we may, since nothing is taken for granted anymore, give up monotheism; or (3) we may try to break the connection, the elective affinity between the two terms. We have seen that we can choose, indeed, some verses from the Bible, from the Qur'an, in order to show that the sources of tolerance are there. We also know that we could choose other verses in order to be intolerant, to show that intolerance is possible and to justify intolerance. We could, and historically we have done so.

This brings me to my last observation on religion and modernity. Yes, religion can and ought, perhaps, be a challenge to modernity, a critique of modernity, but this should not disguise the fact that modernity has been fundamentally a challenge to all our religious traditions. Sometimes, I agree with the attitude of criticizing modernity from religion, but let's be aware of the possibility that there is here a sort of defensive reaction because, in fact, we are the ones challenged. Nilüfer says that religion must not adapt or accommodate to modernity. I'm taking, as a reference model, my own church. The Catholic Church must not accommodate or adapt to modernity. Yes, but let's be careful, it is perhaps only because it is a form of premodern religiosity that it speaks in this way. Catholic bishops say very often these days when they see the way people claim to have voices and share decisions and so on, they say let's not forget the Catholic Church is not a democracy and ought not to be a democracy. I have answered several times, okay, I agree it is not, I even agree it must, perhaps, not be a democracy, but let's be careful. The danger is that we justify that it is not a democracy because it's a banana republic. I do not want a church which is a banana republic. I accept that it is, perhaps, not a democracy. Religion criticizes modernity, perhaps, because it is so absolutely premodern in many cases.

Let me give my last word to the Malinowskian native: You see, those people, many of them, seem to be people who buy a newspaper and have some doubts about what they read in this paper. Then they are advised by their religious leaders to buy five more copies of the same newspaper in order to make sure that what the newspaper says is right. In my church, this is a usual practice. Not in your traditions?

Discussion

Berger

I want to add another footnote to what Joan said about monotheism. A few years ago I read a book by a Japanese philosopher by the name of Nakamura. He said the West has made two fundamental mistakes: one was monotheism and the other was the Aristotelian principle of contradiction. Every sensible person knows, he said, that contrary to the West, of course there must be many gods, and every sensible person knows that something can be both A and non-A. Just a little footnote worth thinking about. The big religious chasm is not between the three West-Asian religions; it is between, if I may use that image, Jerusalem and Benares. I think it is that encounter which is going to be of tremendous significance in the next hundred years or so and will raise the issue of tolerance and pluralism in a new way.

Fisch

I think you are absolutely right in noting that we are very similar, not because that is a true statement, but because we have been behaving as though we are, and in truth we aren't. For example, we haven't been dwelling on the different notion of sacredness. What does a sacred text mean? How does the canon function? Does it function as the source for the true and the good or as something else? Talmudic literature, for example, attempts to come to terms with the *akkedah* (the binding of Isaac), including one midrash that says that Abraham's temptation to sacrifice the son was so great in those ancient times that he pleaded with the angel to at least make a little cut. Those familiar with the literature know this.

I could go on for an hour about the different concepts of Deity one finds only in the talmudic literature. That is just a small segment of our history. The point I am making is that we come to this table with very different religions, and we are coming together in order to find resources to tackle these problems with different resources and joining forces with different tool kits. Some of us are exploring—as I do, in advance—theoretical models by which to do it and then looking back into our knapsacks to see if we have got anything to use, and others are going about it differently. It is worth exploring differences and seeing what each can contribute from one's own legacy and religious metaphysics.

Stone

I think I have to take a stand with Menachem here, in contrast to our usual positions. I think what Menachem is raising in pointing to the different conceptions of the Deity and the differences between the traditions is that this sort of simple equation of the monotheistic religions versus the polytheistic religions is a rhetorical move. I know it is a very interesting argument that has been made. I find it a difficult argument in part because it has led to the equation of polytheism with tolerance and monotheism with exclusivity and intolerance. This argument has been raised in recent feminist discourse in particular, has become a very important argument to actually engage in critically and not just rhetorically because feminist discourse has made a very significant point that people have come to assimilate much too readily—that there is something about the monotheistic, patriarchal, exclusivist tradition that it is in and of itself a kind of intolerant killing. It is an argument that has not been sufficiently and critically investigated. That is one aspect of the problem. I think if we really looked at polytheistic cultures, we would find precisely the same problems. Certainly, I don't think we could hold them up as emblems of tolerance, especially as Momigliano has shown, in the political sphere.[1]

My second point is also that we have very different conceptions of what a monotheistic religion really is. Certainly coming from the Jewish tradition, the question of what is really monotheistic is a very large question. The whole system of intergroup tolerance comes from that moment, within the Jewish tradition, of recognition, and sometimes only partial recognition, that what we consider to be the three religions of the book are, in fact, monotheistic. It is a complicated subject.

Estruch

Of course I do not want to deny or to minimize the difference between the three monotheistic faiths. I know there are differences. I am sure that they are important, but nevertheless, I think it would be the equivalent of what Nilüfer demanded, of decentering the problem. Somehow, we are very centered around different forms and different conceptions of monotheism, but it is perhaps, again, rhetorical. I think it is not just rhetorical. I am perfectly conscious that I belong to a Jewish sect. What is the Church but a sect of Judaism? We have grown different because there are centuries of each going at it his own way.

Berger

I really have to contradict Suzanne. Let me take one simple thing. All the three West-Asian religions, except for very marginal and usually subterranean currents, have not accepted reincarnation as a reality. All the South and East Asian, or most of them, have. This makes an immense difference, not just in terms of some dogmatic formulation, but in terms of how one senses reality. This has enormous ethical implications. Let me just give you one little episode from Hindu literature. It is a legend and a debate, a sort of Socratic dialogue between a guru and Ishvara, who is the Vedic god of creation. This occurs in the heavenly palace.

Suddenly the sage laughs and Ishvara says, "Why are you laughing?" and he says, "The ants," and he points to a train of ants that are crossing the marble floor of the heavenly palace. Ishvara says, "Well, so what?" whereupon the sage replies that "every one of those ants was once Ishvara and will be Ishvara again." This is a sentence one has to let sink in.

Now I would suggest to you that this is a view of reality that is utterly alien, except for some mystical subterranean currents, to Judaism, to Christianity, to Islam. It makes, moreover, a significant difference in how you view morality, the human condition, the status of politics, etc. So I very much agree with Joan, this is an in-house meeting.

Wolfteich

Just a quick observation. It seems to me that we have at least two different ideas that have been out on the table and I think that I am losing a little bit of focus, so I just wanted to reassert them. One is the argument that we are all fairly similar and the real issues about tolerance and toleration have to do with the monotheist versus polytheist, or more radical, differences. The other argument is the one that Dorothee made yesterday, and I believe you also made in a way, which is that no, it is the near difference that is significant. That is the big issue, or the internal pluralism. I think it might be worth discussing especially if we go back to the political issue. What is the real concern? What should we be addressing—the near difference or the more radical difference?

Hashmi
I have yet to meet a Hindu who claims that he or she is a polytheist.

Seligman
I think we have to make a very important distinction between different types of polytheism. There is nontranscendent polytheism, what was called in the ancient world "pagan." Then there are transcendent religions like Hinduism that have multiple gods, but have a notion of transcendence.

Hashmi
Halacha does not recognize the sociological distinction.

Fisch
Of course sociology doesn't recognize many halachic distinctions either.

Fischer
A note on small differences, and that is people tend to construct the following continuum vis-à-vis Jews in other cultures: that Jews have the highest self-bounded self-definition in Christian cultures. In other words Jews are the most distinguished from their surroundings and create the most bounded communities in Christian cultures. In Islamic cultures we know, in Morocco and in other places, that Jews have shared shrines, holy men, saints, etc. with the surrounding population and that there has been a conflation on the level of popular religion, if not on the level of official religion. When you get to places like India and China, Jews disappear. They tend to get entirely assimilated into the environment because there is no tension, there is no conflict. So for instance, the State of Israel had to make a real effort to find Jews from India to bring to Israel, and they got the last ones before they disappeared forever.

Abu Zayd

This brings me to the question of why tolerance has so often characterized people who believe in so many gods. Before Islam there was no religious struggle. There was political struggle, tribal struggle, around the
sources of livelihood, around the water-well and so on. But it was accepted that every community, every one, has his own god. Interestingly,
this position is exactly that of Islamic mysticism. This is Sufism in Islam.
So if we don't vote for real tolerance, I think that the monotheistic God
is the problem.

Fisch

There is an open question about the Bible. Is the God of the Bible one
God or a jealous God? A jealous God allows for polytheism. Does the
Bible believe in idolatry? And some would say yes. But if he is a jealous
God, he . . .

Stone

. . . believes in exclusivity.

Fisch

That is a polytheism that drives to intolerance.

Berger

I think we are getting too much hung up on the notion of monotheism
and polytheism. The point I was trying to make is that the religions that
have come out of the ancient Near East have an awful lot in common.
Not just in terms of some abstract formulations that one god is jealous,
but in terms of fundamental sense of reality, which is very different from
the sense of reality that has come out of South Asia and then developed
in different ways in East Asia, not to mention some primal religions in,
perhaps, Papua but which we know not much about. That commonality
in terms of, not just prepositional possibilities, but in terms of a sense
of reality, is very significant. Now I am not arguing the feminist bill that
monotheism is always repressive, but I think that we have to be aware of
the fact. Here I think the American context is quite important in terms
of our understanding of pluralism and of tolerance. We can not limit
ourselves anymore to what came out of the ancient Near East. If you
don't believe me, I have a very pleasant suggestion. Take a holiday in
Hawaii, which is probably the one state in the union now in which Christians are a minority. Since the U.S. census doesn't count religion, we don't

really know. Go from Honolulu on the Nepali highway to the other side of Oahu, and you will witness an orgy of religious pluralism. There is everything there that you can think of including some things you don't know what they are. Now tell me what it means to be a Jew in Hawaii?

Friedrich Wilhelm Graf's Presentation

Varieties of Interpretation

I would like to go in the direction that Estruch has taken us. I don't like to present my religious tradition as a confessional tradition or as a religious tradition that can help us to be good tolerant citizens in a multiethnic or polyethnic religious society. I am much more interested in the very deep ambiguities of the Protestant German tradition. German Protestantism is an extremely complex, contradictory phenomenon. On the one hand, you have an extremely rich philosophical and theological tradition. Kant, Hegel, Schleiermacher, who were all of the German classical philosophical tradition. They all were students of Protestant theology. They all came out of this milieu, as in a sense did Reformed Judaism.

On the one hand a very rich theological tradition, on the other hand, as we now know through much work on the intellectual history of eighteenth- and nineteenth-century German Protestantism, the cognitive maps that were developed at this time created, in a certain way, modes of conduct that led to the catastrophes of twentieth-century German history. You know those books on the German Mandarins by Fritz Karl Ringer or Eger's about the German conception of history. If you take these analyses seriously, I think one has to say something about the specific contradictions of German tradition. I would like to do that in six points.

My first point: I would like to come back to the question of the specific quality of religious language. My first point would be that religious language is a language of fiction. We are talking of God, Christ, the Messiah, heaven, hell, and the like. Religion speaks of subjects, of entities, that you cannot identify empirically. You can use the same symbols, words, or narratives to build extremely opposite or different cognitive maps. You can use religious symbols or religious terms for constructing very different cognitive maps. Thus you can take the cross as a symbol for suffering man and you can use it as a weapon. The symbol itself doesn't give you a criterion on how to use it.

What do I mean by this? At the very least, you can use religious language in two very different ways. On the one hand, you can create strong images of the self, of social groups or collective actors. All these "God is on our side" theologies. You find it in all European nationalist states since the late eighteenth century. You find it in Zionism and in the American tradition as well—all of which identify God with the aims of a certain group and so on.

On the other hand you can use religious language to stress the finitude of man. You can use it as a language of self-limitation, and as we are interested in tolerance, of course, we have to think about the second way of using religious symbols and religious language. I think it is much more complicated to differentiate between religion and ideology than some of us have suggested this morning. I was quite astonished how easily some of us said well it is religion in this case and ideology in that. I think we must look at the many ways in which traditional religious language and modern ideologies and modern political aims are combined. All interesting ideologies of modernity have always used traditional religious language; even the Nazis did so. We have to think about the fact of syncretism at this point.

My second point: German Protestantism has been deeply transformed by the German Enlightenment. In a certain way the German Enlightenment, in spite of people like Mendelssohn and so on, has mainly been undertaken by German Protestant thinkers. I'm not going into historical details at this point, but one can say we had two reactions to this enlightened transformation of classical Protestantism. We have something comparable to Reform Judaism which we call "Culture-Protestantism," and, on the other hand, we have the creation of a conservative milieu. I am not interested in saying that the one answer to modernity has been a good one and we called it a liberal and the other has been a bad one, but I would say that the different answers to modernity which you can find in the Protestant milieu are both very interesting combinations of traditional elements of Protestant religion with specific modern ideas. Of course the idea of the autonomous self is, for that liberal tradition, very essential. There is no liberal theologian in nineteenth-century German Protestantism who doesn't think that the autonomous self is something specifically Protestant, the essential doctrine of Protestant religion. Peter has shown this in many articles about the doctrine of justification. I will not be going into this.

My third point: In Adam's paper he reminded us of Richard Popkin's *History of Skepticism* [see introduction]. Popkin's book does in fact present an important theory regarding the question of possible connections between the Protestant religion and tolerance by abandoning the idea of an infallible church. By leading religious certainty back to the strictly inner experience of the individual, the reformists opened the way for a culture of skeptical religious consciousness, which constitutes the criteria of true tolerance. This is Popkin's argument. I do not intend to examine his fascinating theories in the context of seventeenth- and eighteenth-century theological programs. Rather I am interested in describing two strategies with which Protestant theologians in Germany have responded to the new challenge of inner-Christian confession of pluralism and the questions concerning coexistence with Jewish minorities. I am interested in the structural ambivalence of this tradition. The fundamental views of reform theology offer a basis for a skeptical theology capable of promoting tolerance. On the other hand, however, specific Protestant ideas or cultural values have often served to base concepts of human coexistence which leave no room for ideas of tolerance or acceptance of the other as the other. The main German idea—you can see this on every level of cultural discourse—has been the idea of confessional parity. This is an essential concept of the old German legal system, and it still constitutes the modern Germany welfare state, the importance of consensus. This is something that is different from tolerance. It is acceptance of the other not as the other, but only in regard to some practical reason.

My next point. In describing the contradictions of liberal and neoclassical liberal theory, I think one can show that a culture of tolerance, of accepting diversity, depends on certain moral premises and religious traditions. Tolerance, we agree, is not just the result of a little sympathy, generosity, and brotherly love. A culture of tolerance remains bound to a shared historical context of experience in which all individual agents have agreed to leave certain problems concerning final reasons unresolved, or relegate them to academic discourse. Perhaps part of the background to this in some societies is tied to a Protestant theology and its concepts of self-demarcation in the faith of a devoutly religious person. In comparison with the Catholic tradition, for example, the Protestant tradition insists very strongly on the elementary differences or discontinuities between created and creator. There is no natural-right conception which allows such continuities. Protestants believe in a good creation. They have no need of strategies to relativize the deep sin of man. On all levels of doctrine, or in nearly all doctrines, Protestant tradition has always been interested in the fact that the human being is not God himself, is not very close to God, that mankind is not in some way bound directly to God and therefore anything like another absolute agent. From the Protestant perspective, man is a notorious sinner and even his Christian faith is as a reborn Christian. One chief distinguishing feature of the Protestant tradition is its doctrine of sin. In contrast to Catholicism, Protestantism takes a more pessimistic, I think more realistic, view of men.

In completely different language games, this can be described as a dramatic theory or doctrine in which the religious subject is warned against pronouncing his subjective perspective as absolute. In other words, in the median of religious language, boundaries or limitations of the finite subject are drawn up. If religious belief can help humans to understand themselves in relative terms, then this faith must enable us to view ourselves skeptically. Skepticism in the face of others is inexpensive, I think. Skepticism towards oneself is something like an expression of a wisdom which you can only find in religious language games.

At this point, I would like to make another short remark. We were talking about mysticism this morning, and Adam recommended us to look at the Islamic traditions of mysticism. We had a mysticism discourse in Germany at the turn of the twentieth century. Important Jewish and Protestant thinkers were part of this discourse. Troeltsch, for example, described the barren model of church and sect and thought that mysticism was a type of religion especially important in modernity. Buber's collections on Jewish mysticism and the like are all illustrations of this trend. I warn you, however, mysticism is an extremely dangerous religious phenomenon because it creates something like an immediate relation between the religious subject and the absolute God. All those politically, extremely totalitarian theologies of the twenties and thirties, all those pre-Nazis theologies, always used the mystical language. My interest would be just the opposite. What we are interested in, or what we should be interested in, are theologies which help us to get to precise limitations of man, to differentiate between God and man, not to allow God to get too close to empirical actors, collective actors, or individual actors. That is what I am interested in.

One more remark: the term "autonomous self" in itself is extremely indeterminate. What we have to think about is which type of autonomous self are we speaking of. Do we think of a very strong agent, or do we think of an agent who has moral or religious intellectual capacities for self-limitation?

Discussion

Abu Zayd
Well, this is a very important point that mysticism could be very dangerous, but so could everything else, I hasten to add: mysticism, theology, and even philosophy (think of Heidegger). I nevertheless agree with you about the nature of the language of religion. It could be used in different ways, and whatever the intention is of a theologian or a mystic or a philosopher, it is not the intention that decides how the discourse will be employed by other powers. Thus again we confront religion and power, religion and politics. This is exactly where religion can be a very dangerous, intolerant weapon. When religion and politics come together, there is no safe place for any individual or group, whether in the Muslim world or other places. So again we return to the deep politicization of religion, and to secularism, and to the separation between religion and politics, between religion and the public sphere as solutions to these dangers. By way of individual autonomy, we thus find ourselves returning to the position from which we were trying to escape. I must admit that I don't have an answer. This is not a response to your paper, but the whole situation. We are trying to get off of a hook and being taken back to the hook because we find that religion or monotheism is simply dangerous.

Graf
I don't think it would be correct to say that what is involved here is a secondary politicization of religious language as you imply. I think we have to accept that all religious language is in a very fundamental way politic. If you speak of the kingdom of God, you speak of something like a good or well-ordered society, and implicit in this is always the terms of inclusion and exclusion and so of politics. For example, the German Catholic modernists at the turn of the twentieth century were very modern because they were extreme nationalists. Yet it was a theological argument that they used, an argument that you can find in Reform Judaism as well as in liberal Protestantism. It is not the theology that creates the difference, it is the context.

Seligman

Not long ago I asked Richard Popkin what he thought of the idea of skepticism as a factor in the development of tolerance. He said, "Nonsense." Actually he used another word which I won't repeat. He added that if you want to look for tolerance in the seventeenth century, look to the Christian millennialists. Look for those who thought that any moment will see the Second Coming. Why? Because until the Second Coming the situation is of a hidden revelation—like that Jewish version of the hidden revelation that Shlomo noted—and so knowledge is occluded, and we have no right to decide on who is just or not. With the Second Coming, God will pass judgment, but it is not ours to judge.

Wolfteich

Just two points or questions. The first is, I somehow feel compelled to defend mysticism here, but I would raise the question—I very much agree with you that it has always been a threat to religious authority for one thing. The crucial threat, I think, was that an unmediated experience of God threatens Church authority. I would push the point about uncertainty and whether an epistemological modesty would also compel one to allow for the possibility that there might be different experiences. And that some people might have a more direct experience, or more certainty, than oneself. That is one question.

The second question is about the implications of your discussion of sin in the Protestant tradition. I agree with your analysis there, but what are the implications of that doctrine of sin for toleration? I could see it going either way. I could see it going toward more intolerance because of a more fearful picture of what people might do.

Fischer

It seems to me that this is a religious equivalent of what we have presented as the Jacobin version of modernity. In other words, Jacobinism can either take a Kemalist, explicitly secular, form (as in Turkey or Israel), or it can take a religious guise, but it is the same idea—that if you don't conform in terms of your cultural assimilation, then you don't belong to the collectivity. Now, if I am not mistaken, Mendelssohn in the discussion around Jewish emancipation in the 1780s and 1790s attempted to produce an alternative model. In *Jerusalem*, if I am not mistaken, he presents a Lockean-type American social contract model, which is that if you don't harm other people then it doesn't matter what you believe in. The question then becomes of alternative forms of modernity not requiring a Jacobin thrust, and if these are limited to the North American reality.

Berger
And that of course brings us to the more analytic question and a very common debate in modern social science, namely, to what extent does a modern society need common values. On the one hand you have what you or Adam I believe once characterized as the Hayekian [from economist Friedrich A. Hayek], or traffic-signal theory of society. In other words, why do most people obey traffic laws—because it is in the common interest. Against this is the Durkheimian view that society requires a collective conscience. I think the answer to that dilemma is rather simple. The traffic-signal view of society holds until there is a crisis. I will obey the traffic lights unless I am in a hurry to get to the hospital, in which case I will drive through all the red lights. It is the crisis that supersedes. Now the analogy limps a little bit, but I would say that the Hayekian model functions very well until sacrifices are demanded of the citizens. It can be extreme sacrifice, risking your life in war, but much less sacrifices as well, taxes on behalf of people you don't like and causes you don't approve of. I think both are right, but under different conditions, and that is relevant to something we have discussed before, which is how tolerant can we be of values which tend to explode society.

Seligman
I agree but would add that crises are always built in. Death is crisis, life is crisis. They are built into the structures of our life. Hence market rationality is never sufficient to explain social reality because there are always crises. Now social choice and rational choice, utility function-type theories will define these crises out of their social calculus, and a religious perspective will admit the fact that crisis is built into existence. This is relevant to our discussion because the life of an individual is always a continual crisis, given the tragic nature of existence.

Berger
But the issue is not the crisis of the individual. I agree with you that everyone faces aging, illness, and so on, that these are sorrowful conditions, but collectively, there can be periods of time where most people feel that society is not in crisis. It is working, it is okay.

Seligman

But I think those traffic lights have to be able to address the crisis in the individual. The collective traffic lights have to address that as well.

Berger

No, because as long as there is no crisis, this can be left to institutions that are not part of the state, part of the public order.

Seligman

While I remain unconvinced, if only because the state does not subsume all of the public order, I would however like to pick up on Shlomo's question of the American model and remind us that American Protestantism was never in contestation with alternative models of social order. What allowed the full flowering of American Protestant assumptions was precisely that it wasn't in tension with Catholic models the way it was in continental Europe. That old insight of Seymour Martin Lipset on the first new nation is I think relevant here. We seem, however, to be coming full circle to one of Shlomo's remarks at our very first session—on the critical role of American Protestantism in the discourse of tolerance (though of course Roger Williams is more important here than Richard Mather—precisely because he uncoupled salvation from the organization of the political realm). Perhaps then this is a good place to end this fascinating discussion and continue the search for alternative languages and discourses that have not perhaps been so privileged historically. Thank you all for coming and for spending these two intense days in discussion of issues that are more and more relevant to both states and public orders in more and more places in the world.

CHAPTER FOUR

Toward a Phenomenology of Religious Tolerance

Je est un autre.
—*Rimbaud*

I am a man, no other man do I deem a stranger.
—*Unamuno*

Translation exists because man speaks different languages.
—*Steiner*[1]

Between these quotes lies our problem, as well as its solution. Like translation, toleration, which is its precondition, is necessitated by the different languages spoken. Both are made possible by the realization that despite these different languages—replete with different, often contrasting, universes of meaning—no one other is, in his or her essence, a stranger.

These themes were broached repeatedly, in different ways, by our interlocutors. Abu Zayd's interpretation of Islam as embracing all monotheists and Mahmutćehajić's strictures on the multifarious ways of knowing God point in this direction. Stone's insights into the plurality of creation and the Jewish valorization of difference and diversity as a feature of created order and its implications on the place of the heretic and sinner within the community all focus on the meaning of the very terms "stranger" and "other." As expressed institutionally in such categories as *dhimmi* or the Noachides, a category of the un-strange stranger or non-strange other is created, one whose language is different, but is yet translatable. And in fact the problems of translation and of tolerance are connected, as are those of ego, and alter, of identity and boundaries.

In its own way, this issue appeared a number of times in the dialogues when the boundaries of traditions were discussed. Stone's exchange with Fisch on the casuistic method as opposed to the allegorical one, addressing how the former kept one within a tradition and the latter allowed for a move beyond, is an example of this problematic. Here too, of course, issues of a religious particularism (as in Judaism) as opposed to more universalistic assumptions (in Christianity or Islam) play a significant role, as we have seen, in determining the boundaries of the tradition and so the terms of its translation.

Not surprisingly, the very salient issue of religion and modernity, and of religion as a modern ideology—an issue broached most clearly in the Islamic conversations by Mahmutćehajić, Göle, and Abu Zayd—illustrates a completely different problem of translation and more especially of its limits, that between a premodern and a modern consciousness. It was, we learned, precisely when religion began to play the role of a modernist ideology that it presented itself in its most harmful, closed, and repressive guise. Moreover, as Graf noted, this dynamic is itself an inherent aspect of modernity. Graf's remarks on the role of various strains of Protestant interpretation in the making of modern German ideology and identity are a helpful reminder that it is not only in Islam, or among radical religious parties in contemporary Israel—such as Shas, which Fischer discussed—that religions seem to violate their own presuppositions and boundaries. On this I believe it may be useful to quote, of all people, Thomas Paine, who, in his *Rights of Man* wrote:

> Toleration is not the opposite of intoleration, but is the counterfeit of it. Both are despotism. The one assumes to itself the right of withholding liberty of conscience, and the other of granting it. The one is the Pope, armed with fire and faggot, and the other is the Pope selling or granting indulgences. The former is the church and state, and the latter is church and traffic.
>
> But toleration may be viewed in a much stronger light. Man worships not himself, but his Maker: and the liberty of conscience which he claims, is not for the service of himself, but of his God. In this case, therefore, we must necessarily have the associated idea of

two beings, the mortal who renders worship and the immortal being who is worshipped. Toleration therefore places itself not between man and man, nor between church and church, nor between one denomination of religion and another, but between God and man; between the being who worships and the being who is worshipped; and by the same act of assumed authority by which it tolerates man to pay his worship, it presumptuously and blasphemously sets up itself to tolerate the Almighty to receive it. . . .

Who are thou vain dust and ashes, by whatever name thou art called, whether a king, bishop, a church or a state, a parliament or any thing else, that obtrudest thine insignificance between the soul of man and his Maker? Mind thine own concerns. If he believes not as thou believest, it is a proof that thou believest not as he believeth, and there is no earthly power can determine between you.[2]

What Paine is arguing here is precisely how the assumption of political functions by religious authorities robs religion of its proper role in matters of ultimate concern. Most of us would not expect such sentiments from Paine, revolutionary as he was. We see him too often only through the lenses of Burke's *Reflections on the Revolution in France,* to which *The Rights of Man* was a rejoinder. Yet Paine maintained his Quaker sensibilities, which were not that far afield from many Sufi currents in Islam—or even in some limited sense from the circumscription of halachic authority that was discussed by Fischer in terms of "occluded revelation." And while I do not know how John Courtney Murray would feel about being included with the likes of Thomas Paine, the truth is that this separation of religious authority from political power (which is very different from isolating religion from the public sphere) is not that distant from the principle of religious liberty that Murray espoused and that Wolfteich brought to our attention. Here then, is a brief exercise in translation.

In much more concrete terms of course, this issue of the boundaries of religion in its interaction with public order stands at the heart of Fisch's intervention and that of Göle as well. Sovereignty, and the role of religion and religious individuals who hold positions of power in an otherwise secular and pluralistic society, is no easily glossed subject. Whether we view the problem as one of public virtue and private vice, or private virtue and public vice, the salient issue—whether for a minister of tourism who must encourage the holiday traffic of idolaters or the division and use of space on a public beach, in either Israel or Turkey—is a matter that goes to the heart of any analysis of the boundaries between the spheres.

Moreover, and as both Fisch and Göle made clear, the very Western and perhaps Protestant distinction between public and private realms, selves, activities, and responsibilities does not hold in all countries and societies. As with the case of the *foulard* in French public schools and in Turkey as well, definitions of selves and of the social actor or citizen do not parse the same in all social settings.[3]

As can be ascertained from von Tippelskirch's discussion, the very idea of the self and its relation to the other is central to the problem of toleration. The ideas of sameness and otherness, which Estruch scrutinized to provide a sense of the problem (whether tolerance is necessitated by sameness or by difference), touch on the very core of tolerance as a way of being in the world. Von Tippelskirch's presentation, which sensitizes us to the importance of the other and the ethical obligations otherhood entails, returns us once again to the issue of boundaries. At stake of course is the very boundary of self and its relation to what is beyond that boundary, whether the other is as different at Estruch's Trobriand islander or rather more along Freud's lines of the "small difference." This is not an insignificant variable in determining the course of toleration in different civilizations and societies. In the following chapters, we shall return to these issues of sameness and difference and of the boundaries of selfhood to understand, compare, and contrast the dynamics of toleration in modern secular thought and in more traditional, religious ideas of self and other.

Much of our discussion did in fact return again and again to the issue of boundaries: for example, the boundaries of tolerance (Berger's question on cannibals and human sacrifice, or the case of Islam and Buddhism—Buddhism being beyond the limits of what Islam could accept as a *dhimmi* religion)—as well as the boundaries of communal membership (Rabbi Kook's attitude towards secular Zionists, the thought of John Courtney Murray, sectarianism in Islam, and the contemporary challenges of Muslim identity between tradition and modernity) are all illustrations of this. Delineating the boundaries of community is, as well, defining the other and defining them as strangers or not—which is precisely what is so fascinating about the categories of *dhimmi* and of the Noachides, both categories which blur these boundaries of stranger and of other, and so, in essence, of the community itself. Delineating boundaries, however, does not simply define the exogenous, but constitutes the endogenous as well. It is of course in the relation between the two, as in the constitutive conditions of the later, that tolerance is to be found (or not).

To unpack this dynamic, however, is no simple undertaking. As explained in the introduction, there exists an all too common contemporary tendency to define toleration in modern, secular terms—taken from the vocabulary of the Enlightenment. This is unfortunate as it blinds us precisely to that understanding of tolerance that we wish to develop, one not predicated on modernist assumptions and sociological and psychological truths. How then to translate from within the more emic, religious discourse, without in so doing transforming the problem of tolerance into the modern language of rights, entitlements, and individual goods? This is the challenge taken up in the following chapters. Using the metaphor of translation and of dialogue, an attempt is made to understand that problematization of existence that transcendent religion affected in the orders of the world. Out of this transformation, new categories of self and of other, of community and of stranger, emerged. As we shall see, these new categories redefined the grid of tolerance, its boundaries and its classificatory codes. By formalizing somewhat the themes of the dialogues along these lines, we will thus be able to appreciate the potential they open up for uncovering and utilizing different religious resources for toleration.

.   .   .

In the early decades of the twentieth century, Hermann Cohen argued the centrality of monotheism to that process by which the stranger was turned into the fellowman. To be sure, however, even Zeus, the highest god in the Greek pantheon, was the god of guest-friendship. Zeus was, therefore, god of something similar to that guest-friendship by which Israel was a stranger in Egypt, and thus mandated to respect the Egyptian. As Cohen points out: "Humanity is already so rooted in the stranger, that the slave, as stranger, can be admonished to the bond of gratitude."[4] It is a bond, we might add, predicated on and in translation (or else wherefore the stranger).[5]

There are strong analogies between the problem of toleration and the problem of translation. The move from stranger to fellowman is analogous to the move from one language to another. Walter Benjamin has compared the translator to one standing outside a forest, calling in to it "without entering, aiming at that single spot when the echo is able to give, in its own language, the reverberation of the work in the alien one."[6] A similar metaphor would hold for toleration if we were to transpose the action from speaking to listening!

Benjamin goes on to claim that "Where a text is identical with truth or dogma, where it is supposed to be the 'true language' in all its literalness and without the mediation of meaning . . . this text is unconditionally translatable," as indeed the Holy Writ has been.[7] If for Cohen the foreigner becomes a fellowman through the community of prayer, for Benjamin the very translatability of the Bible is a function of its revelatory aspect.

Both insights speak to us. Religion (not necessarily the dogmatic forms of organized religion, but rather the gnostic theophany of an Ibn-Arabi for example) may provide the ground for translation, for tolerance—for listening to the reverberations of another's speech in a manner not afforded the denizens of a more liberally appointed tolerance. In the latter, the very self-contained nature of the self, no longer "alone with the alone" but only with itself, precludes either.[8]

Diverse tongues are rooted in the diversity of our mental frameworks. The localism of language necessitates translation. Language which makes us at home in the world can also alienate us from the world in its very mediation. The deeper we delve into the phenomenon of language, as stressed in the writings of Hamann, Humboldt, and Herder, the greater we realize the specificity of each linguistic expression.[9] The localism of language, of all language, parallels the specificity of all forms of human experience. It, therefore, demands translation to be made known. It demands a recognition that the outer forms (what in the Islamic tradition is known as *zahir*) do not fully encompass the core of meaning (*batin* or *gnosis*). If it did, how could translation be possible? Meaning then, or at least full meaning, must lie beyond words.[10]

The precondition, the necessary but insufficient condition for translation, is thus tolerance in its minimalist sense—as bearing, suffering (Hebrew, *nasa*) of the other, bearing the other sufficiently to heed her call, regardless for the moment of its intelligibility. Religion, which recognizes the unity of Being beyond the diversity of phenomenological existence, can perhaps provide a ground for such tolerance that the very modern apotheosis of existence cannot indeed summon.

The first move of tolerance is a move of restraint, of reigning in. What is reigned in first and foremost is judgment. To withhold judgment is to recognize the limits of knowledge (and so of language) and so also to recognize the boundaries of self. This was a theme to which our discussants returned again and again, whether in the Jewish, Christian, or Islamic context. It is a theme deeply rooted in what Gary Remer has termed the "rhetoric of tolerance" among the humanists.[11] This was a view which distinguished between the relatively few "essentials" of faith which required adherence (and which were seen as common to all Christians) and the many non-essential doctrines (within Christianity) where no dogmatic acceptance was to be required. It was an attitude predicated on persuasion, peaceful resolution of disagreements, a stress on ethics over dogma, and a general "reluctance to condemn others for heresy."[12] It is the tolerance of Chillingsworth and of Pierre Bayle, of a recognition that God "impos'd no such Laws on us, nor Duty, but such as is proportion'd to our Facultys, to wit, that of searching for the Truth, and of laying hold on that, which upon a sincere and faithful Inquiry, shall appear such to us, and of loving this apparent Truth, and of governing our selves by his Precepts how difficult soever they may seem."[13] In some ways this recognition of one's limits and indeed of the limits of knowledge itself harks back to Socrates and his claims of ignorance, or rather his claims that true knowledge can begin only in the recognition and avowal of one's own limits. Knowing oneself is knowing what one does not know. From this position one may listen, and only from this position may one learn.

Such a moral compass would seem strikingly antithetical to the claims of Enlightened reason and not that distant from those of religion—hence the claim that a certain model of tolerance can be approached only from a religious perspective. What goes under the name of tolerance in a rationalist discourse is often at best indifference and at worst a stalemate in the calculus of mutual intolerance. Where knowledge is both absolutized and instrumentalized—as it is in the Enlightenment—there can be no room for tolerance. The problem is in fact defined away as irrelevant. How so? Knowledge is absolutized, as there is nothing beyond what is either known or knowable. Being is defined solely as existence, man's essence by his existence, unity only in the diversity of material and empirical forms. Knowledge is instrumental in terms of this existence and the control thereof. As the problem of one's fellowman is posited in the self-same categories, tolerance is defined away: subjected to a Hobbesian (or perhaps Mandevillian) calculus of interests, known, instrumental, and universal. In his *Fable of the Bees*, Bernard de Mandeville expressed most tellingly the rise of that type of individual encompassed in this anthropology:

> Man centers everything in himself, and neither loves nor hates, but for his own Sake. . . . Every individual is a little World by itself and all Creatures, as far as their Understanding and Abilities will let them, endeavor to make that Self happy: This in all of them is the continual Labour, and seem to be the whole Design of Life.[14]

Here too then, the otherhood of alter is defined away in the very universalization of reason. And if otherhood is defined away, so too, by implication, is desire—which is of course the fatal flaw of the whole enlightened edifice. Needless to say, this is what opened the way to the critique of J. G. Hamann, the German theologian and philosopher whom Isaiah Berlin termed "the Magus of the North." In such thinkers as Hamann, the Enlightenment was attacked for its apotheosis of reason and failure to respond to the "whole" person, the unity of body and soul, the passion and the limbs, not solely the calculating brain. "Life" for Hamann was "action" and not only life's contemplation. "Do not forget," he demanded, "for the sake of the cogito, the sum."[15]

With Hamann and other critics of the Enlightenment, desire is not quieted by reason nor subdued in a calculation of reason's handmaiden: interests. Desire is not content with analysis of utility functions or of rents. It demands more. It demands recognition. It is surely no coincidence that the issue of recognition so central to Hegel's *Phenomenology of the Spirit*, as well as to the thinkers of the Scottish Enlightenment, has emerged again at the cutting edge of international politics (not to mention of academic debate). The very globalization of reason (in the rules of commerce) calls forth its antithesis in the myriad local politics of recognition—often it must be noted of particularistic, xenophobic parties and movements. From the Bharatiya Janata party (BJP) in India to Le Pen in France, from Haider in Austria to the Nahdlatul Ulama (NU) in Indonesia, the politics of identity is but the politics of recognition. Behind both is a desire neither recognized nor subsumed by reason.

The problem of recognition and of desire, however, is the problem of restraint: restraint in the face of the other and in the recognition of limits—not least of which are the limits of language. Desire can be gratified only in translation. Only through translation can both desire and its object remain. Only through translation is the one not subsumed by the other. And the problem of translation is, as we affirmed earlier, analogous to that of toleration. Both demand a humility towards our own truth claims; both demand an ontological modesty which was one of the Enlightenment's greatest challenges.

To be sure, the progress of the Enlightenment also transformed the stranger into fellowman—but by radically different means. The fear of the stranger, of the ineluctable other, is overcome by the very terms of citizenship in the nation-state. The universalism of reason, upon which the transcendental edicts of the *Déclaration des droits de l'homme et du citoyen* are predicated, serves to anchor our lives in a shared experience of reason.

The very sameness of interest, posited by Hobbes, or later Hume, provides a new basis for social integration. The phenomenology of fear is transformed into the reciprocity of interests.

Thus the social bonds existing between people were characterized by Hume in this now famous quote:

> Your corn is ripe today; mine will be so to-morrow. 'Tis profitable for us both, that I should labour with you today, and that you shou'd aid me to-morrow. I have no kindness for you, and know you have as little for me. . . . Hence I learn to do a service to another, without bearing him any real kindness; because I foresee, that he will return my service, in expectation of another of the same kind, and in order to maintain the same correspondence of good offices with me or with others.[16]

And the adjudication of disputes between such self-regulating and autonomous agents was, in Adam Smith's words, achieved through appeal "to the eyes of the third party, that impartial spectator, the great inmate of the breast who judges impartially between conflicting interests." In Smith's terms:

> We endeavor to examine our own conduct as we imagine any other fair and impartial spectator would examine it. If, upon placing ourselves in his situation, we thoroughly enter into all the passions and motives which influenced it, we approve of it, by sympathy with the approbation of this supposed equitable judge. If otherwise, we enter into his disapprobation and condemn it.[17]

> . . .

> Before we can make any proper comparison of opposing interests, we must change our position. We must view them from neither our own place nor yet from his, neither with our own eyes nor yet with his, but from the place and with the eyes of a third person, who has no particular connection with either, and who judges impartially between us.[18]

In both Hume and Smith we find that orientation based on the autonomous, contracting individual engaged in exchange with other such individuals as constituents of modern politics and society.

Ideally, the problems for which tolerance is a solution no longer exist, as the concern with ultimate authorities and sacred coda are relegated to the darkest closets of consciousness. They are to be dealt with by the likes of Sigmund Freud and need not concern the theorists of social order—individual phantasmagoria rather than collective consciousness. As we now know, however, a century that began with the horrors of the Belgian Congo, ended with the massacre in Srebrnica, and encompassed horrors too imaginable to describe is surely one where fear, most especially fear of the other, has not been eliminated.

Where desire remains so does fear. No amount of recalibrating human motivation along the lines of simple interest can abrogate either. The problem of the other existing (for us) in fear and desire remain. And so does the need for tolerance. The phantasmagoria of consciousness—what Hamann called *Schwärmerei*—are not solely the fruits of individual imaginings. They are, as well, the very stuff of collective dreams, and nightmares. Fears of miscegenation characterize societies in 2002 no less than in fourteenth-century Aragon. The "*Judensau*" (the medieval image of Jews suckling from a pig's mammae) remains in the stone facade of the Marienkirche in Wittenberg. And the horrible use of mass rape by Serbian forces in Bosnia in the 1992–1995 war is still fresh in far too many minds. We cannot bypass these issues in the autonomy of the liberal self.

This being the case, we must then return to the problem of translation and what I dare to call a phenomenology of toleration. For is not toleration but the act of translation writ large? Are we not, after all, always translating; from the one to the other, from inner to outer, from silence to speech, from the book of nature to the book of man? And does not every such translation, every such act rest on a prior hesitancy? On a prior restraint? Does not the very dialogue of two interlocutors necessitate a manifold degree of self-control, which is the very stuff of civility as it is of tolerance? Today, so often "I hear you" is said—an indication perhaps that no one is, indeed, listening after all. But it nevertheless indexes that acknowledgement which, quite literally, makes room for alter's speech. Something similar must happen in the act of tolerance.

The medieval idea of "bearing with" or "suffering" as defining the tolerant act can be broadened beyond its initial, negative connotations of suffering evil or bearing with that which is distasteful, unpleasant, or wrong. (The sixteenth-century French words encompassing this semantic field were *tolérer, tolérance, souffrir, souffrance, permettre, endurer, endurance, admettre, mettre en publique, dissimuler*.)[19] It can be understood rather as suffering one's own self-restraint. It is bearing within that which must be borne for our very life within society. What must be endured or suffered, tolerated or permitted, is our own bearing of the other.

We must bear the other, both as a burden and in the self-restraint that such support demands—even the other over which we have no control. Hannah Arendt discussed something similar, not tolerance precisely, but the burden of responsibility for the other's acts over which we have no control:

> This vicarious responsibility for things we have not done, this taking upon ourselves the consequences for things we are entirely innocent of, is the price we pay for the fact that we live our lives not by ourselves but among our fellowmen and that the faculty of action, which, after all, is the political faculty par excellence, can be actualized only in one of the many and manifold forms of human community.[20]

The only way to "escape" this aspect of mutual, collective responsibility is "by leaving the community and since no man can live without belonging to some community, this would simply mean to exchange one community for another and hence one kind of responsibility for another."[21] This responsibility for what we did not do, for what is not our own, is close in nature to injunctions for tolerance—for hearing and supporting ideas and positions not our own. Both are predicated on a shared humanity. However different our languages, the voice of the other implicates us.

This other, moreover, remains other even after we have posited a concomitance of interests after the manner of David Hume. Interests unite us momentarily (the "stockholder" model of the polity) and in their presumed rationality (at least of material interests) offer the illusion of, if not control, then at least predictability. This indeed is the rational choice and economist reading of man and society. Interests are, as Max Weber taught us long ago, not only material but ideal, and as ideal interests (in such intangibles as salvation, meaning, recognition) they take us far along the road to desire, a road to where no control and no predictability is vouchsafed.[22] And yet, it is precisely here that toleration must be exhibited, where its presence must be felt.

On what basis? Restraint in the fulfillment of our interests is one thing, both rational and calculable. Beyond this, however, where do we look for the sources of such a tolerance? Where do we learn to listen, to make room for alter's speech and to bear it in silence? Where indeed do we learn that silence which lies as a precondition to the act of translation?

There is, in this context, a famous tale told in the Babylonian Talmud, in the tractate of Erubim (13:b), on a dispute between the two major schools of law, the school of Hillel and that of Shammai.

For three years there was a dispute between Beith Shammai and Beith Hillel, the former asserting, "The *halachah* is in agreement with our views". Then a *bath kol* [heavenly voice] issued announcing, "[The utterances of] both are the words of the living God, but the *halachah* is in agreement with the rulings of Beith Hillel". Since, however, "both are the words of the living God" what was it that entitled Beith Hillel to have the *halachah* fixed in agreement with their rulings?— Because they were kindly and modest, they studied their own rulings and those of Beith Shammai, and were even so [humble] as to mention the actions of Beith Shammai before theirs.

Here then the very creation of *nomos*, of rule-giving order, is tied to the act of listening, to the restraint involved in studying the rulings of one's adversaries.[23]

The centrality of discussion and dialogue, and hence by implication that self-restraint of bearing one's own silence that makes dialogue possible at all, is evident in all traditions and emphasized in all works devoted to the conditions of tolerance.[24] Thus, the injunction of the Apostle James, "let everyman be quick to hear but slow to speak" is quoted in the preface to Peter Abelard's *A Dialogue of a Philosopher with a Jew and a Christian* (1136). This quote, following a similar thought brought from the biblical book of Proverbs, is, I believe, a reference to that silent speech between traditions upon which the understanding of each must rest. The point of Abelard's *Dialogue* was itself less to uphold traditional Christian assumptions than to highlight the thread of common reason in all positions: the Law of the Jews, the natural law of the philosophers, and the supreme Good of the Christian God. As noted by Peter Mews, in Abelard's dialogue he "was primarily concerned not with proving Jews wrong, but with understanding the supreme good and how that supreme good should be reached. In terms of existing dialogue literature this was a novel perspective. By drawing attention to the common ground that was the goal of the philosopher, the Jew and the Christian, Abelard avoided the customary arguments generated by the uniqueness of the Christian claim."[25] Abelard was writing within a distinct genre of medieval dialogue, which included such works as Gilbert Crispin's *Disputatio Judei et Christiani* and *Disputatio cum gentili* (1092–1093) and Ramon Llull's *Liber de gentili et tribus sapientibus* (1275). Mews and Nederman both make the interesting claim that Abelard's dialogues go a step further than most in transforming such a genre from a demonstration of Christian superiority to an exercise in mutual edification (continuing in the work of Llull).[26]

Over four hundred years after Abelard, Jean Bodin wrote his famous *Colloquium heptaplomeres de rerum sublimium aracnis abditis* (*Colloquium of the Seven about the Secrets of the Sublime*), which was a dialogue between a Catholic, a Lutheran, a Calvinist, a Jew, a Muslim, an advocate of natural religion, and a skeptic. As argued by Gary Remer and Marion Kuntz, Bodin's dialogue departs from the accepted humanist script by refusing to reconcile all differences of religion in one single and unitary truth-claim. Though it is judged by many as a "failure" for precisely this reason (failing, that is, of the accepted humanist resolution) Remer and Kuntz show how the dialogue does itself point the way to a vision of toleration seen as "a unity based on multiplicity."[27] Unintentionally resonant with certain Sufi views of religious truth, Bodin's own argument saw "religious truth as composed of distinct elements whose differences cannot be ignored."[28] A vision of the harmony of diverse perspectives ("concordia discourse") is presented as an essential element of religious truth. And religious tolerance is, as explained by Marion Kuntz, a derivative of this harmony.[29] Interestingly, this harmony of beliefs is set off by the physical venue of the meeting, in Venice, which in the sixteenth century was the most international of cities, where the "commensality" of different faiths and religious creeds was more evident that anywhere in Europe.

Not published until the nineteenth century (although Leibniz had prepared a copy for publication in the seventeenth), Bodin's work was circulated in manuscript form for centuries. Its call to religious tolerance preceded many later arguments, including those of John Locke, as it ends with the argument that "no one can be forced to believe against his will." (This was of course the central feature of John Locke's argument for religious toleration in his 1689, *Letter Concerning Religious Toleration.*) Beyond the argument from conscience, Bodin's *Colloquium* makes a subtle, and for our purposes here a critical, point. This is the very valuation of dialogue for dialogue's sake. Valued is not the art of discourse for the sake of achieving a single and unitary truth, but as it were, for itself (something perhaps analogous to the Jewish notion of *torah l'shma*—that is the pursuit of torah for its own sake, rather than for any reward). The exchange of diverse views is for itself valuable. Not the negation of difference, but its very upholding is the point of dialogue. This is not a Millesian use of dialogue to urge on reason in the pursuit of a knowable (though yet unknown) truth. It is rather a use of dialogue to school the interlocutors in the act of living in a "concordia discourse." None of the participants decide to change their position on the basis of the discussion.

None convert. None are bested in the sense of having lost an argument. Nor do they agree that their differences are only in matters inconsequential, marginal, or inessential. Nor, yet again, do they adopt an argument of skepticism towards religious truths, or lack of faith or relativism (which would of course be the modern version of such a dialogue). All keep their faith or their belief in the existence of truth as well as in their own version thereof. Yet, they *tolerate* difference and argument, even revel in it. (What comes to mind as analogy is in fact the metaphor that Bodin puts in the mouth of one of his protagonists, when discussing the meaning of harmony: "the flavor of fresh oil and vinegar is very pleasing but it cannot be mingled by any force.")[30]

To moderns, schooled on the absoluteness of the principle of contradiction, such an approach verges on the incomprehensible. Yet it is precisely here that we have so much to learn on dialogue, on silence, and on that art of translation which is predicative of toleration. We may be schooled in a humility that is not skeptical, a modesty that is not relativist, just as we may learn a belief that is not absolutist. This is really the essence of dialogue, at least of Jean Bodin's *Colloquium*. What I am trying to argue is that such nonabsolutist belief is the essence of translation as well, or at least what makes translation possible. And, further, phenomenologically, it is what makes toleration possible as well. Not the retreat from truth, which is the negation of desire and what the relativism, skepticism, or indifference of so many ideas of toleration seem to imply, but its very recognition is the source of a genuine toleration: that is, of a toleration that endures and suffers, admits and permits of something other than alter's acts, beliefs, and doctrines. What the participants of Bodin's *Colloquium* endure (*tolérer*) are not alter's beliefs but an aspect of their own act of believing and affirming. It is here that the crux of the tolerant act and of its inherent restraint is to be found.

We may recall here Martin Buber's characterization of the three faces of dialogue which I quote at some length, as it well illustrates both the dialogue of tolerance and its opposite—the absoluteness of the self, capable of only a mirrored monologue.

> There is genuine dialogue—no matter whether spoken or silent—where each of the participants really has in mind the other or others in their present and particular being and turns to them with the intention of establishing a living mutual relation between himself and them. There is technical dialogue, which is prompted solely by the need of objective understanding. And there is monologue disguised

> as dialogue, in which two or more men, meeting in space, speak each with himself in strangely tortuous and circuitous ways and yet imagine they have escaped the torment of being thrown back on their own resources. The first . . . has become rare; where it rises, in no matter how "unspiritual" a form, witness is borne on behalf of the continuance of the organic substance of the human spirit. The second belongs to the inalienable sterling quality of "modern existence." . . . And the third . . . a conversation characterized by the need neither to communicate something, nor to learn something, nor to influence someone, nor to come into connection with someone, but solely by the desire to have one's own self-reliance confirmed by marking the impression that is made . . . an underworld of faceless specters of dialogue![31]

The turning to one another with which Buber characterizes real dialogue brings us back to the problem of recognition and the need for recognition, as well as its precondition: that is that lack, that lacuna, which recognition comes to complete. This lack is what Hegel characterized as desire: that which brings self-consciousness into existence through the perceived need to transform Being. Above, we tied desire to recognition, and that is very much Hegel's own argument. Expanding on that connection here will clarify its relevance to the theme of toleration.

In Hegel's chapter on *Lordship and Bondage* (commonly known as the *Master and Slave*), in his *Phenomenology of Spirit*, he parses out the dialectic of self-consciousness as a struggle to the death between two actors. It is a struggle for recognition. If the struggle ends with the death of one of the combatants, nothing is achieved as no recognition can be granted by the dead. Thus recognition and the unfolding of self-consciousness begins when one of the combatants succumbs, short of his death—afraid of his death. He becomes the slave whose fear of death and unwillingness, in the end, to risk all in face of death leads him to servility. The master on the other hand, in his willingness to sacrifice all, to face death unafraid, would seem, on first sight, to have attained that recognition required for consciousness and thus for human existence. This, however, is only an illusion. For in truth the master, as master, is caught in an existential bind. He demands recognition, but the only recognition that matters is that given by another man, that is, from another who was willing to face death, not from the slave who shied away from death. Recognition from the slave is not recognition at all. The master is defeated by his very triumph. He risked all in face of death for recognition by another. The other, the slave, however, in shying away from death became a slave—from whom any recognition is pointless. The master then can triumph only in death (his or his opponent's)—which of course is no triumph at all. The very terms of his success thus defeat the master's attainment of recognition.

The slave on the other hand is in a very different position. True, the slave shied away from death, but that very fear, the very fear of death's nothingness, has a positive element. The dread or terror of nothingness contains the seeds of its overcoming. As opposed to the master's position, which is essentially static, trapped in its own triumph, the slave's position is active; first it opposes the nothingness of death (in its refusal to yield to it), and then, much more significantly, it negates the world through its action: that is, through work, the work the slave does for the master. This work, moreover, is transformative, for it is in line with an idea, it is formed by a concept—admittedly, as yet, the concept of servitude, but a concept nonetheless. A concept is more than anything a blueprint for the transformation of nature. To quote Alexandre Kojève:

> By acting, he negates, he transforms the given Nature, his Nature; and he does it in relation to an idea, to what does not exist in the biological sense of the word, in relation to the idea of a Master—i.e., to an essentially social, human, historical notion. Now, to be able to transform the natural given in relation to a nonnatural idea is to possess a technique. And the idea that engenders a technique is a scientific idea, a scientific concept. Finally, to possess scientific concepts is to be endowed with Understanding, Verstand, the faculty of abstract notions.[32]

It is then the slave's work, not the master's fruitless triumph in battle, that produces historical change, history. It is the slave's work that transforms nature and makes the world human. As nature is transformed so is the slave, and by necessity the nature of the relations between master and slave. Through the transformative work of the slave he becomes other than he was. Changing the world, he has changed himself as well.

For Hegel the course of these transformations is the course of human history, identified as the progress of human freedom through the realization of the Absolute Idea in history. We need not follow its course here. It would take us too far afield. Though the careful reader who, I hope, excuses my summary presentation of Kojève's interpretation of Hegel will immediately be reminded once again of how critical these suppositions were to Marx's own historical anthropology, from the critical role of transforming nature in the coming to be of human existence to the importance of the concept in guiding this transformation. Moreover, when Marx discussed the necessity of turning Hegel on his head, it was to this that he was referring; that is, to the idealist frame in which what Marx nevertheless recognized as the fundamentally true representation of human existence was presented.

With the benefit of hindsight, some may now feel that turning Hegel on his head was not an unambiguously good idea. But that does not diminish the perspicacity of Hegel's own insights into the human condition (rightside up as it were). At very least, I believe, it provides us with an understanding of the dynamics of toleration, of what is involved in the tolerant act. In fact, it yields an understanding of what is involved in any act of real dialogue, of any real turning towards the other. For in each such a turn (and we are not concerned here with Buber's second and third forms) we show the face of both master and slave. We both demand recognition and shy in the face of an ultimate surrender of self. I am, as can be seen, suggesting that Hegel presents us not solely with a philosophical anthropology, but with an existential phenomenology as well. Triumphing as masters leaves us with a recognition we ultimately devalue (hence the need for ever more social triumphs, or, for that matter, conspicuously accumulated durable goods. There is no end to this and no reason to tolerate either, until we come up against the will of a stronger other. This, by the way, would lead to the type of toleration so often practiced both today and in the past—a *politique*—toleration of the balance of forces and of the inability to impose one's will on another, rather than an articulated toleration of principled self-restraint). Succumbing as slave, however, presents other potentialities. The restraint of the slave before death is akin to our own silence, our own ability to listen to the other. Enduring our own silence, reigning in our own desire to force recognition from alter, is analogous to the slave's own hesitancy before nothingness. In both cases a new form of action is called into being. In the case of the slave it is work; in the dialogic situation it is tolerance. Both are predicated on restraint, both transform the situation upon which they act and within which they were engendered. Both open up the historical process. Both, if you will, are timeful. Like the work of the slave, the work of tolerance is transformative, not only of external reality but of the actors as well. And in both cases, this action is formed by an idea and is a critical step beyond nature. In both, the problem, indeed the act of recognition, is wrestled from brute force and repositioned in the transformative action of work in and on the world. Work, again, rooted in self-restraint, founded even on fear.

Toleration, I am claiming, is part and parcel of the work of recognition. This work, as we have seen above, can and does take many forms. First and foremost, it is the very stuff of translation, with its infinite tension between and within languages. Translation itself, which always highlights the limits and insufficiencies of languages, is but a case of the more general problem of dialogue, of establishing a mutuality between present and particular beings. This, we know, is no easy task—if for no other reason than that the particular nature of each individual experience is continually lost in the general and abstract nature of language. Thus, the problems of recognition and of language are, as we have seen, inexorably linked together.

They must, moreover, both be predicated on restraint, on bearing the other, that very concept of *nasa* (to carry or to bear) broached in the writings of Lévinas, which is but another form of that responsibility (perhaps ontological responsibility) that Hannah Arendt ties to our very life in the world, our life in the community of our fellow humans. Without restraint, there is no dialogue; without silence, there is no language; and without tolerance, there is no communal life. Common to all is a reining in of desire, an ability to suffer desire frustrated, rather than a continual calibration of desire quantified. From Mandeville, Hume, and Smith we learn the capacity to bear frustrated desire as a compromise of interest realization (desire delayed). A calculus of delayed gratification is, however, of a very different nature than the bearing, or suffering, the carrying (*nasa*) of unrealized desire that is at the core of tolerance and of its connection to religion.

To turn to the connection of the above discussion to religion is thus to turn from framing our relations with the other in the Hegelian terms of fear to something different. We must in fact turn our attention from *fear* to *awe* and realize that the problem of desire is the religious problem par excellence. For it is religion that recognizes desire, recognizes that is, the problem of Being out of which desire springs (desire, not lust, though it can often take that form). It is after all within a religious consciousness that, following Fisch, we find Abraham struggling with God, or Job demanding of God an accounting. It is in religion that the limits of self become less a matter of mere *techne* and more an ontological position vis-à-vis God and the other. This is the move which Lévinas seeks to delineate and of which von Tippelskirch and Fischer remind us. For

Lévinas, this is the ontological obligation imposed on self by alter, the ethics which precede philosophy and which, as Fischer said, constitute that fissure which fractures existence. With religion, fear of the other is transformed into awe of the radically and transcendent Other, *das ganz Andere* or totally Other in Rudolf Otto's terms. In this move humility and modesty become virtues as they reflect not weakness but recognition (see below on the Islamic idea of *hilm* as juxtaposed to *al-Jahaliyya*). Whether in the Calvinist idea of *deus abscondidus* or in the Jewish idea of the covenant as yet unfulfilled, in epistemic terms or in our inability to know just what God wants—all dimensions brought forth in our dialogues—what emerges with religion is a problematization of existence (and of meaning) out of which desire, as something more than simply "want," emerges.

By religion, I refer to those religions of the Axial Age, that period between 500 B.C.E. and 600 A.D., as defined by S. N. Eisenstadt, in which there emerged and became constitutionalized.

> a conception of a basic tension between the transcendental and the mundane orders, a conception which differed greatly from that of a close parallelism between these two orders or their mutual embedment which was prevalent in so-called pagan religions, in those very societies from which these post-Axial Age civilizations emerged.[33]

The emergence of these Axial civilizations followed a period of institutional breakdown characterized by a similar breakdown of cosmological symbolism. This period, in Eric Voegelin's terms, of "cosmological disintegration" resulted in a new appreciation of the relations between the individual and society to the cosmic order.[34] The change was accomplished through the fundamental restructuring of the relations between mundane and transcendent orders. As Eisenstadt and others have noted, the emergence of this conception in the civilizations of ancient Israel, Christianity, ancient Greece, China, Hinduism, Buddhism, and Islam constituted a major force in the restructuring of the terms of collective life and of the principles of political legitimation.[35] For with the conception of a higher, transcendent order to which the political realm had to orient and legitimize itself, the "King-God" disappeared and was replaced by the notion of the accountability of rulers and collectivities to a higher order.

The Axial break (and the emergence of what has in other contexts been termed the great civilizations or historical religions) presumed a fundamental reordering of the nature of relations between society and "the powers governing the cosmos."[36] Breaking down their mutual inter-penetration, the Axial age posited a new conception of the social order, autonomous of, but in tension with, the cosmic (henceforth conceived of as transcendent) sphere. With the institutionalization of such a conception of chasm between mundane and transcendent orders (between society and the cosmos) and the concomitant search to overcome this chasm, the idea of salvation entered human consciousness.

With the invention (or discovery) of transcendence in this period, the magical, rather unitary and undifferentiated vision of cosmic existence became bifurcated by the ethical, by the call of a transcendent Being. Otherness was no longer represented as the otherness of demons, diverse deities, or wandering souls. That *Hinterwelt*, the "world behind the world" formerly given to magical coercion, was thenceforth projected outward beyond the world of daily affairs and events.[37] In this move, the otherness of enchanted nature took on transcendent properties. Within Western religious tradition, otherness was apotheosized in the logos of a personal creator God. This was achieved primarily in the radical transcendence of the Jewish Yahweh.[38] Against this transcendent being and its authority, totally beyond and outside the cosmos as it was, the very historicity of human existence was defined.

It is the authority of this transcendence that Kierkegaard plumbed in the image of the binding of Isaac and that provided a new moral locus of self-identity. To quote Karl Jaspers:

> For the first time *philosophers* appeared. Human beings dared to rely on themselves as individuals. Hermits and wandering thinkers in China, ascetics in India, philosophers in Greece and prophets in Israel all belong together, however much they may differ from each other in their beliefs, the contents of their thought and their inner dispositions. Man proved capable of contrasting himself inwardly with the entire universe. He discovered within himself the origin from which to raise himself above his own self and the world.[39]

Within the Western tradition the individual came to exist primarily as an individual-in-relation-to God, which as Jaspers noted is precisely what provided the "resoluteness" of "personal selfhood . . . experiencing the highest freedom in the limits of freedom in nothingness."[40] Each individual became a unique entity "immediately responsible to God for the welfare of his soul and the well being of his brother."[41]

The individual, of course, comes to be conceived differently in different traditions, even within the seemingly similar conceptions of Judaism and Christianity. The essential point is that the idea of transcendence provides a new locus of moral authority and selfhood not rooted in ascriptively defined and primordial categories of personhood. However paradoxical it may seem to us, the very authority of the transcendent calls the self into being as moral evaluator, as agentic in a sense other than power. Problematizing existence, transcendence drives the self to encounter Being and so discover desire, as opposed to simple lust.

It is thus in and through transcendence that Being is problematized and the consciousness of that nothingness from which desire springs is made possible. Religion in a sense not only recognizes desire, but generalizes it (in different ways in different civilizations.) It is therefore only in and through religion that a true tolerance can be sought—neither indifference nor relativism nor the tolerance of a balance of power between mutually absolute masters, but a tolerance predicated on the work of restraint in the face of desire. It is in this context of course that the mutually *politique* balance of power within a society of masters is shown to be not a tolerance predicated on the dynamics of desire and its recognition, but one of interaction eviscerated of desire and characterized only by lust (and its pleasures.) Tolerance becomes an almost personal virtue or attribute, an indicator of purely personal pluralism or worldliness in matters of taste, art, cuisine, sexual mores, religion, or olfactory stimulants.

Where desire resides, fear does as well. Fear of the other can, however, be transformed into awe of the other, *das ganz Andere* which was the generalization of desire achieved by Axial, or transcendent, religions. As we have seen, the absolutist rule of reason ignores both and attempts to define desire away. The ghosts of reason, however, always return, as desire is not to be denied. What *is* defined away though is the dynamic of tolerance, of restraint and endurance—of the work of the slave, of the dialogue of suffering. A position of tolerance can only emerge within the crucible of recognition. It can only be expressed in the face of desire. It is, as we have said, expressed primarily in the work of translating desire, rather than in imposing recognition.

And this work can only exist, can only begin (indeed only makes sense), in a world where the problematic nature of Being is recognized. This recognition is religious by definition. The moral autonomy of self-regulating agents in a secular world is of a different order of existence, as is what goes under the rubric of toleration. What we have termed above the principled indifference towards what pertains to the private in liberal regimes is not tolerance. It is rather simply what it is, principled indifference—which may shade off at times into relativism, at other times into a Hobbesian balance of power. It is not the translation of desire. And that is, of course, why the arguments and appeals of indifference do not work when the issues in dispute are those of recognition and of desire.[42] To appease these claims, we must find a language rooted in the self-same problematic. This is the language of religion, from which a dialogue (rather than an exchange transaction) may be effected.

To effect such a dialogue and the translation it necessitates is, however, no simple task. Precisely because the language of religion addresses Being and seeks to satiate desire always in very particular idioms is its translation difficult. Even assuming an openness to the other, to the stranger (which cannot always be assumed), the paths of translation are unclear. Symbols, as Mary Douglas has taught us, "are the only means of communication. They are the only means of expressing value; the main instruments of thought, the only regulators of experience. For any communication to take place the symbols must be structured."[43]

The particular ways this structuring has taken place in different world religions has influenced the dynamics of toleration. In fact, viewing religious traditions as particular types of symbol systems, each with its own particular internal architecture or structure, will give us insight into their respective modes of toleration. In slightly different terms: Desire generalized is always desire generalized along very particular paths with particular implications on the structure of symbol systems. We explore below only two dimensions of these symbol systems: of the symbolic classification they express and of their relevance to the dynamics of tolerance in different religions.

.   .   .

Drawing on the work of Mary Douglas and Basil Bernstein, I would like to posit two dimensions of symbolic classification. The first (A) pertains to the boundaries of the group. The second (B) pertains to the classificatory code, that is, to the nature of what is classified. As can be seen, these dimensions have much in common with Mary Douglas's schema of "group" and "grid" that she developed in her work on *Natural Symbols*. Each dimension can be further distinguished. Dimension *A: Boundaries of Group* can be viewed as relatively permeable or impermeable and as relatively inclusive or exclusive (broad or narrow). Though seemingly similar, these are analytically separable dimensions: the one having to do with the nature of the boundaries and the other with their extent. Dimension *B: Classificatory Code* can be seen as limited or expanded (applying to fewer or to greater aspects of life and social organization) and as leaning to a greater degree of inflexibility or a greater degree of malleability. Again, two similar but separable dimensions: the one pertaining to the extent of classification and the other to its modes. To schematize:

Dimension A: Boundaries of Group
　　a1) permeable or impermeable
　　a2) inclusive or exclusive
Dimension B: Classificatory Code
　　b1) limited or expanded
　　b2) inflexible or flexible

Thus, for example, along axis (A) Hinduism can be seen as having relatively exclusive or narrow definitions of membership (in the importance of ascription, the holiness of the subcontinent itself to religious practice, the sacrality of the land, the role of Brahmins in sacralizing other land), yet relatively permeable boundaries (they can assimilate other gods into their pantheon). The sharp divisions between Islam and Christendom, with clearly delineated borders, rarely characterized the interstices of Hinduism with other religions. Islam, on the other hand, is seemingly characterized by an inclusive, universal, and broad definition of group membership. Yet, at the same time it is one which is relatively nonpermeable. One can be a lax Muslim, but not a lapsed one.

To move to dimension B, we may, for example, compare Islam to Judaism and see how they both have relatively expanded classificatory codes. Both the Jewish halacha and the Muslim sha'aria are much more precise, detailed, and densely girded in their organization of the intricacies of daily life than analogous codes in Christianity (except perhaps for the rules of monastic orders in Catholicism). Yet, their degrees of malleability are quite different. Judaism, with its tradition of continually developing interpretation, is much more flexible than is Islam. And within Islam, Shi'ite Islam, which maintains that the gates of *itjihad* consensual interpretation are always open, has more flexibility than most Sunni versions. On the other hand of course, Judaism is much more exclusive than is Islam. The idea of covenant as organizing metaphor for religious experience provides not only that openness of interpretation, but also a very different sense of boundaries and definition of community than universal submission (*islam*) to the will of God.

Sectarian Protestantism in the seventeenth century was, for example, characterized by exclusive group boundaries that were nonetheless permeable. Judaism by contrast is exclusive but not very permeable. And if the classificatory codes of Judaism can be seen as expanded but malleable, those of Protestantism would be limited (at least in their heyday), and inflexible, as witnessed by the continual exclusionary practices of sectarian groups—precisely the sort of disassociation of the medieval *universitas* of which their Catholic critics warned.[44]

Of course this type of classification can be implemented not only between religions, but within one religion as well. We have briefly mentioned differences between Sunni and Shi'ite Islam. One could also classify differences between ancient Zadokites, Pharisees, and Essenes along the same grid; or differences between different groups of Sufis in Islam or of world renouncers in Christianity or Buddhism. Similarly and perhaps more interestingly, one could focus on different types of practices and orientations; say an emphasis on ritual purity (as one Islamic *hadit* states: "purification is one half of the faith") or on intentionality (*kavanah* in Hebrew, *nir* in Arabic) and analyze what role, if any, they have in the construction of these two dimensions of symbolic classification. One could usefully query what sort of classificatory codes have an "elective affinity" (to use Max Weber's phrase) with a high emphasis on intentionality in religious doctrine. There would, at first sight anyway, seem to be a high correlation between a privileging of intentionality (over ritual, say) and a limited (explicit) classificatory code (which in turn would expand the areas and actions to be judged by individual conscience) that is nevertheless relatively inflexible. This would seem to be the generalization taken from say, seventeenth-century Christian Protestants, Islamic Mutazilites, and Jewish Hasidim. On the other hand, a stress on ritual purity would in some cases indicate an exclusive and narrow articulation of borders (Judaism, Hinduism), but not in all cases (Islam). Yet, in both Judaism and Islam it would seem to bespeak a concern with maintaining nonpermeable borders with outsiders.

Interesting is certainly the case of heterodox insiders as well. For all religions have seen movements to reassert a sense of ritual (and social) purity, a return to the pristine terms of the religious message. Sometimes these movements have been incorporated within the religious traditions (Sufism in Islam, as well as the Mahdi movement of the nineteenth century, Hasidism in Judaism, Catholic Franciscans, and so on). Sometimes such movements have simply disappeared historically (as many Christian heresies have or the Jewish Karaites, though some groups of the latter did persist as communities in the Crimea until the Nazi occupation). Sometimes they have emerged as new religions (Buddhism, Christianity from Judaism, Ba'hai from Shi'ite Islam). And sometimes they occupy a strange in-between position, as Protestantism does, or Shi'ite Islam in its relation to majoritarian Sunni interpretations. Just how heterodoxies were treated within the traditions would seem a critical function of the definition of boundaries as well as classificatory codes (and also historical conditions).

Along the same lines one could look to rituals of restoration, purification, and reintegration as pointing to a form of internal tolerance that is far from those of liberal/individualist societies and indeed a form that would be rejected as intolerant in modern terms. Yet, maintaining the integrity of the group (its boundaries), rituals of restoration and reintegration nevertheless do not exclude. Certain religions are more concerned with such rituals than others: Hinduism more than Protestantism, for example. Certainly early Christianity, which existed in expectation of the eschaton, had relatively few of such rituals. The eternal delay of that event and the universalization and generalization of the Christian message (and boundaries of community) led of course to a new concern with such rituals. Protestantism, in reformulating the terms of the Christian commonwealth, in effect did away with the necessity of such rituals, replacing the reintegration of self to community with a reintegration of self to itself (by the end of the seventeenth century). This is, however, no longer reintegration, but a whole different idea altogether. It changes the problem of tolerance from that of group boundaries to the acts of individuals, which we shall take up shortly.

My own concern with these symbolic dimensions, however, is not to develop yet another taxonomy of religions or of religious experience. It is rather to operationalize the previous remarks on toleration, on its nexus in the relation of the self to other and of my argument that the problem of toleration is really one of translation, of a translation of symbols and symbol systems rather than anything else. For what we find on simple reflection is that these two dimensions studied, of group boundaries and of classificatory codes, are the two grids of toleration as well: that is toleration of the other (individual or group) (A) and toleration of discrete sets of acts (B). This is not surprising, especially if we recall the origin of these dimensions in Basil Bernstein's categories of *speech* (elaborated and restricted, analogous to our idea of classificatory codes) and the nature of *family control* (analogous to our idea of group boundaries). We can in fact illustrate these grids of toleration with the following diagram:

+ outside group

|
(A) | - (*Limits of Tolerance*) +
(Boundaries of Group) | (B)
|

+ inside group

One can immediately notice that the dimension of group boundaries (vertical axis) has in fact two aspects; degrees of tolerance towards those outside the group, that is, members of other religious groups and, critically, degrees of tolerance towards internal dissidents, heretics and those considered deviants by the given categories of the religion in question.

This way of representing the problem of toleration is useful for a number of reasons. Most importantly perhaps, it cuts across the distinction between medieval and modern modes of tolerance (and intolerance). For the medieval problem of tolerance revolved around group identities, while the modern problem is oriented towards individuals and their acts. Making use of the above grid thus gives us a language within which we can speak of, indeed conceptualize, two very different types of historical problems without reducing the one to the other. For what usually happens is that the traditional problem of toleration (of groups) is reduced to the modern problem (of individual or acts), and the specificity of the former is lost. Dis-aggregating the terms of toleration in both traditional and modern contexts allows us to juxtapose them. In so doing we thicken our understanding of the problem of toleration in all contexts by showing where the difficulties lie in any act of translating the relevant symbol systems as a whole (given their very different orientations to the critical two axes of symbolic representation).

Moreover, and well within the premodern terms of the problem, we can see just how critical a number of the tolerant "moves" referred to in our dialogues were. A concern with maintaining group boundaries (axis A) and with tolerance as an affair of groups rather than individuals does not have to preclude the development of tolerant attitudes. The concept of the *dhimmi* in Islam or the developing notion of tolerance to those who abide by the Noachide laws in Judaism—critically as expanded by Ha'meiri as both Fisch and Stone have shown, are moves to blur somewhat the nature of those group boundaries, to establish intermediate categories of "fellow travelers" if you will.[45] Tolerance towards those outside the group is thus extended and recognition accorded on the basis of a new category, which valorizes without totally subsuming the alter into ego. Similarly, and as pointed out by both Stone and Fischer, moves can be found to accept difference within the group and thus extend somewhat its own boundaries—which is a move echoed in different ways by the Catholic Church in the Second Vatican Council.

Along axis B (of classificatory codes) various premodern mechanisms of tolerance were also teased out in our foregoing discussion. One of the most interesting of these was the idea of casuistry—as a mode both of maintaining the boundaries of a tradition and at the same time of developing new orientations and injecting a lability into the tradition and its classificatory codes. Here too we find similarities in Judaism, Islam, and the Roman Catholic Church—of the need to accommodate change and reframe codes of conduct and behavior while maintaining the coherence of the tradition and of the community. Of course the whole discussion of epistemological modesty, in all three traditions, whether rooted within mystic or rational orientations, also bears directly on this axis and on our self-reflection towards our own classificatory codes. We take our bearings from Job (who questioned divine justice) no less than from the Deuteronomist (who classified its rules). As Abu Zayd made clear however (and he spoke from within the Islamic tradition, but the insight holds for all religions), it is always very specific historical and geopolitical contexts that will influence the privileging of one mode over the other.

As tolerance is, in the end, not a matter of either people (or types of people) or of acts, but of symbols, an approach based on an appreciation of these symbols permits us a greater degree of insight into the dynamics at work in different cases. Most especially it helps us to understand that the problem is not one of a traditional/intolerant attitude posited over against a modern/tolerant one but rather of different dimensions of tolerance and intolerance in both (indeed in all) societies. Tolerance of course must always be rooted in a value position. If not, then there is, by definition, nothing beyond that value position and so no realm that must be tolerated. It is only in and from a value position (and the symbol system expressing such values) that the problem of tolerance, of its modes and its limits, can emerge.

To reiterate briefly, religion, which engages the terms of Being, problematizing it in the face of transcendence, thus engages desire in its most elemental forms. To a great extent, the work of religion (often in ritual) is the work of translating desire, transforming its modalities and suffering its mediation, in the growth of new forms of recognition. Not all of these can be institutionalized. Thus the Sufi martyr Mansur Hallaj's

(d. 309 c.e.) dictum *Ana'l-Haqq* (I am God), which led to his execution
for blasphemy, was in fact, as illustrated by the great mystic Rumi, an act
of supreme submission (and hence recognition of the Divine)—though
it was hardly seen as such by the caliph.

> People imagine that it is a presumptuous claim, whereas it is really
> a presumptuous claim to say *Ana'l-Abd*, I am the servant of God and
> *Ana'l-Haqq*, I am God is an expression of great humility. The man
> who says *Ana'l-Abd*, I am the servant of God affirms two existences,
> his own and God's but he that says *Ana'l-Haqq*, I am God, has made
> himself non-existent and has given himself up and says I am God, i.e.
> I am naught, He is all: there is no being but God's. This is the ex-
> treme form of humility and self-abasement.[46]

Hallaj's recognition, however, negated the orders and structures of the
world (and of its power centers), hence his execution. Crucial to the act
of recognition within the orders of the world must therefore be its ability
to develop along the concrete venues of group definitions and classificatory codes, as matrixes of translation. The particular forms of their institutionalization have come to shape the dynamics of both tolerance and
its absence in different societies, including the secular West.

It is as well at the core of the above-noted distinction between the
medieval and early modern European problem of toleration—that is, toleration of groups—and the modern version of the problem—that is,
toleration of individual acts and/or proclivities. For the medieval definition of community was that it was in possession of truth. The boundaries of the group were deemed to be congruent with the boundaries of
truth. All groups, we may note, have an element of "intolerance" inherent in their very constitutive conditions (even if they are not explicitly
identified with transcendent truth-claims as they were in the medieval
and early-modern periods and as certain religious groups, such as Jews and
Muslims, continue to be). For groups to exist, they must have boundaries.
And while one can perhaps meaningfully discuss the issue of tolerance
to those beyond the boundaries of the group, the issue of tolerance towards insiders becomes somewhat more problematic. While evangelical
and missionary activity towards those of other faiths would be a prime
form of intolerance towards those "others" beyond the boundaries of the
group, often a mediated form of indifference can be found (as for example, in the attitude of observant Jews towards most all non-Jews). This
attitude of mediated indifference, however, becomes, at least on some

level, difficult to maintain internally. At some point, if a group is to maintain its boundaries, it must be intolerant of behavior that threatens to abrogate those boundaries. (Thus the problem of tolerance for the Orthodox community of Jews is not towards Roman Catholics but towards Reform Jews.) If a minority of the members of the West Roxbury Numismatic Society began devoting their energies to philately and began to bring stamps rather than coins to the weekly meetings and thus attempted to change the group's focus, one would hardly condemn the other members for demanding of these stamp-bearers to desist or cede to form a different organization. We may not wish to call such behavior intolerance, but whether we condemn it or not, view it in a positive or negative light, it does contain no small degree of intolerance (at least to modern sensibilities). Yet, this "intolerance" is in essence mandated by the very constitutive definitions of the group as the West Roxbury Numismatic Society. It is tied to the very identity and self-definition of the group. About such matters, groups are often less than tolerant, though to be sure we do not usually view such matters as bearing on the problem of tolerance.

At least we do not when it is a matter of a stamp society. Yet, when it is a matter of a religious group acting in such terms to its internal dissidents, we do most often view it in precisely such terms of tolerance and intolerance. Thus, when the groups in question are defined in modern, instrumental terms, we do not tend to see the matter of group inclusion or exclusion as bearing on matters of tolerance (and hence with a bearing on individual rights—except of course on an instrumental level, where relevant). On the other hand, when groups are defined in traditional terms, of having boundaries coeval with those of a set of truth-claims, then processes of exclusion are viewed as forms of intolerance inimical to modern values and desiderata.

Given this orientation of ours, it is useful to review, however briefly, its own history, which was in the Protestant Reformation of the sixteenth century. After all, the original purpose behind the Council of Trent (1541) was to find a *modus vivendi* between the Catholic and Reforming Protestants, an irenic attempt to maintain the unity of the Church (that is, maintaining its boundaries) after the failure of the Diet of Regensburg. Failure to reach agreement on the issues of original sin, transubstantiation, and penance spelled the end of such attempts to maintain Christian unity—precisely those nonessential, or what were termed adiophoric, beliefs that the Humanists believed were unnecessary to maintain Christian unity. We have, however, all been thoroughly transformed by those events, regardless of our religious beliefs or lack thereof, and that is why we tend to view stamp collectives one way and membership in a religious collective somewhat differently. For in a fundamental sense, we have all assimilated the deeply individualistic tenor of sectarian Protestant beliefs, which privilege the principle of individual autonomy, the freedom of conscience, and the self-regulating agency whose roots are in the belief in the inner light and the immediacy of the Holy Spirit as espoused by numerous Protestant sects in the sixteenth and seventeenth centuries (and whose heir Thomas Paine was). It is, interestingly enough, among many of these sects (though by far not all) that the first principled and explicit arguments for religious toleration can be found.

The path of toleration that eventually led to modern positions on the privatization of belief, freedom of thought, and individual rights is rooted in Protestant beliefs, in the privatization of grace and the internalization of conscience that developed most saliently among groups of sectarian Protestants—Moravians, Quakers, Baptist, Anabaptists, Collegiants, Socinians—in the late sixteenth and seventeenth centuries. Such religious thinkers as Hans Denck (d. 1527) and Sebastian Franck (d. 1542) played an important role in developing an attitude of toleration of different Christian sects not just to one another, but to all of humankind. Sebastian Franck's belief in religious freedom, the opaqueness of all ultimate truths, and the common nature of the human predicament continued to be influential much beyond his lifetime.

The writings of thinkers such as Jean Bodin (d. 1596) and Pierre Bayle (d. 1706) developed less explicitly religious bases for toleration and provided a critical bridge between the explicitly religious discourse of the sixteenth century and the increasingly natural-law arguments of the late seventeenth and early eighteenth centuries.[47] Pierre Bayle, who himself converted to Catholicism in 1668 and back to Protestantism less than two years later, was exceptional for his time, extending toleration even to atheists, which neither Jean Bodin nor, later, John Locke was to do. (Locke also refused toleration to Catholics.) Bayle indeed anticipated a very modern approach to toleration predicated on individual liberty and freedom of expression. Samuel Pufendorf's (d. 1694) writings on toleration within the context of the early modern natural-law tradition (though less radical than Bayle) must also be noted in this context.

More critically, we are heirs to the ideas of political community that emerged concomitantly (and necessarily perhaps) with ascetic-Protestant ideas of individuality. This was the idea of the political community as a voluntary compact between self-willed agents, the political community as an act of will achieved by individuals who exist in a position of metaphysical equality. The self-evident truth of created equality and the natural rights of man are all, as has been attested to by many, the political derivatives of a new *societas* of individual agents imbued with grace (or rights, depending on one's orientation towards transcendent or transcendental truths). And it is within this reading of community that the issue of boundaries and group identity becomes transformed. With the idea of constitutive groups essentially defined out of existence (in the idea of the contract as the basis of community) the issue of tolerance arises with a saliency and conscious self-reflexive quality it had not had before. The problem of tolerance is no longer one of groups towards other groups, but instead of every individual to each and every other. It is no longer the problem of a judging public defined as a community of truth which constitutes the very terms of self identity, of self in community and so of its own boundaries. Rather the problem of tolerance becomes the logistical problem of directing the discrete acts of autonomous self-regulating agents in a market (of goods and later of ideas). It becomes the problem of individuals and their acts.

The problem of tolerance and that of civility thus emerge concomitantly. They are both, in a sense, necessary to the emergent eighteenth-century bourgeois culture of the nation-state. In fact, to some extent it is only in this period that the issue of tolerance emerges in a form that we can perceive as our own. Interestingly, it is also the period when tolerance becomes a positive virtue rather than the lesser of two evils, as it was in medieval Catholicism. As individuals are valued in their individuality, the problem of toleration becomes one of tolerating different forms of this individuality. This is registered in the language of civility, acts of which, for their part, are meant to blunt the edges of individual self-regarding acts and provide a symbolic language of mutual recognition between metaphysically equal individuals—the institutionalization of the Hegelian dialectic of recognition. With the universalization of this view of the self as self-willed agent, the medieval approach to toleration is transformed into the quintessential modern one. What this entails on the level of ideal types is in fact a transformation of the problem from one dealing primarily with axis (A), group boundaries, to one dealing primarily with axis (B), individual acts and where they fall within a classificatory code. The differing saliency of each axis in the medieval and modern systems reflects the different aspects of symbolic classification, indeed the vast difference in the primary dimension of symbol systems organizing reality in the different civilizational frameworks.

The universalization of the modern terms of individual identities effectively defined away the whole problem of group boundaries, removing them from the problem of tolerance. Groups are no longer constitutive of individual selves, no longer identified with transcendent truth-claims (despite perhaps Georg Lukacs's attempt in the 1920s to argue precisely this role for the world proletariat and, in a somewhat different mode, attempts of certain radical feminists and lesbians to make that claim on the purely ascribed criteria of gender), but are seen as increasingly of a purely instrumental nature: the stockholder model of the social order. True, even in modern societies certain forms of group membership are seen as effectively delineating the boundaries of self-identity and making transcendent claims of ultimate truth, but these are ideally relegated to the private realm, with no or few, claims to the public sphere of the organization of the political community or regulation of the division of labor. Charity is fine; prohibition on interest-taking is something quite else again. (Interesting here are the attempts of such Muslim modernists as Mohamad Iqbal [d. 1938], one of the "fathers" of modern Pakistan, to base what we think of as certain forms of citizen entitlement on the Muslim decree of *zakat*, that is, the poor-rate.) And of course when such groups do dare to make claims on the public sphere, typically not in Western Europe or the United States, but more frequently in countries such as Israel, Iran, Turkey, Egypt, Pakistan, or India, they are seen as invoking a rhetoric of intolerance, as indeed they are in many cases, when judged by modern standards of culture and society.

The problem is that simply defining them as such does not lead us anywhere. For, as I have attempted to argue, the terms of the problem with which they are dealing is substantively different from the modern one. Moderns tend to ask: The truth for whom? Is it a clear truth or an ambiguous one? An absolute or a relative one? And so on. We tend to discount the idea of truth standing in any relation to group boundaries and are willing to recognize such boundaries only in so far as they define an instrumental entity (the American Medical Association or the West Roxbury Numismatic Society), but not as a truth-collective, except again, in so far as such collectivities voluntarily refrain from engaging the public sphere. Again, tolerance is not about truth-claims (for moderns) but about the limits of certain forms of behavior and how they are countenanced by the collective. Laws against sodomy are not about the truth-claims of the individuals involved but about the limits and extent of individual freedoms. This is a very different issue from the one confronting Muslims, or a Christian or Jewish minority existing in their midst; or from the problem for Christian civilization of the continued existence of the Jew in their midst; or for that matter from Huguenots in France in the sixteenth and seventeenth centuries. And it is not that one or another set of issues is more or less humane, more or less "emancipating" than the other, it is that they are a fundamentally different set of issues, with different stakes, with different symbolic concerns at stake, and it is a category mistake to treat them both as the same problem. They are not. Unfortunately, and all too often, we read back chronologically and reinterpret problems of group boundaries and of the contesting truth-claims of different groups and the conflict they engender in terms of more modern individual concerns with personal freedom and expression. As long as we do so, we remain deaf to the language being spoken.

If the problem existed only in the terms in which it is posited by modern notions of self and society, we would not need to draw on other traditions and ways of thought. Yet, it is precisely because modern readings of self and society do not (indeed cannot) fully encompass the human dilemma (as indeed no one reading can, including the traditionalist), we must as well tap the language of traditionalist readings to provide answers that are less than forthcoming in our modernist tongue.

As a first step in this procedure we may well posit modern readings of the problem of toleration along the same two axes that we used to understand traditional/religious readings. True, as noted, the relative saliency of the problem does, in most general terms, move from axis (A) to axis (B), but that is because of the very terms in which axis (A) is posited. In modern liberal societies axis (A) is defined in universal terms that are relatively nonpermeable. The relegation of other than universal identities to the purely private realm is of course the foremost example of this lack of permeability (intolerance really) of alternative forms of identity. Its classificatory code (axis B) is, on the other hand, limited. That is, it makes relatively few claims on the organizing symbols of daily life; those that are made, however, are inflexible. Of course, as in different religions, the different modernities of different global societies, even of different European countries, or North American ones, will show significant differences of relative emphasis in these four categories. As ideal types however, I believe they hold up under scrutiny. The critical point here, of course, is that the progress of toleration in modern societies is not along axis (A), as the universalization of boundaries essentially defines away the idea of group, and any threat to such identity threatens the very constitutive conditions of modernity and hence is not countenanced. Nor is it along the lines of increased flexibility of axis (B), though there is no prima facie reason to rule that out. Rather, and historically, the growth of tolerance in modern and especially in modern liberal societies has been by *limiting ever more the range of activity that the classificatory code is responsible for organizing*. Of course, the problem with this is that at a certain point and in conjunction with the universalization of boundaries along axis (A), society threatens to define itself out of existence as a *nomos*-governed entity. Predicating tolerance on the increasing self-reflexive self-limiting of the symbolic code is a dangerous endeavor. It, in the end, threatens to undermine the very shared universe within which self and alter reside. Tolerance becomes indifference with a vengeance—a vengeance that can take brutal forms when the terms of mutual interest (which, through contract, is now all that is holding ego and alter together) are transformed. Desire is neither restrained nor satiated, nor translated, but denied. The very return to myriad forms of group-based identities (religious, ascriptive, gendered, ethnic, etc.) calls such solutions into question; questioning if such solutions can be achieved at all.

New forms of group-based identity arise again in the language of desire, in their very vocal and public demands for recognition. And this, in fact, is the social significance of such holidays as Kwanza, or of a Boston rabbi lighting a Channuka menorah on Boston Common (or a French rabbi on the Champs de Mars for that matter). All betray the demand for group-based recognition, for a recovering of one's identity framed collectively. Not surprisingly, these demands are most often framed religiously. This is the case not only over prayer in school or placing the Ten Commandments in a courthouse. It is not surprising that in contemporary America, the struggle over identity, community, class, and status (i.e., over recognition) often takes the form of a struggle over religious symbols. For the language of religion is that language in which the problem of recognition was first framed and through which alternative sources for a language of tolerance can be found. These must be those that recognize restraint, endurance, and suffering—tolerance in its original sense (however politically incorrect this may sound to contemporary ears.) Better the learning of self-restraint and tolerance (in its original sense) of what we think is wrong, than the lie of false agreement and desire denied.

A world denuded of desire is denuded of truth-claims as well. After all, it is through truth-claims—originally of a religious and/or philosophical nature—that Being was problematized in the dynamic which called forth desire. The privatization of desire (reminiscent of Max Weber's insights into the privatization of charisma in the modern world) is part of the privatization of truth-claims discussed above, concomitant on the belief in a purely instrumental organization of the shared public realm. We may recall Walter Benjamin's insights on the oxymoronic nature of the term "public opinion." "Opinions" he notes, "are a private matter. The public has an interest only in judgements. Either it is a judging public or it is none."[48] And of course the progress of modernity, indeed its globalization, has been characterized by just this evisceration of the public.[49] Again, what I am pointing to is the solution of indifference to the problem of tolerance through the ever-increasing restriction of a shared public *nomos*. Quite apart from whether this solution can be translated into Hindi or Punjabi or Arabic, is the question if it is even a viable solution in what we have come to think of as modern societies. *Nomos* can only be circumscribed so much without threatening anomie. Yet if this restriction of *nomos* has been the modern route to toleration, and if in its very definition it must be self-limiting, then we must resurrect other languages and other modes—those rooted in a recognition of desire and in the competency to make truth-claims, but also those which evince a restraint towards those very claims.

Tolerance in modern societies, I have argued, rests on both the evisceration of group-based identities and the radical circumscription of shared classificatory codes. Radical universalism requires an equally radical individualism. This makes it exceedingly difficult for members of these societies to understand the terms of desire and its translation (and so the term of toleration or even its failure) in other societies, not so constituted. It also, however, transforms the very terms of tolerance from the work of recognition and translation, from the dialogue of mutuality, to a simple interest calculation along the lines laid out by David Hume. The inherent limits of this approach are made clear in the Channuka menorah on Boston Common, in the celebration of Kwanza, and for that matter in the backlash to gay marriage in Vermont and the riots of young Muslims in England, or the vote for Le Pen in the runoffs to the 2002 French presidential elections. On the global level, we witness the same limits in the failure of the Oslo Peace agreement in the Middle East, in the 1992–1995 war in Bosnia and the violence in the Sudan; the list is endless.

All are examples, admittedly, not particularly pleasant ones, of the inherent limitations and insufficiencies of an appeal to tolerance and mutual acceptance, which seeks to elide the core of existing problems (by doing away with groups and shared *nomoi*) rather than face the painful work of recognition and so translation. Just how to approach the latter work is, needless to say, the challenge facing us all.

Some light can, I feel, be shed on this, at least in metaphor, by recalling the reality of Sarajevo before the 1992–1995 war and the nature of commensality there: the move between the particular *mahalas*, or neighborhoods, and the city center, the *Charshiya*. As explained in an evocative work by Dzevad Karshasan:

> Upon leaving the Charshiya, all Sarajevans retreat from human universality into the particularity of their own cultures. Namely, every *mahala* continues the enclosed lifestyle of the culture that statistically prevails in it. Hence, Byelave, for example, is distinctly a Jewish *mahala*, whose everyday life completely realizes all the particularities of Jewish cultures, life in Latinluk goes on in accordance with the particularities of Catholic cultures, in Vratnik in accord with Islamic cultures; and in Tashlihan according to the particularities of Eastern Orthodox cultures.[50]

In this move between cultures, with its almost enforced pluralism, a new/old form of tolerance may perhaps be found. It would be one that abjures the false universalism of Jacobin modernity. It would be one that must admit of the particular as well as of the universal and which in the move between them would bracket that certitude of knowledge upon which all tolerant attitudes must in the end founder. It would be, in Bob Scribner's words (used to describe events in the sixteenth century) a "tolerance of practical rationality . . . of ordinary people . . . a tolerance found frequently in daily life which made little fuss about difference in belief and accepted it as a normal state of affairs."[51] That such a tolerance could also be easily overturned should, however, not escape us either, not in the period of the Reformation and not today.

Needless to add, the conflation of ethic and religious identities in the Balkans is also a potent reminder of the dangers of all group-based and identity politics in the modern world. This was as true in the period of the Reformation (for example, in the popular anti-Jewish riots in Regensberg in 1519 and Frankfurt in 1614) as it is today. The rising tide of certain forms of Islamic identities in Bosnia and Herzegovina, as indeed in other societies (and religions), also reminds us of the myriad ways religious fundamentalism is implicated in the project of modernity itself. Abu Zayd made that point most saliently. The very search for self-certainty and absolutist religious truth that characterizes fundamentalism of all stripes (Christian, Hindu, Islamic, Jewish, or Sikh) is itself part and parcel of modernity. Such absolutist and totalizing orientations, always inherent in religions (as indeed in all nomological positions), develop both in tandem with and in protest to the impingement of modern political-ideological centers on enclave cultures: from Quom in Iran to Bnei Brak in Israel, or Lakewood, New Jersey, to Gujarat State in India. As both Mahmutćehajić and Graf noted, it may also be the case that religion will combine with nationalist movements and ideologies in very different permutations—a religiously sanctified ethno-nationalism has, unfortunately, been an option in more than one country over the course of the last century. Many of these movements resurrect a language which we have come to associate with the larger project of modern liberal individualism, with which they articulate a protest to modernity as well as a strikingly intolerant position in the political arena.

Yet the language of will and of moral choice, of freedom, is and has always been a religious language, one in fact that was made possible by the very diremption of religion from the world. This is the moral freedom granted by transcendent religion in which the religiously ordained self henceforth exists in an irreconcilable tension with the call of transcendence. As explained by Eric Voegelin:

> These experiences [of transcendence] become the source of a new authority. Through the opening of the soul the philosopher finds himself in a new relation with God; he not only discovers his own psyche as the instrument for experiencing transcendence but at the same time discovers the divinity in its radically non-human transcendence. Hence, the differentiation of the psyche is inseparable from a new truth about God. The true order of the soul can become the standard for measuring both human types and types of social order because it represents the truth about human existence on the border of transcendence. The meaning of the anthropological principle must, therefore, be qualified by the understanding that not an arbitrary idea of man as a world-immanent being becomes the instrument of social critique but the idea of a man who has found his true nature through finding his true relation to God. The new measure that is found for the critique of society, is indeed, not man himself but man in so far as through the differentiation of this psyche he has become the representative of divine truth. . . . The truth of man and the truth of God are inseparably one.[52]

Transcendence provided a locus of heteronomy that neither hitherto existing group solidarities provided—one that constituted authority as such. It is this authority that provides what Charles Taylor termed that "constitutive good" upon which individual selves as moral evaluators came to rest.[53]

It is this very authority of the moral will that, taken in one direction, may evolve into a fundamentalist religiosity, but that is not its sole trajectory. Other responses to modernity are possible and have evolved in all religious communities in their respective encounters with modernity. We discussed in the introduction the case of Castellio and of a position of skepticism towards ultimate truth-claims which came to characterize certain Christian thinkers (and sects) in the early modern period. Similar moves can be found in other traditions as well. Within Judaism, one can look to a somewhat similar notion of epistemological modesty as sustaining not modern pluralism, but a degree of tolerance which can be culled from the writings of a number of ultra-Orthodox thinkers. One such scholar, the Chazon Ish (R. Avraham Yeshayahu Karelitz, d. 1958), the main ideologue of ultra-Orthodoxy in contemporary Israel, argued that since we live in a time when the sources of revelation are occluded, there is no authority for implementing divine commandments. As explained by Fischer, since the epistemological condition of exile sustains unbelief, adherents thereof cannot be held culpable.[54] While such a position does not perhaps support a positively privileged pluralism, it does maintain a position of principled tolerance and restraint which is a critical component of religious traditions not inculcated with Christian, and most especially Protestant, notions of individual moral autonomy.

Similarly Ayatollah Shariatmadari protested the reintroduction of drastic criminal penalties (such as the cutting off of hands) in postrevolutionary Iran. Short of the construction of the perfect society and the coming of the Hidden Imam, no justification for such actions could be offered, he claimed, as there was always the possibility that "Satan could be held to have misled the criminal."[55] Shariatmadari's argument resonates with the claims of the medieval Jewish philosopher Maimonides on the tolerance one must hold toward Jews who have lost their knowledge of the laws and the codes of communal worship.[56] This was an argument used by many Rabbis to understand the place of secular Jews in modern-day Israel. It was explicitly used by such thinkers as R. David Hoffman of Berlin to see modern public violation of the Sabbath in terms of the existence of a plurality of value positions, which must abrogate the severity of halachic norms, and has been since developed by different religious thinkers in Israel and abroad.

Maintaining the truth of the community, rather than the individual terms of truth-claims in modernity, these thinkers—Jewish and Muslim alike—provide principles for toleration culled from within traditional doxa. It is a language that continues to address the terms of Being, and yet, as we can see from Shariatmadari to the Chazon Ish, it is a language that can be translated rather than eviscerated.

CHAPTER FIVE

Conclusion

Languages of Tolerance

One argument that can be drawn from the analysis in chapter 4 is the somewhat counterintuitive notion that tolerance, understood not as rooted solely in power differentials and the inability to impose one's will on the other, is far from being all of a modern virtue. Clearly, the dictates of realpolitik may make us "tolerant" in the absence of alternatives, and that would be true of any society at any time—true in modern as in premodern times. We know too that tolerance, at least within the canon law of the West, was no more than a second-best solution used to define the position of Jews and prostitutes. It defined a status where one had to suffer (*tolérer, souffrir*) an "evil," for extirpating either Jews or prostitutes would have had consequences more severe for Western Christendom than suffering their presence. Or so, at least, the redactors of the law believed.[1]

Premodern societies were often not particularly tolerant ones, and marginal and minority groups, groups who were not part of the regnant definitions of community, were often persecuted and subjected to no small degree of violence. The position of the Jew in medieval Christian societies was not an enviable one; neither was the role of *dhimmi* in Islam particularly sought after. The degree and nature of the violence was different in different places, and here is not the place to compare Islamic and Christian or Western and Eastern Christianity as civilizational forms in terms of their tolerance or acceptance of the other. Such an exercise often turns polemic in nature, and the quite sensible historical comparison often becomes a politico-moral jousting match.

What we can learn from all premodern societies, however, is that tolerance is very much about groups and about group identities.

Tolerance—as understood and as practiced, even as not practiced—was a matter of attitudes and behavior towards corporate groups and so toward individuals as members of those groups, rather than towards individuals in their unique individuality. Given the terms of membership and identity in premodern and in religiously organized societies, this is not surprising. We should recall that "rights" were, in this world, not anything accorded to individuals, but to corporate groups.[2] Such were the categories of medieval law and society, and it is only sensible that such were the terms of tolerance in these societies. While there is nothing startling or original here, it should give us pause for thought, for what I want to claim is that tolerance—and intolerance for that matter—does inherently have to do with groups and with individuals as existing within groups, rather than with individuals as autonomous, self-regulating moral agents, endowed with individual rights and acting as such on the public stage.

My point is not that premodern societies were, in any quantitative sense, *more* or *less* tolerant than modern ones, but rather that their form of social organization was one that made the whole problem of tolerance relevant. Modern societies have elided the whole problem of tolerance rather than solved it. Occasionally this works, but not always; one cannot simply add "modernity" to the mix, as one would add salt to vegetable soup. Moreover, and this is a good deal more to the point, modern identities are themselves changing, and the type of individual selves which were long seen as the necessary concomitant to the nation-state are also changing, as is the nation-state itself.[3] As subnational and transnational identities are growing apace, religious, ethnic, and ethno-religious identities are making new claims on individuals' sense of self and society. Given these developments, the quintessentially modern moves that obviated the problems of tolerance and intolerance no longer hold. For these reasons, we must mine other sources and perspectives. Here, however, let us work out some of the analytic aspects of this issue not fully addressed above.

First, it is important to point out that tolerance is a very circumscribed virtue. It is not the solution to all evils. It is not a panacea. It is not without boundaries. Clearly, some types of behavior are intolerable, though it is not absolutely clear how one would go about defining what is beyond the pale. Certain religious and philosophical categories come to mind: ideas of natural law, or in Jewish context the Noachide commandments, present some useful general orientation. However, within these limits there is certainly great room for disagreement, for disgust, for rejection of much of what one considers as wrong, misguided, immoral, reprehensible, and hence for the need to tolerate what one believes to be wrong and that which makes one uncomfortable.

Certainly one cannot be expected to tolerate a clearly defined threat to one's own identity. When that threat is directed at one from outside, let us say through the barrel of a rifle, one cannot be tolerant. There is no serious analytic problem there. But what if that which is considered a "threat" comes from a different direction, from inside, as was the case with our numismatic society? Having met for decades, discussing, analyzing, and trading coins, all of a sudden a few members begin to bring in stamps, refuse to even look at a coin and proceed to take up meeting space and time with matters philatelic—must the numismatics tolerate them? Do they not equally present a threat to who we are as the West Roxbury Numismatic Society? Surely we do not have to exterminate our budding stamp collectors; we may politely tell them to leave and perhaps join the Philatelic Society that meets down the street. We may tolerate their existence in the greater Boston area, but not as part of our identity, of who we are.

The relatively simple point I am trying to make with this example is that groups have boundaries. They cannot exist without boundaries. One cannot make claims to any type of identity without that identity being defined, which in some sense involves it being bounded and circumscribed as well. To ask a group to tolerate what threatens that identity is to ask the group to dismantle itself, to make itself cease to be, and if anything is a model of intolerance it would be this eradication of existence. Tolerance, then, is a virtue that has everything to do with boundaries and with margins. It does not have to do with all-out threats to who we are, whether those threats come from outside or from inside, or whether those threats are physical or symbolic in nature. Rather, tolerance has to do with behaviors and/or beliefs that exist on "the margins" of the group's identity. Again, we may think of Jews and prostitutes in medieval canon law as presenting good examples of precisely this type of marginality (along with lepers, sometimes Muslims, beggars, strangers, etc.). All existed on the borders or margins of society, not beyond and not fully within.[4]

If we follow this logic to its conclusion we reach a very interesting finding: the thicker the boundaries, the greater the number of individuals, behaviors, and attitudes that reside on that boundary; the thinner that boundary, the fewer. Hence, the thicker the boundary, the more issues of tolerance and intolerance are raised and became relevant, as the greater chances are that one will come into contact with behaviors and beliefs that one finds objectionable without them necessarily threatening one's identity (though perhaps causing one to make endless calculations as to the existence or nonexistence of such a threat). And of course it is once again clear why tolerance was such an important theme in societies with strong group identities—they are societies with very thick boundaries, with very wide corporate identities and group definitions which necessitate such tolerance, however often and tragically they may be defined by its empirical absence or failure.

Now my point here is that modern societies—defined let us say by the *Declaration des droits de l'homme et du citoyen* and the American Constitution—do not so much make societies more tolerant; rather, they do away with group boundaries. In a sense, this has been a project of modern states (in their liberal form even more than in other more romantic-national forms). Within the public sphere, boundaries are, in these societies, parsed into razor-thin edges and individuals interact not as members of groups, but as bearers of rights (citizen right, social rights, human rights, and so on). Group identities have been, in the public sphere, replaced by individual identities, and the problem of tolerance of difference has been replaced by the legal recognition and entitlements of rights. This is what I mean when I say that modernity has elided the problem of tolerance, obviating the necessity to be tolerant rather than make people tolerant. It has replaced tolerance with rights.

Critically, this development has more than political dimensions. It is also the basis of social and economic life in most Western liberal societies and is a critical aspect of globalization. This is the difference between what Ernest Gellner termed multi-stranded and single-stranded relations. In multi-stranded relations we see that "a man buying something from a village neighbor in a tribal community is dealing not only with a seller, but also with a kinsman, collaborator, ally or rival, potential supplier of a bride for his son, fellow juryman, ritual participant, fellow defender of the village, fellow council member."[5] This situation is very different from the single-stranded relations we enter into when purchasing a commodity, wherein our calculations are, on the whole, orientated around purchasing the best possible commodity for the least price.

And this difference has huge implications for matters of tolerance as well. Let me illustrate with a small example. My relations with my car mechanic are single-stranded: He fixes the catalytic converter and I pay him a few hundred dollars. That is all there is to the relationship. When he has completed his job and I have paid him, the relationship is over;

there is nothing "left over" as it were. We need not be tolerant of one another, and our interaction before, during, and after is controlled solely by matters of legal rights to property, equality of access to market resources and exchange, and so on.

My relationship with my acupuncturist, however, is somewhat different. She is a member of my synagogue. I see her every Saturday. A number of times in the past I came to their home at very odd hours of the morning and night to help her husband fulfill religious obligations when his father died. They have been to our house for dinner. I give references to her son, a student of philosophy at Princeton University. She gives us all a discount for her treatment, and in some cases my wife gives her yoga lessons rather than cash payments. In short, our relationship is complex, multi-stranded, and with broad boundaries. And if, let us say, her son was not a wonderful, pleasant, and bright young man, but rather a foul-mouthed, insensitive, and boring lout, I would still have to tolerate his presence because my relationship to his family is made of thick stuff rather than a single-stranded act of exchange guaranteed by legal rights.

Tolerance is all about the type of relations that exist on these thick boundary lines of identity—identity that must by definition be a group identity of sorts. Much of the economic and political thrust of the modern world order is, however, about replacing group identities with individual ones, replacing tolerance with rights, and replacing a relatively small number of multi-stranded relationships with an almost infinite number of single-stranded ones. In the process, tolerance goes from being a community-centered act to an individual, almost psychological, attribute or personal characteristic.

Of course there is nothing wrong (practically or morally) with "solving" the problem of intolerance by removing the social conditions that make tolerance necessary. On the contrary, when it is possible, it seems to work well. But my feeling is that the conditions which defined the "high modernity" of the Western European and North Atlantic nation-state—and which allowed this particular solution, or rather elision of the problem—are changing. A return to group-based identities and to religious commitments in many parts of the world and the growth of trans-national identities predicated on religion, ethnicity and nationhood not dependent on statehood are calling into question the type of individual identities that stood at the core of the revolutionary idea of citizenship. The globalization of economic relations has not, however, led to a restructuring of collective ideology along the lines of mid-eighteenth-century Glasgow or Boston.

To the extent that it is the case, we will have to reinvent a language of tolerance not predicated on liberal and modernist ideas of the self and of the interaction between selves. To do so, we will, I believe, need to have recourse to religious foundations for tolerance. Here we have been explicating possible sources for these in the foundational texts of the three Abrahamic religions, all of whom recognize this problem of otherhood and do not attempt to define it away but, with greater or lesser skill, meet the problem of tolerance of difference head-on. The study of each and a greater comparison than that afforded by the preceding dialogues, an assessment of the different monotheisms' relative strengths and weaknesses in this regard, must remain the concern of future inquiry.

We have noted here, however, that religious languages of toleration develop along the axes noted in the previous chapter—that is, of group boundaries or of classificatory codes. The tension underlying all arguments over boundaries (external as well as internal) is over the relation between the individual and the community. The tension underlying all contrasting claims over classificatory codes is over knowledge and its sources (in reason and/or in revelation). This came out clearly in the dialogues. Stone's insights into the process of casuistry (mirrored in the Islamic tradition by other interlocutors), Graf's points on human self-limitation, Fisch's claims on epistemic modesty in Judaism, and Göle's description of the changing lifestyle commitments of contemporary Muslims in Turkey all turn on issues of classificatory codes. Von Tippelskirch's contribution too turned on the issue of classification and the different modes of its possible elaboration. In contrast, Abu Zayd's insights on the relation of Islamic religious and national identity, Hashmi's discussion of modes of tolerance in Islam, and Mahmutćehajić's claims on the correct understanding of what Islam is all point to the issue of boundaries. Similarly, Wolfteich's analysis of the thought of John Courtney Murray as well as the Jewish discussion, whether of Ha'meiri's thought or those of more contemporary rabbinic authorities such as the Chazon Ish, all turn on the relative permeability and meaning, extent, and nature of existing boundaries between insiders and outsiders, and indeed on the very definition of insiders.

As religious traditions evolved, different groups took different positions on these issues, and some came to provide important resources for tolerance (as well as for intolerance) within the different religious traditions. To be sure, some arguments for tolerance are much more articulated and fully developed and have a stronger relation to the core values of certain traditions rather than others. Thus, for example, an argument for tolerance predicated on a pluralism of ways of knowing God is strongly felt in the Islamic mystical or Sufi tradition. Jewish mystics, by contrast, were hardly known for their tolerance of non-Jews, who were seen by some mystics as being without souls.

On the other hand, the Islamic idea of *hilm* is mirrored in the Jewish idea of modesty (*anva*) and is one that in the Talmudic discourse provided a strong argument for that hesitancy in the face of the other and the other's arguments that we are claiming as the core of the tolerant act. As we saw in the introduction, similar ideas can be found in the Christian tradition, one of the most important early modern examples of which was the case of Sebastian Castellio in his arguments against the burning of Miguel Servetus as a heretic.

Not all traditions developed these arguments along the same lines and in similar manners. The example of epistemological modesty, as opposed to humility *simpliciter*, as standing at the core of the tolerant attitude is, I would claim, a particularly Jewish approach that is not mirrored to the same extent in other traditions. As we have seen, however, a number of different arguments for tolerance were (and can be) used from within the religious idiom. We must be cautious not to elide these arguments into a more modern and secular or liberal discourse, which, while a natural move, would also defeat our purposes. The horizons of our inquiry are, moreover, circumscribed by the three Abrahamic religions, for they all work with a similar tool kit: all are monotheistic, all believe in a creator God and so in some valuation of the world and this-worldly activity. All have soteriologies of some combination of this-worldly and other-worldly orientations. All struggle with the problem of theodicy. All uproot the individual (albeit to different extents) from primordial and ascribed statuses. All seek to remake the world to different extents. All share, to some degree, common sources, prophets, and textual contexts. All have been engaged in mutual dialogue (and hostility) since their inception. And while Judaism has not had the power (until recently and in an extremely mediated fashion) to promulgate its own modes of intolerance (except towards insiders), all, as Estruch noted, have a history of intolerance, hatred, and much blood on their hands. Finally, all are undergoing some manner of worldwide resurgence. Though taking different forms in different countries—from evangelical Christianity in Latin America to Orthodox Judaism in mid-Manhattan to the Turkish Welfare Party in Istanbul—all point to a renewed saliency of religious identities and commitments that few would have believed possible a scant decade ago.

As noted earlier, this return to religious identities is sometimes characterized by a fundamentalism of belief, a wish to find the safest possible haven from the anxieties of the secular world and its dissonant belief structures and heterogeneous claims of a "transgressive reason." Needless to say, these often lead to a very particular and rather closed religious attitude, often dangerous as well. Hence, our concern here to resurrect older languages and idioms. We cannot aim at achieving historical comprehensiveness but only at providing a rough framework for analysis and understanding. We do hope, however, to enrich a language rendered artificially mute by the constraints of time.

One of the most obvious places to begin inquiry in the religious languages of toleration is with the idea that man is created in the image (Hebrew: *b'tzelem*) of God. (Interestingly, the word *b'tzelem* is the name of a secular human-rights group in contemporary Israel.) The idea of a person as transcendentally constituted may provide a certain moral compass and grid of behavior that is not readily available in more secular renditions of the human condition. Not that the idea of autonomy does not in itself provide a powerful force for human validation—the myriad achievements of the modern world are monuments to precisely that force. Yet such an orientation carries with it a "default" position that is not always salutary. The English historian R. H. Tawney, who was himself both a member of the Labour Party and a close friend of the Anglican Church, put it well in the verses quoted earlier in the dialogues.

There we noted how loss of the transcendent anchor has, while validating the individual, also normatively privileged different capabilities, skills, and fungible resources of these individuals to an unprecedented degree. In making each an *other*, it has not so much solved the problem of toleration as defined it away, translating it, in most cases, to the problem of individual rights. It is rights then that provide the ground of mutuality and recognition in the contemporary world. Yet rooted as they are in political communities, rights themselves are severely mediated by these very terms (in the case of the stateless persons, refugees, citizens of states defined in the West as "rogue states," citizens of states with poorly institutionalized legal systems, and so on).

What can be countenanced from a religious position is a grounding of the individual not in a socially determinant and yet accidental community of his or her birth, but in a set of "ultimate concerns," to use Paul Tillich's phrase. This has provided an argument for human dignity and worth in all the monotheistic traditions. It is rooted in the very breakthrough to transcendence that characterized the Axial Age. Within the

Western tradition and its modes of institutionalizing the Axial chasm, the individual came to exist primarily as an individual-in-relation-to God, which as Jaspers noted is precisely what provided the "resoluteness" of "personal selfhood . . . experiencing the highest freedom in the limits of freedom in nothingness."[6] Each individual became a unique entity "immediately responsible to God for the welfare of his soul and the well being of his brother."[7] The valorization of the individual is through his "consecration to God." It is, in Troeltsch's words, "only fellowship with God which gives value to the individual."[8] As pointed out by Marcell Mauss, the notion of the person—as a rational substance, individual and indivisible—owed its metaphysical foundation to Christianity.[9] And while I would not agree with Mauss about Christianity *tout court*, the connection to the Axial Age and the emergence of transcendence is not to be doubted.

Thus, the transcendent, the first fully generalizable other, becomes the basis for a non-negotiable sacred, one seen to exist beyond all possible social constructions, beyond all negotiation. It provides the definitive description to reality, especially to normative reality, or rather the normative aspects of our material reality. Transcendence, or rather the authority inherent to it, reorganizes the relations within the mundane realm. In this, it is quite distinct from magic, which relates to the supernatural precisely as another form of the natural that requires its own set of tools to mediate the impact of the supernatural on the world. Magic effects such change in the realm of the supernatural. Thus, one may, in particular circumstances, need to sacrifice one's daughter in order to get the wind up to continue the course of the fleet to Ilium.[10] Indeed, a comparison of the sacrifice of Iphigenia and that of Isaac highlights precisely this difference between a magical manipulation of the cosmos and the bending of the will to the dictates of a transcendent Deity. For transcendence is not concerned with building houses or keeping the wind in one's sails, but rather with reorganizing the mundane world in accordance with principles now deemed transcendent in nature.

In this reorganization the individual emerges as a moral evaluator (as for example in the prophet Nathan's admonishment of King David or Fisch's example of Abraham arguing with God). The idea of transcendence provides a locus of moral authority and selfhood, albeit one foreign to modern sensibilities. It does so, moreover, without falling back on ascriptively defined and primordial categories of selfhood. However paradoxical it may seem to us, its very authority calls the self into being as moral evaluator, as agentic in a sense other than power. Problematizing existence, transcendence drives the self to encounter Being. In this encounter, agency can become an existential and moral endeavor rather than simply the exercise of power. A heteronomously constituted self is constructed in tension with transcendent dictates.

It is, moreover, this truth that for philosophers such as Hermann Cohen (quoted at the beginning of the previous chapter) provided the basis for ethics in general, of which tolerance is an instance. Thus he notes:

> The correlation of man and God is in the first place that of man, as fellowman to God. And religion proves its own significance first of all in this correlation of the fellowman to God, in which, indeed, man as fellowman becomes a problem and is engendered through this problem. The share of religion in reason is the share of religion in morality, and no problem of morality takes precedence over this problem of the fellowman. The possibility of ethics is tied to this problem.[11]

The problem of the "fellowman" is the problem of tolerance. And here we find a very different basis for human validation, mutuality, respect, and tolerance—one predicated not on any set of "ontological" rights that the human subject carries, but rather on the very constitutive conditions of human existence in the world. This is an idea shared among all the monotheistic, Axial religions in whose image of a creator God the human was formed. Whether we look to Qur'anic injunctions against coercion in matters of religion, or to biblical decrees on justice for the stranger, or yet to the Sermon on the Mount, all give expression to a shared and fundamental truth of human existence as somehow correlative to God and Being.

It is, however, equally important not to reify too much the very concept of *b'tzelem* and with it projections of a high degree of commensurability between different religious traditions. As pointed out in our dialogues, the idea of *b'tzelem* appears in Jewish law only in terms of forms of execution and rules pertaining to burying the dead—that is, in the most corporeal of incarnations and not as part of any broader ethical claims to individual or human dignity. The problem of Being that transcendence forced on individual conscious is not, and was not, articulated historically in similar forms in the different religious civilizations. Quite the opposite. The nature of the tension between universal and particular injunctions, the definition of individual and collective identities, of nominative and realist understandings of religious dicta, all are different and not always commensurate. Traditional rabbinic understandings of the role of law are after all somewhat different from those of St. Paul. Islamic understandings of bodily impurity differ greatly from those of Unitarians. What we have in fact seen is that issues of commensurability and incommensurability are matters of degree. Yet a certain degree of the latter does not preclude translation. If anything, this was the lesson of the *dhimmi* and natural law and of the Noachide commandments. Ethical ideas come "thin" as well as "thick," as do ideas of the individual, social obligations, and of our position vis-à-vis the other.[12]

In this context one could usefully argue that it is precisely the particular Christian concept of the Passion (as expressive of man's relation to God) and of the miracle of the incarnation which makes the idea of the creation of man in the image of God so central in the development of an individual ethical conscience. (Here the useful comparison would be with the Jewish idea of covenant, *brit*, and the Islamic idea of submission, *islam*.) And while this is not the place to enter into extensive comparison, we should realize that many scholars have argued that the very contemporary concern with individual rights, choice, and the freedom of conscience upon which so much of what we consider morally, even ethically, irrevocable in the modern world, rests on these very foundations. Indeed, many of our secular and liberal political orientations owe a large debt to religious injunctions, in the forms of Protestant belief.[13] An important example of this, which illustrates just how indebted modern ideas of individual right are to religious principles, can be found in the interweaving of religious and secular dimensions that came to characterize the reconstruction of natural-law doctrines in eighteenth-century America and the related idea of the individual as constitutive of the political community. This development was analyzed by George Jellinek, whose work served as an inspiration for Max Weber. Already in 1895, Jellinek compared the American Bill(s) of Rights (from different states), the French *Déclaration des droits de l'homme et du citoyen*, and, more significantly, the English Bill of Rights of 1689, the Habeas Corpus Act of 1679, and the 1628 Petition of Right. His conclusions are worth quoting, as the United States has become in so many ways the "ideal" type of Western modernity:

> The American bills of rights do not attempt merely to set forth certain principles for the state's organization, but they seek above all to draw the boundary line between state and individual. According to them the individual is not the possessor of rights through the state, but by his own nature he has inalienable and indefeasible rights. The

English laws know nothing of this. They do not wish to recognize an eternal, natural right, but one inherited from their fathers, "the old, undoubted rights of the English people."[14]

As Jellinek sees it, English law offers no autonomous grounding of individual rights in a set of natural principles but grounds them solely in tradition, in "the laws and statutes of this realm."[15] He looked to the defining traits of Congregational Puritanism to explain how the "inherited rights and liberties, as well as the privileges of organization, which had been granted the colonists by the English kings" became transformed in the New World to "rights which spring not from man but from *God and Nature*."[16]

The very success of natural-law doctrine—based on self-sufficient individuals endowed with reason—as the foundation of the American political community rested on the synthesis of these ideas with the tradition of the Holy Commonwealth of visible saints, the transcendent subject of Protestant belief. Not only (transcendental) reason but also (transcendent) grace, redefined in the inner-worldly terms of individual conscience, continued throughout the eighteenth century to define the terms of individual and social existence in the civil polity. It was the very continuity of this religious heritage that made the positing of a political community of individuals—united by compacts—possible in eighteenth-century America and beyond. And so Jellinek concluded:

> In the closest connection with the great religious political movement out of which the American democracy was born, there arose the conviction that there exists a right not conferred upon the citizen but inherent in man, that acts of conscience and expressions of religious conviction stand inviolable over against the state as the exercise of a higher right. This right so long suppressed is not "inheritance," is nothing handed down from their fathers, as the rights and liberties of Magna Carta and of the other English enactments—*not the State but the Gospel proclaimed it.*[17]

As Jellinek realized, individual rights in America were not derived solely from positive law, but had acquired a transcendent justification unique in the modern world. Indeed, this situation constituted the foundation of modernity itself. It is then the religious or transcendent grounding of rights in that polity most defined by their existence—the United States—

that has provided rights with their charismatic force in organizing the institutional aspects of social life.

This understanding of human rights, and so also of tolerance in terms of individual rights within formerly Christian politics, well illustrates the type of categorization developed above. The breakdown of the medieval Catholic *universitas*, its replacement with a *societas* of compacting or contracting individuals, brought said individuals to the fore as the primary boundary marker in the classification system: no longer the group and its limits but rather, as defined by Benjamin Nelson, that move from "tribal brotherhood to universal otherhood" which came to define the "group" axis of the classification system.[18]

The idea of individual rights is the secular, political instantiation of this *societas*. It delineates on the one hand the prime axes of modern social tolerance—as tolerance to individuals—and, critically, on the other hand the ever-expanding nature of this tolerance. Rights are, as we have witnessed over the past one hundred years, of an accordion nature. They can be expanded or contracted and do not, in themselves, posit their own boundaries. Not only can we, following T. H. Marshall, trace how juridical rights were extended into political rights and these into social rights, but the precise content of any of these (but most especially the latter in the contemporary Western world) is given to infinite elaboration. This fits well with the individualistic nature of rights, which can, sensibly enough, be elaborated according to different individual needs and desiderata. Both dimension (A) of *Group Boundaries* and dimension (B) of the *Classificatory Code* intersect in a discourse of rights, thus revealing an "elective affinity" with a very particular set of civilizational premises. These premises have, in turn, been characterized by their locus in individual salvation, the primacy of faith, and the working of the "inner light" as the central soteriological arenas. The very stress on internality, *Innerlichkeit*, and the calculus of intentionality correlate with an only limited shared or societal classificatory code (leaving most areas of decision making to the autonomous judgment of the individual.) This is precisely the dynamic of rights: a limited but relatively inflexible classificatory code. Here then the Protestant origins of secular rights are most easily assessed, origins which, however, lent the new gospel its very strength and saliency.

Yet, this strength is also a weakness. The very "elective affinity" between Christian, or more properly Protestant, ideas of self and interiority, of the privileging of conscience in ethical life and the autonomy of the Kantian moral self, all do well to root our ideas of rights within a certain (more broadly defined) religious civilization. Judaism, Islam, and Christian Orthodoxy, to say nothing of the East Asian religions, may all have very different beliefs pertaining to the constitutive conditions of individual rights—beliefs pertaining to the individual, society, and the transcendent order. Given a shared recognition of transcendence, what alternative to a code of rights can be found? More generally:

- If the shared recognition of human validation is to be found in all religious traditions, and
- the contemporary (and secular) understanding of this validation (and so tolerance of difference and otherhood) is articulated most saliently in the language of rights, and
- that language is uniquely resonant in only one set of religious assumptions, then
- we would do well to view how other religious traditions understand this entity which we term *rights*, and
- consider what alternative modes of expressing individual worth, validation, and tolerance exist in other religious traditions.

Just as the Christian or Protestant articulation is not the only form of religious expression, so is an understanding of human validation in terms of rights not the only possible one. Tolerance may indeed be predicated on an appreciation of the sanctity of individual life, without that appreciation necessarily taking the form of rights. After all, the inviolability of rights in those parts of the contemporary world where it exists—primarily in the United States, Canada, and Western Europe—owes not a little to the Christian concept of grace as constitutive of individual identities. Other traditions, however, view the self somewhat differently, without, for all that, invalidating self-worth and the corollary vision of tolerance.

Thus, other sources or resources for tolerance can be found within religious traditions. One of these, noted above, is predicated on a position of existential and epistemological humility that the very encounter with the transcendent generates. The Tawney quote above touches on parts of this, as does the excerpt from Tractate Erubim in the Babylonian Talmud quoted earlier (chapter 4). The idea of *anva*, humility, is central in all monotheistic religions, and we have already noted the role of an epistemological modesty in the arguments posed by Sebastian Castellio to John Calvin in the case of Miguel Servetus.

In Islam, a similar concept provides a similar repertoire. [The con-]cept of *hilm* combines qualities of "moderation, forbearance an[d leniency] with self-mastery and dignity." In some ways it is surprisingly akin to the idea of civility among the eighteenth-century Scottish Moralists. According to the great Islamic scholar Ignaz Goldzhier, *hilm* combines moral integrity with mildness of manners and is juxtaposed to *al-Jāhilīya*, that pre-Islamic period of Arab tribal warfare where emotions governed actions and where "haughtiness, arrogance and insolence" ruled, rather than the humble submission of Islam.[19] Toshihiko Izutsu's study of *Jāhilya* and of *hilm* provides us with a good sense of how central these terms are to appreciating the inner phenomenology of Islam, how the "haughtiness" of the *Jāhilya* is contrasted with the forbearance of the *halim* (he who is characterized by *hilm*) in defining the idea of Islamic behavior.[20] In the Prophet's transvaluation of values wrought on Arab society, the practice of forgiveness and leniency was considered *halim*—an attribute of the Patriarch Abraham, and ultimately of Allah. In this move, the Prophet replaced the values of tribal vengeance with that of forgiveness. Existential modesty and humility, no less than epistemic doubt, exists within religious traditions as principles of tolerance rooted in the very term within which we face the other—again, Buber's dialogue of mutual relation.

Two questions insert themselves into the argument at this point. The first is whether a stance of humility or epistemological modesty is a sufficient basis for tolerance. Some of our interlocutors, such as Fisch, clearly think it is. I am more comfortable presenting it as a necessary condition. I am somewhat unclear if it is a sufficient condition. It is necessary, for it radically displaces the self from its centrality in relation to others. This was the point brought up in our discussion of Lévinas. It is a position that can even be found in the American pragmatist John Dewey, whose social method called for asking the other what he thinks about whatever matter is standing for consideration by the two interlocutors or actors.[21] It is very similar to that putting of oneself aside or in a bracketed position that is necessary to the act of translation, to the very dialogic situation, and, as the foundation for a principled toleration, where tolerance is understood not as a *politique* act of accommodation, but as a moral stance.

The problem modern societies have struggled with for over two centuries now is whether this move is possible without an idea of transcendence.[22] For transcendence presents that absolute in the face of which the self's measure can be taken irrespective of material social position and status. This then is the submission of Islam, as precondition to humility that despite different resonances can indeed be translated into different religious languages and civilizations.

The second question to ask is whether these virtues are in some way unique to religious civilizations or traditional worldviews in a manner that cannot be reproduced in modern secular societies. The sense comes out of at least a number of the dialogues that that is indeed the case. Mahmutćehajić's insights into the sacred plurality of premodern communal life in Bosnia, which resonate so well with Stone's presentation on forgiveness and on the moral pluralism that correlates with a created nature, form one such sets of arguments. The position taken by Fisch and to an extent by Graf and Fischer on the sources of an epistemic modesty rooted in the very nature of a religious understanding of the world is yet another, as is the type of development of doctrine expressed by the Catholic Church during the Second Vatican, especially in its relation to religious pluralism, to which Wolfteich sensitized us. All suggest the close connection between epistemic and existential levels of tolerance. In the modern world, however, both dimensions are so bound up with the workings of reason and its own totalistic assumptions that room for a principled humility is severely circumscribed.

The linkage of epistemological and existential levels is, moreover, not arbitrary. Both define central axes of our being-in-the-world. In fact, both relate back to the two axes of social classification we discussed in the preceding chapter: boundaries of community and classificatory codes. Both in fact are illustrative of the remarks on casuistry broached by Stone, Hashmi, and Fischer—on the critical role of casuistry as a method for maintaining communal boundaries and boundaries of identity and inclusion while, at the same time, transforming its classificatory codes. Moreover, and as I believe we learn from von Tippelskirch's presentation of Freud, Levinas, and Barth, the terms of self-hood and of our epistemologies do in fact refer back, if somewhat obliquely, to these codes as well. Humility or modesty in one realm would seem to carry over to the other. Though, of course, we would do well not to forget Berger's strictures on an arrogance of moral positioning and the possibility of being, at one and the same time, epistemically modest and morally arrogant, and whether such is not in fact desirable. We can in turn query whether this is the same as being humble in one's personhood and arrogant in one's knowledge. Or could one be truly humble in one's epistemic claims and yet arrogant as a person? I would think not, for the terms of Being and of Knowing are too interwoven to allow such separation of effects. Yet, it is a religious attitude that roots both in a true humility. Without a transcendent authority, there exist but the differentials of powers and the deference that such differentials bring forth. Deference, however, is not humility.

What can be found in the Christian trope of meekness, in the Jewish concept of *anva*, and in the Islamic virtue of *hilm* is no less than an existential positioning of the knowing subject vis-à-vis what is unknown, what is other. Here then are the roots of Hermann Cohen's correlation of the fellowman to God, and here a source of tolerance in all religious civilizations. This is, of course, the message of the Book of Job, and it resonates not only with Sufi beliefs in Islam but with the modesty that must come vis-à-vis creation in all its multiplicity—that plurality that Stone noted in her opening remarks on the Jewish tradition. Faith can humble reason or, if not reason itself, then the arrogance which is often its commitment. Of course when faith *replaces* reason (whether in the trial of Galileo or, as noted by both Fisch and Fischer, in government practices in contemporary Israel, or as Abu Zayd pointed out in the Islamic world) it loses its own attributes of modesty and suffers the consequence of all intolerant positions: it defeats itself.

If the transcendent in its transcendence cannot be approached solely through reason, neither can alter. That, I believe, is the real meaning of such concepts as *anva* and *hilm*. That is the truth of the religious perspective and what the modern world explicitly denies. We seek to make the other approachable through reason, and to a great extent, when that is not possible, we redefine other (and hence ourselves) to make that possible. All of economics, of rational-choice theory, if not the social sciences *tout court*, is, precisely, this attempt to redefine the other (and so, always, also ourselves, as alter's other) in terms of general and universal interests that then make such an approach possible. The problem of translation is transformed into one of conversion, fungibility, and exchange (of quantifiable properties), and so the problem of difference is reduced to the greatest possible extent. Again, too, the evisceration of desire.

What transcendence provides, or perhaps only permits, is the continued existence of otherness, of the very category of what cannot be known and is, by definition, unknowable. *Ein begriffener Gott ist kein Gott.* (A knowable God is no God.) A touchstone of what is beyond calculation (for the knowable is the calculable) is as well a continual touchstone of humility and so of a modesty of claims and of selfhood. This is significant if a real toleration, one that maintains the inviolability of what is tolerated, is to be apprehended.

Approached through reason (mutuality of interests, political calculation, resource conversion, and the fungibility of value positions), the problem of tolerance is defined away (along with all else that is unknown) as somehow not a real problem. Difference is here reduced to an underlying sameness (which is what permits the calculation of interests and exchange) or trivialized (marginalized) beyond the realm of that which must or must not be tolerated. At best it is, as noted above, privatized and hence principally separated from the realm of what is or is not tolerated. With this, however, it is also removed from the realm of shared meanings, that realm through which we represent ourselves to ourselves. So much is this the case that issues involving tolerance of diverse practices and behavior are in contemporary Western, liberal democracies debated not in terms of tolerance but in terms of their public or private character. What is deemed private need not be tolerated. One's taste in the bathroom tiles, for example, is beyond public scrutiny. An illustrative case in point is homosexuality in the United States. Successfully moved (conceptually and legally) into the private arena, it no longer became a matter of tolerance. Consensual sexual acts between adults were simply no one else's business. This in itself is not tolerance. Whether it leads to a greater degree of real tolerance is as yet open to question. It is no doubt an elegant "solution" to the intolerance towards homosexuality, but its limits are made quite clear when the private nature of the relation can no longer be taken for granted. This has been the case in the state of Vermont, when in the summer of 2000 the legislature legalized homosexual unions and the previously private (and tolerated) relation entered the public realm, to a huge uproar and protest by people whose "tolerance" was tried beyond its limits.[23]

No less important is the question whether such a solution (the privatization of difference) can hold in societies where the public/private distinction and its concomitant definitions of the individual and of society do not hold the same valences as they do in the United States. If, for example, homosexual acts cannot be privatized due to very different definitions of individual selves, of society and the nature of their connection, can sources for tolerance be found in other realms? This no doubt is a difficult endeavor. Yet true tolerance is a difficult position to maintain, and to do so we may have need of precisely those structures of thought that have all too often in history provided a bastion of intolerance and oppression. Such cannot be denied. The recently approved social doctrine of the Russian Orthodox Church, which condemns homosexuality in no uncertain terms, is an example of just how difficult such a position of tolerance is to beget.[24]

Yet the restructuring of the problem in modernity, essentially as the attempt to define it away, is also no solution, because most of the world has not adopted uniquely post-Protestant liberal democratic and secular assumptions. And even in many of those societies which have adopted these assumptions, from Wyoming to Marseilles, the reemergence in so many polities of vocal collectivities and religious identities challenges the very idea of privatized religion, demanding its public recognition and public role. It demands a public tolerance as well. This can be provided only by revisiting Enlightenment assumptions on the rule of reason and the privatization of Desire. Just possibly then, the necessity to rethink the assumptions of modern politics will permit a dialogue with those religious orientations whose contributions to a tradition of tolerance must be sustained.

Recall the classical liberal Enlightenment response to "the Jewish Question," that was given by Count Stanislav de Clermont-Tonnerre in 1789: "We must refuse everything to the Jew as a nation and accord everything to the Jew as an individual."[25] This became perhaps the paradigm statement of attitudes toward the other, *the* modern alternative to real tolerance that could not be vouchsafed. As we all now know, it did not work, not for the Jews as a nation and not for the Jews as individuals. Contemporary politics, of Jews and Muslims in France or of homosexuals and the disabled in the United States, all take as their premise the failure of this "solution" and demand public recognition of their private selves. This is the meaning of the famous slogan "The personal is political." All challenge accepted pieties and demand more than the classic liberal solution allows. In these demands, the nature of politics in the nation-state is changing. This is the real significance of the politics of recognition. The demand for recognition is always a demand for the public recognition of the particular, which is precisely why it is such a problem in countries such as France, where the universal terms of equalitarian citizenship leave no public room for such particulars. We need only recall Article I of the Declaration of the Rights of Man and of the Citizen (August 26, 1789) of the French National Assembly—"All men are born and remain free and equal in rights: *social distinctions can not be found but on common utility*" (emphasis mine)—to realize how inimical such recognition is to the terms of modern citizenship. Yet, a politics of recognition is also always a politics of meaning, of "strong evaluations" in Charles Taylor's terms. It is a politics predicated on a "vocabulary of worth" and of "qualitative constraint." Ultimately, it is a politics of expressive identities as well, for unexpressed, unrepresented, in some deep sense, we simply do not exist.[26]

The recognition of this has fueled much of the current movements of multiculturalism and what is called the politics of identity. When Lubavitz Jews defiantly light a Channuka menorah in the Champs de Mars in Paris or in Boston Common, when Kwanza is accorded the public recognition of Christmas and Ebonics taught as a language, these issues are at the forefront. Existing liberal accommodations of the privatization of difference are overthrown. What all too often takes their place is a trivialization of difference or, alternatively, its rearticulation as political "pork"; so instrumentalized, it is again reduced to the shared common denominator of interest. And again elided.

An alternative solution, I am suggesting, is one that involves precisely its recognition. For that recognition to take place, difference must itself be established and accepted. He or she, bearers of recognition, must do so from their own particularity and not from an assumed or latent or carefully disguised universalized position. One of the only ways to make such a move is from a position of humility and modesty—not weakness, not passivity (from which one could not be tolerant). This approach is very much part of the Islamic idea of *hilm*, as it is the Jewish concept of *anva* and injunctions against the use of force in arriving at the truth. It is to be found in the self-limiting discourse related by Graf as well as in that Levinasian attitude towards the other broached by von Tippelskirch. All recognize the existence of particular positions and the need for such to coexist without their reduction to a generalized universal.

One could, of course, argue that it was a precisely the failure of such mutually particular recognition that led to the liberal, Enlightenment solution of a universalization of all difference in the public realm. What we are witness to at present, however, is the increasing difficulty in maintaining this accommodation and the return to particular identities, commitments, and desiderata that religious communities do in fact encourage.

With the spread of globalization and the increasingly interconnected nature of the world's population, the saliency of these issues only grows from day to day. The inherent conflict between local, in many cases religious, identities and a broader, global political agenda has in fact served to restructure and reconfigure existing conflicts in new and often dangerous ways. One recent example of this is the anti-Muslim activity in the city of Lodi in Northern Italy, near Milan. There, on October 15, 2000, the local Catholic inhabitants desecrated a site upon which a mosque was to be built by pouring pig urine all around it.[27] The idea was that by rendering the site impure they would be able to stop the mosque from being built. On hearing of this, one's immediate association is the construction of a Moslem graveyard opposite the Old City Gate in Jerusalem to prevent the Jewish Messiah from appearing, as he would be of the priestly class and so unable to pass through a graveyard. Anti-immigrant sentiment is taking a religious form—the failure of the bishop of Bologna to count non-Catholic births in the city's natality rate and the issuance by the mayor of Rouato of a municipal ordinance on November 24, 2000, forbidding non-Christians from approaching within fifteen meters of a church are but a few additional examples of the type of dynamic to which I am pointing.[28]

Similarly, one may look to the current conflict between the State of Israel and the Palestinian National Authority for other permutations of this dynamic. Over the course of its many decades, the conflict between Israel and the Palestinians has taken many forms: from inter-ethnic to inter-state to again inter-ethic conflicts. On the whole, and until relatively recently, it has not taken an explicitly unambiguous religious dimension, though such dimensions were of course present and for some on both sides do in fact define the terms of conflict. The rise of Gush Emunim in Israel after the 1973 War and the more recent increase in the strength of Hamas are of course indications of such religious framing of the conflict. But they are also reminders of how circumscribed that idiom has been and how strongly the conflict has remained rooted in a politics of simple interests and conflicts of interests rather than of ultimate religious truth-claims—between which, we should recall, little compromise is possible.

It is therefore all the more tragic that at this very historical juncture when some form of settlement appeared on the horizon, when a politics of interest appeared to be yielding for the first time, when a mediated agreement (for many an unjust and only partial agreement, though an agreement nonetheless) seemed possible—that at this very time the religious arguments are gaining currency, making compromise and understanding ever so much more difficult and even perhaps unattainable. Beyond the Middle East, of course, what we have been witnessing since the fall of 2000 has been, to some extent, the expansion of the Palestinian-Israeli conflict beyond its geographical boundaries and national solidarities. This was a significant change from previous modes of conflict. The physical attacks on Jewish citizens of France, Germany, Belgium, and Canada by Muslims who are fellow citizens (and this is what distinguishes this from earlier attacks on Jews, such as the bomb placed in the Rue de Rosiers in the 1970s) illustrate all too painfully this new articulation of the conflict along religious lines.

Howsoever it stands in relation to the recent violence, the reemergence of religious identities among Jews and Palestinians does seem to be a critical component of recent politics. The decline of Chadash, the Israeli Communist Party, in Israel has led to a reemergence of the politics of *chamulot*, kin-groups, and at least according to some to a reassertion of religious identities—Christian and Muslim—within the Palestinian population, which is in turn characterized by great tensions, animosities, and often murders between villagers. Some of these events have reached the media (such as the violent conflict in Nazareth over the building of a church and a mosque on the same site), but the phenomenon is apparently more widespread than what is reported in the Hebrew and English media. The continuing strength of the ultra-religious party Shas—of which Fischer spoke—is itself enough to show how salient are the new terms of religious identities and self-definitions. At no time within local Israeli politics had an ethnically based party ever been successful electorally. Shas, which is a party of ethnic protest (of the sepharadim, that is, oriental Jews, against the hegemony of the European-born Israeli elite), is successful precisely because it unites ethnic protest with religious identities, values, and commitments. The heart of a heartless world—not only in Turkey, Egypt, and Gaza, but in Israel as well.

Given these developments, and others, over many parts of the world from Ireland to Indonesia and the Sudan to Chechnya, it thus becomes critical to take religion seriously as a site not only of conflict, but perhaps of resolution as well. Religion provides a bedrock of identity and hence a cause for conflict around unassailable positions, providing alternative forms of politics and understandings, not rooted in an Enlightened idiom of individual interests and calculations. This very reaction to liberal modernity may, however, provide as well a solution afforded neither by the terms of Enlightened reason nor of fundamentalist faith, but rather through a dialogue between faith and reason that has not been assayed for centuries.

It is of course not at all clear that this will indeed be the case. Yet it is becoming clear that any simplistic "outsourcing" of the North American model of toleration simply does not work in many parts of the world—

precisely those parts where non-Protestant religious identities and commitments are salient. This being the case, it behooves us to attempt other approaches to the problem of toleration, to try both to conceptualize the problem in new terms and to posit new solutions, of however tentative and provisional a nature.

These solutions will need to emerge out of religion itself. They will need to posit some point between the absolutism of what is often termed fundamentalist faith on the one hand and the nihilism of postmodern relativism on the other. (Both, we should note, leave only the power of a third-party enforcer to mediate conflicts.) Whereas we cannot recollect the naïveté of pre-Enlightenment religion, we need not settle for what Mahmutćehajić has termed the sentimentality (in all of its romantic associations) of post-Enlightenment religion. Religion via the Enlightenment is a very different phenomenon than religion in retreat before the Enlightenment. It was the latter that characterized so much of religion in the nineteenth century—whether the growth of Orthodoxy among Hungarian Jewry in mid-century or the First Vatican Council in 1869.[29] And if orthodoxy was religion's reaction to the first phase of modernity, fundamentalism is religion's reaction to the later phase of what is often termed postmodernity.

However, what has been made so irrevocably clear by our interlocutors is that these are far from the only possible responses. Moreover, as Göle and others have noted, it may just be the case that genuine tolerance can only be afforded from within a religious perspective that recognizes the category of the sacred and stands in awe before it. What the dialogues and accompanying chapters present is just a beginning, a hesitant and sketchy framework—to continue our metaphor of translation and language, a stuttering towards an answer, rather than a fully articulated answer. Yet, there is an answer, one that has very clear contours and parameters. The beginning of any new understanding of tolerance *must*, and, as we learn from the dialogues, *can*, be predicated on a recognition of identity, and of particular identities that stand in self-limited recognition of their own finiteness before the infinite plurality of creation. Maintaining their own beliefs and boundaries, they do nevertheless eschew the narcissism of small difference to recognize the other and bear, or suffer, or tolerate the very phenomenon of otherhood, of ego and of alter both. Boundaries are maintained, though also elaborated. Neither the concept of *dhimmi* nor of the Noachides involves the move from *universitas* to *societas* that accompanied the transformations of modernity.

Both seek to maintain particular identities of group (and so, by definition, of other) while also endowing other with value, mediated and partial though it may be. In both an intermediary category is posited that allows the existence of both self and other. Of course, the concrete modes in which these categories are articulated (who is included in these categories and who is not, and how) are not given in any finite sense of the term, but are dependent on contingent historical circumstance and the global array of political forces. The destruction of the statues of the Buddha in Bamiyan, Afghanistan, in March of 2001 by the Taliban (after their security was vouchsafed for earlier—and critically, as the international situation of the Taliban became more isolated and they became more desperate) presents a good case in point (as does its near universal condemnation by Muslim intellectuals throughout the world). Thus, while no one is advocating the reintroduction of the *dhimmi* as a legal category to further contemporary problems of tolerance, it is the concern with boundaries that exists within religious traditions that we wish to stress.

Not only are boundaries maintained within these traditions, but knowledge is not absolutized. Or perhaps it is precisely because the boundaries of communities—which present themselves as communities of truth—are maintained that human knowledge cannot be absolutized. Some mode of what we termed above as practical rationality has always been an aspect of such communities. A built-in self-limiting orientation, an epistemic modesty and humility towards one's own truth-claims, has also always been an aspect (not the only one to be sure) of such communities. (Again, it is often exogenous political developments that will determine if at any particular time it is this humility that is stressed within the tradition, or very different types of more aggressive and aggrandizing orientations.) Within a grammar of casuistry, a tradition maintains itself and its truth-claims while at the same time recognizing the inherently finite and limited nature of its knowledge. Casuistry itself, as noted by Albert Jonsen and Stephen Toulmin, is predicated on the recognition of the discrepancy between general and universal moral rules and their concrete and particular implementation—which is, of course, itself precisely the situation in which the believer stands in relation to the truths of his or her revelation.[30] If the modernist attempt to remove the conditions (of difference and particularity) that made tolerance necessary is indeed untenable (as it seems to be), a return to this grammar and to the self-limiting acts of translation that make language possible at all may well become necessary. The alternative fundamentalisms, of reason and of revelation, in religion as in politics, are, as we know, less than salutary in their social effects.

. . .

It is, finally, through this very concept of boundaries and limits that we can arrive at a definition of just what this idea of tolerance involves. It helps us move beyond the metaphor of translation and enrich the idea of dialogue with a more analytic understanding. In some ways this understanding takes us back to the case of Jews and prostitutes, who, as we learned earlier, were those categories of individuals whose toleration in medieval canon law was nothing more than a second-best solution. And Jews and prostitutes, we would do well to recall, were the marginal or liminal people par excellence of medieval Christian society. They existed very much on its boundaries (not, I hasten to point out, totally beyond them). Existing at the boundaries, however, also meant that in a sense they patrolled boundaries. Their existence on the margins did not make of them marginal categories. Quite the opposite, for on the margins the "whole" was represented. In general terms, this is a truism we know well from the anthropological work of Victor Turner on liminal or marginal states and statuses.[31] Marginal states, of pilgrimage or of a change in social status and so on, become precisely those social spaces where the whole of society is represented and the solidarity of the group as a whole expressed. It is in that role that the margins carry the potential to provide an ongoing challenge and critique to society and its received opinions (a point which resonates with our discussions of the outsider, the sinner, and the boundaries of community in respect to the near-other and the absolute antagonist). It is, as we were led to realize in our dialogues, not the total other and outsider or antagonist with whom the issue of tolerance emerges (for most often with them we either have no interaction, are indifferent, or are threatened), but rather, precisely that near-other, that marginal entity, towards whom the issue of tolerance emerges. Buddhism provides much less of a problem to Orthodox Judaism than do Christianity and Islam, let alone Reform Judaism. This we recall was a salient theme in our discussions—echoing Freud's concept of the "narcissism of small difference"—and it bears remembering as we begin to reposit our understanding in terms of boundaries and margins.

David Nirenberg illustrates this issue wonderfully in the case of prostitutes in the Christian Middle Ages. The prostitute, who belonged to no man, neither father nor husband, but was the receptacle of all men's lust, thus became "a concrete representation of a community of men united to each other by a common sexual bond. In the case of the four-teenth century Crown [of Aragon] this was a community delimited in

terms of religious identity. All Christian males could, in the words of
St. Paul, 'become one body' with a Christian prostitute, but through her
(and this St. Paul did not say) they also became one with each other."[32]
It is no wonder that prostitutes were known (and continue to be known
in certain societies) as public women, *les femmes publique*. It is also no
wonder that, as Nirenberg makes clear, miscegenation across the lines of
religious communities (those of Christians, Jews, and Muslims) was of
such great concern in the fourteenth-century Kingdom of Aragon—
especially in terms of the prostitutes. The different communities maintained their own prostitutes, and the granting of sexual favors across
confessional lines was punished by death. The prostitute, the public woman, whose public nature was itself a function of her marginality, thus,
in a sense, patrolled the boundaries of the community—that very community or public that in a strange, counterintuitive way she came to represent. Note the irony, that it is precisely the marginal or peripheral
prostitute who plays a role in defining and maintaining the boundaries of
the center and of the community. Perhaps, though, the irony is more
apparent than real, for indeed there is no center without its boundaries
and no public without its margins, within which its very own definition
resides. The point is that the prostitute, who could deny her sexual favors
to no man within the community, was barred on pain of death to granting them to anyone beyond the community. Prostitutes had to be tolerated precisely because their role on the boundaries of the public defined
and in some sense maintained that very public.

And here of course the case of the Jews, that other tolerated and
marginal group, comes to mind as playing a somewhat similar role. For
the Jew also, as it were, patrolled the boundaries of Christendom. The
Jew did not so much define the Christian other as define the Christian
self.[33] Christianity had, after all, defined itself in terms of the rejection of
Judaism and of Jewish law and posited alternative terms of fulfillment in
the form of Jesus as Christ. More importantly, Christianity itself could
be realized only at the eschaton, where the Jews came to accept Jesus as
Messiah. In some sense then, the very triumph of Christianity did indeed
rest (in fact until the Second Vatican Council) on the elimination of the
Jews—not their corporeal elimination (which was why Jews were protected by canon law edicts on toleration) but their ideal or symbolic elimination in accepting the tenets of the Christian faith. Again, we see how
the very core of a community (the Christian *ecclesia*) is intimately tied to
and dependent upon those existent on its boundaries. Christians cannot
be free of the Jews, whose final eschatological acceptance of Jesus as

Christ will prove the truth of Christianity. And of course this was precisely the reasoning behind medieval canon laws on tolerance—the need to maintain the Jewish presence as witness to the Second Coming. The Jew was hated, reviled, demeaned, and often attacked. But he could not be destroyed, precisely because of his role vis-à-vis the very central tenets of Christianity.

Both Jews and prostitutes in different ways did provide a similar function: both patrolled (to continue the metaphor) the boundaries of the Christian community. They were those near-others, with whom "dialogue" could provide an internal critique (to follow Fisch's earlier remarks), whether of the family and sexuality or faith and community. Precisely their existence on the boundaries is what defined them as existing in Freud's "small difference," to the majoritarian society. They are not so far removed as to preclude interaction and dialogue, but far enough distant to provide the crux of that definition of self by other and other by self that is the encounter with desire—reigning it in or not as the case may be, but not negating it. Of course, rather than critique, Christian anti-Judaism served as a theological self-affirmation of the Church. Miriam Taylor, summarizing the work of many scholars, has analyzed just how intrinsic this need for self-affirmation and the legitimation of Christian identity was, as well as how deeply tied it was to an anti-Jewish orientation.[34]

The margins, the boundaries, in a very strong sense then maintain the center. And tolerance, I am positing, is the ability to live with the fact that others control or patrol our boundaries—or at least have a say in their constitution without the type of destructive reaction that characterized Christian attitudes towards Jews until the Second Vatican. Rather, the other must become the live embodiment of that skeptical consciousness to which Graf pointed, without then becoming a target of anger, hatred, and violent impulses. As we saw in the previous chapter, this is resonant with the Hegelian issue of recognition.

To have another patrol one's boundaries is an inherently unstable situation, one involving a great expenditure of psychic energy to maintain. Often, there is a tendency to do away with the other who has such power over us. This also is evinced all too often in the fate of minorities within majority cultures, and for that matter in many cases of postcolonial violence in Africa, including the genocidal attack on the Tutsi by the Hutu in Rwanda in 1994.[35] To do away with the other, by either eliminating or incorporating them, thus allows us to patrol our own boundaries. However, doing so means, by definition, destroying the other who is necessary for the very constitution of self. In Hegel's terms, it is turning the other into a slave from whom no recognition is possible or worthwhile. The move to incorporate the other grants us perhaps safety (and control) but not recognition (needless to say, this is a dynamic that can happen as well among couples—to the detriment of the relationship). Living with the reality of other's control is thus a situation of great fragility and uncertainty. The fact that our own boundaries are in the hands of another presents us with a frightening situation: less than total control over our very own constitutive terms of ordering, meaning, and integration.

There is, I believe, no final way out of this tension, and the burden of living with the uncertainty of the other patrolling the boundaries of our own selves, whether collective or individual, is no small burden to bear. Tolerance must be understood not as suffering the other, but as suffering our own discomfort. Tragically, all attempts to overcome this tension, to relieve us of this burden of the other—in the forms say, of messianic and millennial movements, religious or secular in nature—have been disastrous in their consequences.

All attempts at foreshortening this tension have led to either the physical elimination of the other, or, what was sometimes only slightly less horrible, the myriad attempts to incorporate the other by denying his or her existence as other. Different forms of religious commitment, to the extent that they refuse to accept this tolerance—that is, they refuse to acknowledge the role of the other in defining self and community—are no less murderous than the myriad fundamentalisms of reason have been in this regard.

I would like to end this inquiry with a rather long quote from the Swiss author Max Frisch on the subject of jealousy, which he penned in 1949. It will, I hope, help us realize that the issues of boundaries and of tolerance are as important on the intimate and individual no less than communal and collective levels of existence. As we see, the boundaries and indeed what is bounded may be very different here, but the underlying dynamic is strikingly similar.

.　　.　　.

When the time comes: when the look in two eyes, the lighting up of a familiar face, which for years you took to mean you, when all this suddenly belongs to another; in exactly the same way. Her hand, ruffling that other's hair; you have known it. Only a lighthearted impulse, a playful gesture, but you knew it. In this hand lay things shared and familiar, beyond words, and suddenly you see its playful moments from the outside and feel that for this hand of hers it makes no difference whose hair it is ruffling, that everything you felt to be our very own can be done without you; in exactly the same way. Although you know from your own experience how interchangeable the love partner is, you are appalled. And not just because for you it has ended. What appalls you is a suspicion concerning all that had been, a mocking sense of loneliness: it is as if it had never been you with whom she had lain (already you are thinking of her without a name) but only your hair, your sex, which all of a sudden revolts you. It is as if, every time she uttered your name, she had betrayed you. . . .

On the other hand you know exactly:

Neither is she the only possible partner of your love. If she had never come along, you would have found love with another. And there is something else you know, which concerns nobody else, only yourself: I mean your dreams, which push interchangeability to the verge of complete facelessness, and, if you are not completely deceitful, you will not deny that all the things you experienced together and felt as a symbol of your utter togetherness, could have happened without her in exactly the same way. That is to say, within the range of your possibilities. Perhaps after all it is not this interchangeability that gives you such a devilish jab the moment her hand grasps that other head of hair but, on the contrary, the fear that for her hand there may indeed be a difference. There is no question of it: you are not interchangeable, you and he. Sex, which is common to all, has many provinces, and you are one of them. You cannot go beyond your limits, but she can. She certainly cannot go beyond her limits either, but beyond yours she can go; as indeed you can go beyond hers. Surely you knew that we are all limited? It is a bitter recognition, even when unspoken, kept to oneself. Now you have the feeling—like all whose limits have been overstepped and thus, so to speak, identified—the feeling that she has put you in a pillory. Thus it is not only grief that remains, but also rage, the anger of shame which often makes a jealous man mean, revengeful, and stupid, the fear of being inferior. All of a sudden you yourself no longer believe that she ever really loved you. But she really did love you. You! It is just that you are not, as I have already said, all that is possible in love. . . .

Neither is he!
Nor is she!
Nobody is.
This is something we must learn to accept, I believe, if we are not
to become ridiculous, deceitful, not to stifle all that love really is.[36]

.　　.　　.

Here, I think we find presented very poignantly and correctly the themes
discussed above with a clear exposition of how what we hold most dear
and intimate, precisely in its intimacy rests, ultimately, in the hands of
the other. For the man's own boundaries are revealed to be defined by the
other, the woman. The self, fragile and circumscribed, finds its limits,
its boundaries, in the other. And while Frisch is here discussing the realm
of sexuality, the truth of his insight goes far beyond this one realm—
however critical it is—of self-identity. Only, in fact, in this other (and in
other's potential) are the boundaries of self made visible. Frisch seems
here to realize that we are both dependent on that other who posits our
own boundaries and that we bridle at that very dependence. We are condemned, however, to coexist in the mutual tensions of these relationships.

To accept this on the individual level is what psychoanalysts would
term ego-maturity, an eschewal of infant narcissism. To accept it on the
collective level is what I am calling tolerance, an eschewal of group certainty (whether religious or secular). To engage with it intentionally
may well be the form of therapeutic or remedial action best suited to
our present situation—an ethic of responsibility and not, as Max Weber
warned against, of "ultimate ends." A return then to the dialogue with
which we began our analysis and to tolerance as dialogue, but in ways
greatly exceeding metaphor, may well be the imperative of our times.

And so we are left with tolerance, as indeed only a second-best solution, but as one which preserves the integrity of self, of the other, and
of their interaction. The idea of second-best solution is hence redefined
as we come to realize that the eradication of difference which inhers to
all attempts at overcoming difference is but a succumbing to a form of
narcissism, whether collective or individual. A mature discipline in the
face of the human condition is the best we can do if we are to avoid doing
ill. This is perhaps not far from an idea of civility, of proper behavior,
perhaps even approaching the Confucian virtue of *li*, that is, of a pro-

priety that "sets reasonable limits to the satisfaction of desires."[37] Translation—we see—can go well beyond the confines of Western monotheisms. Only, in our cases, whether of the Western monotheisms we have been discussing or of other religious traditions such as Confucianism, these limits are rooted less in the discipline of the market (as civility was for the Scottish moralists) and more in the discipline of tradition, or rather traditions: each with its own set of claims and its own concepts of modesty and propriety. More we cannot do. Less we must not do.

The plurality of truths is untrue at the moment when they are seen externally as many, as determinable standpoints; for every standpoint can also absorb him who thinks it. They become even more untrue when they become mutually indifferent and simply rest alongside one another. What will not and what can not become the same, nevertheless, become related through Transcendence which touches the One, which, even if our gods be different, discovers the God, which requires of us not to relapse into the distraction of warring multiplicities related only by indifference or the struggle over room to exist. There is the sophistry of easy tolerance which wishes to be valid, but not to be really touched. On the other hand, there is the truth of tolerance which listens and gives and enters into the unpredictable process of communication by which force is restrained; in such a process, man reaches from his roots to the heights possible for him.

Karl Jaspers, *Reason and Existenz*

NOTES

Preface and Acknowledgments

1. Works in this area include Marc Gopin, *Between Eden and Armageddon: The Future of World Religions, Violence, and Peacemaking* (Oxford: Oxford University Press, 2000); David Heyd, ed., *Toleration: An Elusive Virtue* (Princeton: Princeton University Press, 1996); Henry Kamen, *The Rise of Toleration* (New York: McGraw Hill, 1967); John Christian Laursen and Cary J. Nederman, eds., *Beyond the Persecuting Society: Religious Toleration before the Enlightenment* (Philadelphia: University of Pennsylvania Press, 1997); John Christian Laursen, *Religious Toleration: The Variety of Rites from Cyrus to DeFoe* (New York: St. Martin's Press, 1999); David Little, John Kelsay, Abdulaziz A. Sachedina, and Frederick Denny, eds., *Human Rights and the Conflicts of Culture: Western and Islamic Perspectives on Religious Liberty* (Columbia: University of South Carolina Press, 1988); Susan Mendus, ed., *Justifying Toleration: Conceptual and Historical Perspectives* (Cambridge: Cambridge University Press, 1988); Cary J. Nederman, *Worlds of Difference: European Discourses of Toleration c. 1100–c. 1550* (University Park: Pennsylvania State University Press, 2000); Gary Remer, *Humanism and the Rhetoric of Toleration* (University Park: Pennsylvania State University Press, 1996); Abdulaziz Abdulhussein Sachedina and Joseph Montville, *Islamic Roots of Democratic Pluralism* (Oxford: Oxford University Press, 2000). Graham N. Stanton and Guy G. Stroumsa, eds., *Tolerance and Intolerance in Early Judaism and Christianity* (Cambridge: Cambridge University Press, 1998); Michael Walzer, *On Toleration* (New Haven: Yale University Press, 1997).

Introduction

1. Bernard Williams, "Toleration: An Impossible Virtue?" in *Toleration: An Elusive Value*, ed. David Heyd (Princeton: Princeton University Press, 1996), pp. 18–27.

185

2. José Casanova, *Public Religions in the Modern World* (Chicago: University of Chicago Press, 1994).

3. See Susan Mendus, *Toleration and the Limits of Liberalism* (London: Macmillan, 1989), p. 108. See also John Horton, "Toleration as a Virtue," in *Toleration: An Elusive Value*, ed. David Heyd (Princeton: Princeton University Press, 1996), pp. 28–43.

4. Williams, "Toleration: An Impossible Virtue?" p. 25.

5. Horton, "Toleration as a Virtue."

6. On this see Adam B. Seligman, *Modernity's Wager: Authority, the Self, and Transcendence* (Princeton: Princeton University Press, 2000). See also Oliver O'Donovan, *Desire of the Nations: Rediscovering the Roots of Political Theology* (Cambridge: Cambridge University Press, 1999), and John Milbank, *Theology and Social Theory* (Oxford: Basil Blackwell, 1990).

7. Michael Ignatieff and Amy Gutmann, eds., *Human Rights as Politics and Idolatry* (Princeton: Princeton University Press, 2001).

8. For some works in this area, see Ernst Troeltsch, *The Social Teachings of the Christian Churches* (Chicago: University of Chicago Press, 1960); Max Weber, *The Protestant Ethic and the Spirit of Capitalism* (New York: Scribner and Sons, 1958); Georg Jellinek, *The Declaration of the Rights of Man and of Citizens: A Contribution to Modern Constitutional History* (Westport: Hyperion Press, 1979); Louis Dumont, *Essays in Individualism: Modern Ideology in Anthropological Perspective* (Chicago: University of Chicago Press, 1986); Benjamin Nelson, *The Idea of Usury* (Chicago: University of Chicago Press, 1969); Hans Blumenberg, *The Genesis of the Copernican Revolution* (Cambridge: MIT Press, 1987); Wolfgang Schluchter, *The Rise of Western Rationalism* (Berkeley: University of California Press, 1981); J. G. A. Pocock, *The Machiavellian Moment* (Princeton: Princeton University Press, 1975).

9. Ernest Tuveson, *The Imagination as a Means of Grace: Locke and the Aesthetics of Romanticism* (Berkeley: University of California Press, 1960), and *Redeemer Nation: The Idea of America's Millennial Role* (Chicago: University of Chicago Press, 1968).

10. Richard Popkin, *The History of Skepticism from Erasmus to Spinoza* (Berkeley: University of California Press, 1979).

11. Servetus is interesting to us for a number of reasons. He was one of the major anti-Trinitarian thinkers of his age and has been described by some as having developed a "sort of Jewish-Christianity" as he "came to perceive Pharisaic Judaism as the root of Christianity." Matt Goldish, "Patterns in Coverso Messianism," in *Jewish Messianism in the Early Modern World*, ed. Matt Goldish and Richard Popkin (Dordrecht: Kluwer Publishers, 2001), pp. 41–56. See also Howard Hotson, "Arianism and Millennarianism: The Link between Two Heresies from Servetus to Socinus," in *Continental Millennarianism, Protestants, Catholics, Heretics*, ed. John Laursen and Richard Popkin (Dordrecht: Kluwer Publishers, 2001), pp. 9–37.

12. Thomas Weld, "Preface," in *A Short Story of the Rise, Reign, and Ruin of the Antinomians, Familists, and Libertines That Infected the Churches of New-England*, ed. J. Winthrop (London: Tho. Parkhurst, 1692), p. 74.

13. Miguel de Montaigne, *The Essays of Miguel De Montaigne*, trans. George Ives (New York: Limited Editions, 1943), p. 813.

14. Ibid., p. 589.

15. Stephen Toulmin, *Cosmopolis: The Hidden Agenda of Modernity* (Chicago: University of Chicago Press, 1990).

16. Menachem Fisch, *Rational Rabbis, Science and Talmudic Culture* (Bloomington: Indiana University Press, 1997).

17. John Clayton, "Common Ground and Defensible Different," in *Religion, Politics and Peace*, ed. Leroy Rounder (South Bend: University of Notre Dame Press, 1999), pp. 104–27.

18. Søren Kierkegaard, *Fear and Trembling* (Princeton: Princeton University Press, 1941).

19. In the Middle Ages, philosophers and theologians debated nominalist and realist positions: that is, the existence of general categories (with, in varying gradations, the realists affirming and the nominalists denying such existence. Attempts at a synthesis of positions were presented by philosophers such as William of Ockham). The debate between Protestants and Catholics over the real presence in the Eucharist is an example of the difference between nominalist and realist positions.

An interesting debate in Judaism refers to the Red Heifer, which was to be burned and its ashes, mixed with water, sprinkled on those who had contact with the dead, as an act of purification. The heifer had to be totally red, and there are fascinating debates in the rabbinic literature over what "totally" means: one non-red hair, five, fifty, a non-red eyebrow, and so on. The claim that even five non-red hairs would disqualify the heifer would rest on a realist interpretation of scripture. The claim, made by R. Akiva, that red means "mostly red," and the rest you can pull out, rests on a nominalist understanding (H. S. Horowitz, ed., *Siphre D'BE RAB* [*Siphre ad Numeros adjecto Siphre Zutta*] *Hebrew* [Jerusalem: Shalem Books, 1992], p. 301). Many such examples and controversies can be found in all religious traditions. The example Shlomo Fischer offers below, in his discussion of the video of the Temple and the offering of the first fruits, is a prime example of the type of realist understanding of religious categories that is so prevalent today in many religious communities, of all faiths.

19. On fundamentalism, see Martin E. Marty and R. Scott Appleby, eds., *Fundamentalism Observed* (Chicago: University of Chicago Press, 1991), and *Fundamentalisms and Society: Reclaiming the Sciences, the Family, and Education* (Chicago: University of Chicago Press, 1992).

Chapter One　The First Dialogue

1. The Noachide commandments consist of seven basic obligations that are binding on all humanity, including refraining from murder, robbery, incest, blasphemy, idol worship, and eating a limb torn from a live animal, and establishing a system of justice. Non-Jews are not obligated to fulfill the 613 particularist commandments of the Torah, which are binding only on Jews; rather, they are obligated only to fulfill the Noachide commandments. Non-Jews who fulfill these obligations merit salvation and are deemed righteous. These universal obligations are also the markers of a civilized society, with whom Jews may interact. See Suzanne Last Stone, "Sinaitic and Noahide Law: Legal Pluralism in Jewish Law," 12 *Cardozo Law Review* 1157 (1991).

2. *Tikkun olam* (literally, repairing the world) is best translated as "improving the world." The term first appears in *Mishna Gittin* as a justification for social legislation designed to improve conditions in Jewish society. In recent usage, it connotes actions to improve society in general and refers to the idea that Jews bear a responsibility, derived from a variety of different sources, for the moral, spiritual, and material welfare not only of Jewish society but also of the larger society which they inhabit. See generally David Shatz, Chaim I. Waxman, and Nathan J. Diament, eds., *Tikkun Olam: Social Responsibility in Jewish Thought and Law* (Northvale, N.J.: Jason Aronson, 1997).

3. Beginning in the Talmud, there is a tendency to mitigate punishment or ostracism of sinners, Jewish and pagan, on the ground that the sinner was not fully responsible for his or her acts. The sinner may be depicted as a "captured child" raised among gentiles, or under duress, erring through lack of adequate education, or misled by desire. Thus, the act itself remains a sin, but the sinner is excused or tolerated. In the modern era, this tendency in the tradition is relied on heavily. See Aviezer Ravitzky, "The Question of Tolerance in the Jewish Tradition," in *Hazon Nahum: Studies in Jewish Law, Thought, and History*, ed. Yaakov Elman and Jeffrey S. Gurock (New York: Yeshiva University Press, 1997).

4. In a story in the Babylonian Talmud, Tractate Erubim (13:b), in a dispute between the two schools of law, of Hillel and Shammai, a heavenly voice is heard to declare that both are the words of the living God—thus sanctifying the process of debate and discussion as value in itself. See chapter 4 for an explanation of the story.

5. Rabbi Emmanuel Rackman was former chancellor of Bar Ilan University (the religiously inspired university in Israel). He is known for his liberal interpretations of certain critical halachic issues, most especially those dealing with the law of the family.

6. Rabbi Shaul Israeli, a Rabbinic Supreme Court Justice in Israel, head of the Merkaz Harav Yeshiva, died in 1996. Rabbi Abraham Isaac Kook (1870–1935) was the Chief Rabbi of Palestine and, along with Franz Rosenzweig, one of the most

important Jewish theologians of the twentieth century. Rabbi Avraham Yeshayahu Karlitz (Chazon Ish) was one of the most important rabbinical figures of the twentieth century. He composed commentaries on the *Shulchan Aruch* and Maimondes' *Yad Hachazaka*. He was one of the founders of Charedi society in Israel and died in Bnei Brak, Israel in 1958.

7. Jacob Katz, *A House Divided: Orthodoxy and Schism in Nineteenth-Century Central European Jewry* (Hanover: Brandeis University Press, 1998).

Chapter Two   The Second Dialogue

1. These would include such works as the following: W. St. Clair Tisdall, *The Original Sources of the Qur'an* (London: Society for the Promotion of Christian Knowledge, 1911); Charles Torrey, *The Jewish Foundation of Islam* (New York: Jewish Institute of Religion Press, 1933), pp. 41–43, 78; Abraham Geiger, *Was hat Mohammed aus dem Judenthume aufgenommen* (*Judaism and Islam*), trans. F. M. Young (New York: Ktav Publishing House, 1970); Abraham Katsh, *Judaism and the Koran* (New York: A. S. Barnes, 1962); William Muir, *The Life of Mohammad from Original Sources* (New York: AMS Press, 1975); A. J. Wensinck, *Mohammed en de Joden te Medina* (*Muhammad and the Jews of Medina*), trans. Wolfgang Behn (Freiburg: K. Schwarz, 1975); C. H. Becker, *Christentum und Islam* (*Christianity and Islam*), trans. H. J. Chaytor (New York: B. Franklin Reprints, 1974); Carl Brockelman, *Geschichte der Islamischen Völker und Staaten* (*History of the Islamic Peoples*), trans. Joel Carmichael and Moshe Perlmann (New York: Capricorn Books, 1960); Julius Wellhausen, *Reste arabischen Heidentums* (Berlin: De Gruyter, 1961); Richard Bell, *The Origin of Islam in Its Christian Environment* (London: Frank Cass, 1968), p. 15.

2. Bahais and Ahmadiyya both subscribe to the view that their founder received revelation. Thus they have been persecuted as heretics. The Bahais have now declared themselves to be a separate religion, but the Ahmadiyya based in Pakistan still continue to insist that they are Muslims and ought to be treated by the state as such.

3. Sigmund Freud, *Civilization and Its Discontents* (London: Institute of Psychoanalysis, 1945), p. 91.

4. E. Lévinas, "Questions et réponses," in *De Dieu qui vient à l'idée* (Paris, 1986), p. 145.

5. J. Winter and D. Joslin, eds., *R. H. Tawney's Commonplace Book* (Cambridge: Cambridge University Press, 1972), p. 54.

6. *Tannaitic* means relating to the *tannaim*, the commentators on the Mishnah, the code of law redacted by R. Judah the Prince in 220 C.E.

7. Beith Shammai and Beith Hillel are two schools of legal commentary, named after their respective founders, Shammai and Hillel, who lived in the first decades of the Christian era.

Chapter Three   The Third Dialogue

1. See Arnaldo Momigliano, "The Disadvantage of Monotheism for a Universal State," in *On Pagans, Jews and Christians* (Hanover: Wesleyan University Press, 1987).

Chapter Four   Towards a Phenomenology of Religious Toleration

1. Arthur Rimbaud, *Une saison en enfes, Illuminations* (Paris: Gallimard, 1973), p. 202; Miguel de Unamuno, *Tragic Sense of Life* (New York: Dover, 1972), p. 1; George Steiner, *After Babel: Aspects of Language and Translation* (Oxford: Oxford University Press, 1998), p. 49.

2. Thomas Paine, *The Rights of Man* (New York: Doubleday, 1961), p. 324.

3. For examples and analysis of these issues, see "The End of Tolerance: Engaging Cultural Difference," *Daedalus* (Fall 2000).

4. Hermann Cohen, *Religion of Reason: Out of the Sources of Judaism* (Atlanta: Scholars Press, 1995), p. 120.

5. We can find indications of this in the ancient practices, dating back to the third millennium B.C.E., of translating or interpreting the names of foreign divinities. The Mesopotamian Listenwissenschaft listed Akkadian and Summerian gods in two or three languages. Later, Bronze Age lists were expanded to include Amorit, Hurritic, Elamite, and Kassite names as well. As explained by the Egyptologist Jan Assman: "Treaties had to be signed by solemn oaths and the gods that were invoked in these oaths had to be recognized by both parties. The list of these gods conventionally closes the treaty. They necessarily had to be equivalent as to their function and in particular as to their rank. Intercultural theology became a concern of international law." Here by the way are the historical rudiments of generalized symbolic exchange as a condition of more particular economic exchange predicated on an idea of the deity as—if not yet fully generalizable—at least translatable. Jan Assmann, *Moses the Egyptian: The Memory of Egypt in Western Monotheism* (Cambridge: Harvard University Press, 1998).

6. Walter Benjamin, *Illuminations* (New York: Schocken Books, 1969), p. 76.

7. Of course the Qur'an and its believed untranslatable nature would seem to question Benjamin's insight. Though, to be sure where the line between translation and what are termed "interpretations" is drawn is somewhat hard to tell.

8. See Henry Corbin, *Alone with the Alone: Creative Imagination in the Sufism of Ibn 'Arabi*, trans. R. Manheim (Princeton: Princeton University Press, 1998), on the thought of Ibn Arabi.

9. See, for example, Larry Vaughan, *Johann Georg Hamann: Metaphysics of Language and Vision of History* (New York: Peter Lang Publishing, 1989); Terence J. German, *Hamann on Language and Religion* (Oxford: Oxford University Press, 1982);

Jean-Jacques Rousseau and Johann G. Herder, *On the Origin of Language: Two Essays*, trans. A. Gode and J. H. Moran (Chicago: University of Chicago Press, 1990); Wilhelm von Humboldt, *On Language: On the Diversity of Human Language Construction and Its Influence on the Mental Development of the Human Species*, trans. P. Heath (Cambridge: Cambridge University Press, 1999).

10. On Jewish mystical language with its endless interpretations, see Yoseph Dan, *Al Hakedusha* (Hebrew) (*On Sanctity: Religion, Ethics and Mysticism in Judaism and Other Religions*) (Jerusalem: Magnes Press, 1998).

11. Gary Remer, *Humanism and the Rhetoric of Toleration* (University Park: Pennsylvania State University Press, 1996).

12. Ibid, p. 3

13. Quoted in Remer, *Humanism and the Rhetoric of Toleration*, p. 240.

14. Bernard Mandeville, *The Fable of the Bees: Or Private Vices, Publick Benefits*, vol. 2 (Indianapolis: Liberty Classics, 1988), p. 178.

15. Isaiah Berlin, *Magus of the North: J. G. Hamann and the Origins of Modern Irrationalism* (London: John Murray Publishers, 1993), p. 58.

16. David Hume, *A Treatise of Human Nature* (Oxford: Clarendon Press, 1960), p. 520.

17. Adam Smith, *The Theory of Moral Sentiments* (Indianapolis: Liberty Press, 1982), p. 110.

18. Ibid., p. 135.

19. William Hauseman, "The Expression of the Idea of Toleration in French during the Sixteenth Century," *Sixteenth Century Journal* 15, no. 3 (1984): 293–310.

20. Hannah Arendt, "Collective Responsibility," in *Amor MUNDI: Explorations in the Faith and Thought of Hannah Arendt*, ed. J. W. Bernauer (Dodrecht: Martinus-Nijhoff Publishers, 1987), p. 50.

21. Ibid., p. 45.

22. Max Weber, *Economy and Society: An Outline of Interpretive Sociology* (Berkeley: University of California Press, 1986), and *The Protestant Ethic and the Spirit of Capitalism* (New York: Scribner and Sons, 1958).

23. True, the dispute concerns disagreements within the halls of the academy. The degree that one can extrapolate from this to disputes outside of the academy, to disputes with strangers, pagans, or converts, is a matter of some contention.

24. Cary J. Nederman, *Worlds of Difference: European Discourses of Toleration, c. 1100–1550* (University Park: Pennsylvania State University Press, 2000); John Christian Laursen and Cary J. Nederman, eds., *Beyond the Persecuting Society: Religious Toleration before the Enlightenment* (Philadelphia: University of Pennsylvania Press, 1997).

25. Peter Mews, in Laursen and Nederman, *Beyond the Persecuting Society*, p. 39.

26. Nederman, *Worlds of Difference*, pp. 25–37.

27. Marion Kuntz, in Remer, *Humanism and the Rhetoric of Toleration*, p. 219, n. 37.

28. Remer, *Humanism and the Rhetoric of Toleration*, p. 219.

29. Marion Kuntz, "Dialogue," in J. Bodin, *Colloquium of the Seven about Secrets of the Sublime*, trans. M. L. Daniels (Princeton: Princeton University Press, 1975), p. lxv.

30. Jean Bodin, *Colloquium of the Seven about Secrets of the Sublime*, p. 145.

31. Martin Buber, *Between Man and Man* (Boston: Beacon Press, 1955), pp. 19–20.

32. Alexandre Kojève, *Introduction to the Reading of Hegel: Lectures on the Phenomenology of Spirit* (Ithaca: Cornell University Press, 1980), pp. 48–49.

33. S. N. Eisenstadt, "The Axial Age: The Emergence of Transcendental Visions and the Rise of Clerics," *European Journal of Sociology* 23 (1982): 294, 296.

34. On the symbolization of cosmic order and on times of troubles, see Eric Voegelin, *Order and History*, vol. 1 (Baton Rouge: Louisiana State University Press, 1954), pp. 1–13, 52–110.

35. Eisenstadt, *Axial Age*, pp. 300, 301.

36. For this terminology and additional perspectives on religious evolution, see Robert Bellah, "Religious Evolution," *American Sociological Review* 29 (1964): 358–74.

37. Wolfgang Schluchter, "The Paradox of Rationalization: On the Relations of Ethics and the World," in *Max Weber's Vision of History, Ethics and Method*, ed. G. Roth and W. Schluchter (Berkeley: University of California Press, 1979), p. 23.

38. On this, see Peter Berger, *The Sacred Canopy* (New York: Anchor Books, 1969), pp. 113–18.

39. Karl Jaspers, *The Origin and Goal of History* (New Haven: Yale University Press, 1953), p. 3.

40. Ibid., pp. 65, 63.

41. Benjamin Nelson, "Self Images and Spiritual Directions in the History of European Civilization," in *On the Roads to Modernity: Conscience, Science and Civilizations*, ed. T. Huff (New Jersey: Rowman and Littlefield, 1981), p. 43.

42. One infamous modern example of such political disputes is the destruction of the Ayodhya mosque in 1992. On this, see Ashis Nandy, et al. *Creating a Nationality: The Ramjanmabhumi Movement and Fear of Self* (Oxford: Oxford University Press, 1996). See also T. N. Madan, *Modern Myths, Locked Minds: Secularism and Fundamentalism in India* (Oxford: Oxford University Press, 1998).

43. Mary Douglas, *Natural Symbols: Explorations in Cosmology* (New York: Routledge, 1996), p. 60.

44. On the idea of *universitas*, see Otto Friedrich von Gierke, *Natural Law and the Theory of Society, 1500–1800* (Cambridge: Cambridge University Press, 1950).

45. See Remer, *Humanism and the Rhetoric of Toleration*.

46. Fihi-ma-Fihi, p. 49, quoted in Afzal Iqbal, *The Life and Work of Jalaluddin Rumi* (Karachi: Oxford University Press, 1999). p. 95.

47. On Ha'Meiri's tolerance, see also Remer in Laursen and Nederman.

48. Walter Benjamin, "Karl Kraus," in *Reflections: Essays, Aphorisms, Autobiographical Writings* (New York: Harcourt, Brace Jovanovich, 1978), p. 239.

49. Richard Sennett, *The Fall of Public Man* (New York: W. W. Norton, 1992).

50. Dzevad Karshasan, *Sarajevo, Exodus of a City* (New York: Kodansha International, 1993). p. 9.

51. Bob Scribner, "Preconditions of Tolerance and Intolerance in Sixteenth Century Germany," in *Tolerance and Intolerance in the European Reformation*, ed. O. P. Grell and B. Scribner (Cambridge: Cambridge University Press, 1996), p. 38.

52. Eric Voeglin, *New Science of Politics* (Chicago: University of Chicago Press, 1952), pp. 66–69.

53. Charles Taylor, *Sources of the Self* (Cambridge: Harvard University Press, 1989), p. 93.

54. Shlomo Fischer, "Intolerance and Tolerance in the Jewish Tradition and Contemporary Israel," *Journal of Human Rights* 2, no. 1 (2003).

55. Roy Mattahedeh, *The Mantle of the Prophet: Religion and Politics in Iran* (New York: Penguin Books, 1986), p. 389.

56. *Hilchot Mamrim* 3:3. See Fischer, "Intolerance and Tolerance."

Chapter Five   Conclusion

1. See István Bejcz, "Tolerantia: A Medieval Concept," *Journal of the History of Ideas* 58, no. 3 (1997) 365–84.

2. See Otto Friedrich von Gierke, *Natural Law and the Theory of Society, 1500–1800* (Cambridge: Cambridge University Press, 1950), and *Political Theories of the Middle Age*, trans. F. W. Maitland (Boston: Beacon Press, 1958).

3. Daniel Lerner, *The Passing of Traditional Society* (New York: Free Press, 1964).

4. David Nirenberg, *Communities of Violence: Persecution of Minorities in the Middle Ages* (Princeton: Princeton University Press, 1996).

5. Ernest Gellner, *Plough, Sword and Book: The Structure of Human History* (Chicago: University of Chicago Press, 1989).

6. Karl Jaspers, *The Origin and Goal of History* (New Haven: Yale University Press, 1953), pp. 63, 65.

7. Benjamin Nelson, "Self Images and Spiritual Directions in the History of European Civilization," in *On the Roads to Modernity: Conscience, Science and Civilizations*, ed. T. Huff (New Jersey: Rowman and Littlefield, 1981), p. 43.

8. Ernst Troeltsch, *The Social Teaching of the Christian Churches*, vol. 1 (New York: Harper and Row, 1960), p. 55.

9. Marcell Mauss, "A Category of the Human Mind: The Notion of the Person, the Notion of the Self," in *The Category of the Person*, ed. M. Carrithers, S. Collins, and S. Lukes (Cambridge: Cambridge University Press, 1985), pp. 19–20.

10. See Adam B. Seligman, *Modernity's Wager: Authority, the Self, and Transcendence* (Princeton: Princeton University Press, 2000).

11. Hermann Cohen, *Religion of Reason: Out of the Sources of Judaism* (Atlanta: Scholars Press, 1995), p. 114.

12. Michael Walzer, *Thick and Thin: Moral Argument at Home and Abroad* (Notre Dame: University of Notre Dame Press, 1994).

13. A recent example of such in the case of human rights can be found in Michael J. Perry, *The Idea of Human Rights: Four Inquiries* (Oxford: Oxford University Press, 2000). See also my critique of these very assumptions in Adam B. Seligman, "Review of *The Idea of Human Rights* by Michael Perry," *Human Rights Review* 1, no. 3 (2002): 140–44.

14. Georg Jellinek, *The Declaration of the Rights of Man and of Citizens: A Contribution to Modern Constitutional History* (Westport: Hyperion Press, 1979), p. 48.

15. Ibid., p. 53.

16. Ibid., p. 80.

17. Ibid., pp. 74–75.

18. Benjamin Nelson, *The History of Usury: From Tribal Brotherhood to Universal Otherhood* (Chicago: University of Chicago Press, 1969).

19. Ignaz Goldzhier, *Muslim Studies*, vol. 1 (London: George Allen, 1967), pp. 201–8.

20. Toshihiko Izutsu, *Ethico-Religious Concepts in the Qur'an* (Montreal: McGill University Press, 1966), and *God and Man in the Koran: Semantics of the Koranic Weltanschauung* (Tokyo: Takeio Institute of Cultural and Linguistic Studies, 1964), pp. 198–229.

21. James Gouinlock, *The Moral Writings of John Dewey* (New York: Prometheus Books, 1994), introduction and especially pp. xliv–xlv.

22. See Seligman, *Modernity's Wager*.

23. *New York Times*, August 3, 2000.

24. *New York Times*, August 16, 2000, A-10.

25. Michael Shurkin, "Decolonization and the Renewal of French Judaism: Reflections on the Contemporary French Jewish Scene," *Jewish Social Studies* 6, no. 2 (2000): 156–76.

26. Charles Taylor, "What is Human Agency," in *Human Agency and Language*, vol. 1 (Cambridge: Cambridge University Press, 1985), p. 24.

27. "Lodi, la lega alla guara santa," in *La Republica*, October 15, 2000.

28. "Il sindaco Alla larga dalle chiese infedeli," in *Il Giorno*, November 24, 2000.

29. On the growth of Jewish Orthodoxy see Jacob Katz, *A House Divided: Orthodoxy and Schism in Nineteenth-Century Central European Jewry*, trans. Z. Brody (Lebanon, N.H.: University Press of New England, 1998).

30. Albert R. Jonsen and Stephen Toulmin, *The Abuse of Casuistry: A History of Moral Reasoning* (Berkeley: University of California Press, 1988).

31. See Victor Turner, *Dramas, Fields, and Metaphors: Symbolic Action in Human Society* (Ithaca: Cornell University Press, 1974), and *The Ritual Process: Structure and Anti-Structure* (New York: Aldine de Gruyter, 1995).

32. Nirenberg, *Communities of Violence*, p. 155.

33. These remarks of course summarize a substantial literature, often contentious, on the relations of Jews and Christians over the past two millennia. An excellent recent volume that surveys this literature is Miriam Taylor, *Anti-Judaism and Early Christian Identity: A Critique of the Scholarly Consensus* (Leiden: E. J. Brill, 1995). One of the classics of this literature, upon which some of my arguments are based, is David Flusser, *Jewish Sources in Early Christianity*, (*Hebrew*) (Tel Aviv: Siphriat HaPoalim, 1979). An excellent study of how Christian liturgy and practice presented a set of boundaries upon which Judaisim defined itself is Israel Jacob Yuval, *"Two Nations in Your Womb": Perceptions of Jews and Christians* (*Hebrew*) (Tel Aviv: Am Oved, 2001). See also David Rokeah, *Jews, Pagans and Christians in Conflict* (Jerusalem: Magnes Press, 1982); James Parkes, *The Conflict of the Church and the Synagogue: A Study in the Origins of Antisemitism* (New York: Athenaeum, 1969).

34. Miriam Taylor, *Anti-Judaism and Early Christian Identity*, pp. 128–29, 178–79.

35. On this theme, especially on the construction of the Tutsi as a racial other to be eliminated, see Mahmood Mamdani, *When Victims Become Killers* (Princeton: Princeton University Press, 2001).

36. Max Frisch, *Sketchbook 1946–1949*, trans. G. Skelton (New York: Harcourt Brace, 1977), p. 272–73.

37. Fredrick W. Mote, *Intellectual Foundations of China* (New York: Knopf, 1971), p. 64. On *li*, see also Donald Munro, *The Concept of Man in Early China* (Stanford: Stanford University Press, 1969), pp. 26–35; Benjamin Swartz, "Some Polarities in Confucian Thought," in *Confucianism and Chinese Civilization*, ed. A. Wright (Stanford: Stanford University Press, 1964), pp. 3–15.

BIBLIOGRAPHY

Arendt, Hannah. "Collective Responsibility." In *Amor MUNDI: Explorations in the Faith and Thought of Hannah Arendt,* edited by J. W. Bernauer. Dodrecht: Martinus-Nijhoff Publishers, 1987.

Assmann, Jan. *Moses the Egyptian: The Memory of Egypt in Western Monotheism.* Cambridge: Harvard University Press, 1998.

Becker, C. H. *Christentum und Islam (Christianity and Islam).* Translated by H. J. Chaytor. New York: B. Franklin Reprints, 1974.

Bejcz, István. "Tolerantia: A Medieval Concept." *Journal of the History of Ideas* 58 no. 3 (1997): 365–84.

Bell, Richard. *The Origin of Islam in Its Christian Environment.* London: Frank Cass, 1968.

Bellah, Robert. "Religious Evolution." *American Sociological Review* 29 (1964): 358–74.

Benjamin, Walter. *Illuminations.* New York: Schocken Books, 1969.

———. *Reflections: Essays, Aphorisms, Autobiographical Writings.* New York: Harcourt, Brace Jovanovich, 1978.

Berger, Peter. *The Sacred Canopy.* New York: Anchor Books, 1969.

Berlin, Isaiah. *Magus of the North: J. G. Hamann and the Origins of Modern Irrationalism.* London: John Murray Publishers, 1993.

Blumenberg, Hans. *The Genesis of the Copernican Revolution.* Cambridge: MIT Press, 1987.

Bodin, Jean. *Colloquium of the Seven about Secrets of the Sublime.* Translated by M. L. Daniels. Princeton: Princeton University Press, 1975.

Brockelman, Carl. *Geschichte der islamischen Völker und Staaten (History of the Islamic Peoples).* Translated by Joel Carmichael and Moshe Perlmann. New York: Capricorn Books, 1960.

Buber, Martin. *Between Man and Man.* Boston: Beacon Press, 1955.

Casanova, José. *Public Religions in the Modern World.* Chicago: University of Chicago Press, 1994.

Clayton, John. "Common Ground and Defensible Different." In *Religion, Politics and Peace,* edited by Leroy Rounder. South Bend: University of Notre Dame Press, 1999.

Cohen, Hermann. *Religion of Reason: Out of the Sources of Judaism*. Atlanta: Scholars Press, 1995.

Corbin, Henry. *Alone with the Alone: Creative Imagination in the Sufism of Ibn 'Arabi*. Translated by R. Manheim. Princeton: Princeton University Press, 1998.

Dan, Yoseph. *Al Hakedusha (Hebrew) (On Sanctity: Religion, Ethics and Mysticism in Judaism and Other Religions)*. Jerusalem: Magnes Press, 1998.

Douglas, Mary. *Natural Symbols: Explorations in Cosmology*. New York: Routledge, 1996.

Dumont, Louis. *Essays in Individualism: Modern Ideology in Anthropological Perspective*. Chicago: University of Chicago Press, 1986.

Eisenstadt, S. N. "The Axial Age: The Emergence of Transcendental Visions and the Rise of Clerics." In *European Journal of Sociology* 23 (1982): 294, 296.

"The End of Tolerance: Engaging Cultural Difference." *Daedalus* (Fall 2000).

Fisch, Menachem. *Rational Rabbis, Science and Talmudic Culture*. Bloomington: Indiana University Press, 1997.

Fischer, Shlomo. "Intolerance and Tolerance in the Jewish Tradition and Contemporary Israel." *Journal of Human Rights* 2, no. 1 (2003): 65–80.

Flusser, David. *Jewish Sources in Early Christianity (Hebrew)*. Tel Aviv: Siphriat HaPoalim, 1979.

Freud, Sigmund. *Civilization and Its Discontents*. London: Institute of Psycho-analysis, 1945.

Frisch, Max. *Sketchbook 1946–1949*. Translated by G. Skelton. New York: Harcourt Brace, 1977.

Geiger, Abraham. *Was hat Mohammed aus dem Judenthume aufgenommen (Judaism and Islam)*. Translated by F. M. Young. New York: Ktav Publishing House, 1970.

Gellner, Ernest. *Plough, Sword and Book: The Structure of Human History*. Chicago: University of Chicago Press, 1989.

German, Terence J. *Hamann on Language and Religion*. Oxford: Oxford University Press, 1982.

Gierke, Otto Friedrich von. *Natural Law and the Theory of Society, 1500–1800*. Cambridge: Cambridge University Press, 1950.

———. *Political Theories of the Middle Age*. Translated by F. W. Maitland. Boston: Beacon Press, 1958.

Goldish, Matt. "Patterns in Coverso Messianism." In *Jewish Messianism in the Early Modern World*, edited by Matt Goldish and Richard Popkin. Dordrecht: Kluwer Publishers, 2001.

Goldzhier, Ignaz. *Muslim Studies*. Vol. 1. London: George Allen, 1967.

Gopin, Marc. *Between Eden and Armageddon: The Future of World Religions, Violence, and Peacemaking*. Oxford: Oxford University Press, 2000.

Gouinlock, James. *The Moral Writings of John Dewey*. New York: Prometheus Books, 1994.

Hauseman, William. "The Expression of the Idea of Toleration in French during the Sixteenth Century." *Sixteenth Century Journal* 15, no. 3 (1984): 293–310.

Heyd, David, ed. *Toleration: An Elusive Virtue*. Princeton: Princeton University Press, 1996.

Horowitz, H. S., ed. *Siphre D'BE RAB* (*Siphre ad Numeros adjecto Siphre Zutta*) (*Hebrew*). Jerusalem: Shalem Books, 1992.

Horton, John. "Toleration as a Virtue." In *Toleration: An Elusive Value*, edited by D. Heyd. Princeton: Princeton University Press, 1996.

Hotson, Howard. "Arianism and Millennarianism: The Link between Two Heresies from Servetus to Socinus." In *Continental Millennarianism, Protestants, Catholics, Heretics*, edited by John Laursen and Richard Popkin. Dordrecht: Kluwer Publishers, 2001.

Humboldt, Wilhelm von. *On Language: On the Diversity of Human Language Construction and Its Influence on the Mental Development of the Human Species*. Translated by P. Heath. Cambridge: Cambridge University Press, 1999.

Hume, David. *A Treatise of Human Nature*. Oxford: Clarendon Press, 1960.

Ignatieff, Michael, and Amy Gutmann, eds. *Human Rights as Politics and Idolatry*. Princeton: Princeton University Press, 2001.

Iqbal, Afzal. *The Life and Work of Jalaluddin Rumi*. Karachi: Oxford University Press, 1999.

Izutsu, Toshihiko. *Ethico-Religious Concepts in the Qur'an*. Montreal: McGill University Press, 1966.

———. *God and Man in the Koran: Semantics of the Koranic Weltanschauung*. Tokyo: Takeio Institute of Cultural and Linguistic Studies, 1964.

Jaspers, Karl. *The Origin and Goal of History*. New Haven: Yale University Press, 1953.

Jellinek, Georg. *The Declaration of the Rights of Man and of Citizens: A Contribution to Modern Constitutional History*. Westport: Hyperion Press, 1979.

Jonsen, Albert R., and Stephen Toulmin. *The Abuse of Casuistry: A History of Moral Reasoning*. Berkeley: University of California Press, 1988.

Kamen, Henry. *The Rise of Toleration*. New York: McGraw Hill, 1967.

———. "Toleration and the Law in the West 1500–1700." In *Ratio Juris* 10, no. 1 (1997): 36–44.

Karshasan, Dzevad. *Sarajevo, Exodus of a City*. New York: Kodansha International, 1993.

Katsh, Abraham. *Judaism and the Koran*. New York: A. S. Barnes, 1962.

Katz, Jacob. *A House Divided: Orthodoxy and Schism in Nineteenth-Century Central European Jewry*. Translated by Z. Brody. Hanover, N.H.: Brandeis University Press, 1998.

Kierkegaard, Søren. *Fear and Trembling*. Princeton: Princeton University Press, 1941.

Kojève, Alexandre. *Introduction to the Reading of Hegel: Lectures on the Phenomenology of Spirit*. Ithaca: Cornell University Press, 1980.

Kuntz, Marion. "Dialogue." In J. Bodin, *Colloquium of the Seven about Secrets of the Sublime*. Princeton: Princeton University Press, 1975.

Laursen, John Christian. *Religious Toleration: The Variety of Rites from Cyrus to DeFoe*. New York: St. Martin's Press, 1999.

Laursen, John Christian, and Cary J. Nederman, eds. *Beyond the Persecuting Society: Religious Toleration before the Enlightenment*. Philadelphia: University of Pennsylvania Press, 1997.

Lerner, Daniel. *The Passing of Traditional Society*. New York: Free Press, 1964.

Lévinas, E. "Questions et réponses." In *De Dieu qui vient à l'idée*, 128–57. Paris, 1986.

Little, David, John Kelsay, Abdulaziz A. Sachedina, and Frederick Denny, eds. *Human Rights and the Conflicts of Culture: Western and Islamic Perspectives on Religious Liberty*. Columbia: University of South Carolina Press, 1988.

Madan, T. N. *Modern Myths, Locked Minds: Secularism and Fundamentalism in India*. Oxford: Oxford University Press, 1998.

Mamdani, Mahmood. *When Victims Become Killers*. Princeton: Princeton University Press, 2001.

Mandeville, Bernard. *The Fable of the Bees: Or Private Vices, Publick Benefits*. Vol. 2. Indianapolis: Liberty Classics, 1988.

Marty, Martin E., and R. Scott Appleby, eds. *Fundamentalism Observed*. Chicago: University of Chicago Press, 1991.

———. *Fundamentalisms and Society: Reclaiming the Sciences, the Family, and Education*. Chicago: University of Chicago Press, 1992.

Mattahedeh, Roy. *The Mantle of the Prophet: Religion and Politics in Iran*. New York: Penguin Books, 1986.

Mauss, Marcell. "A Category of the Human Mind: The Notion of the Person, the Notion of the Self." In *The Category of the Person*, edited by M. Carrithers, S. Collins and S. Lukes. Cambridge: Cambridge University Press, 1985.

Mendus, Susan. *Toleration and the Limits of Liberalism*. London: Macmillan, 1989.

Mendus, Susan, ed. *Justifying Toleration: Conceptual and Historical Perspectives*. Cambridge: Cambridge University Press, 1988.

Milbank, John. *Theology and Social Theory*. Oxford: Basil Blackwell, 1990.

Momigliano, Arnaldo. "The Disadvantage of Monotheism for a Universal State." In *On Pagans, Jews and Christians*. Hanover: Wesleyan University Press, 1987.

Montaigne, Miguel de. *The Essays of Miguel de Montaigne*. Translated by George Ives. New York: Limited Editions, 1943.

Mote, Fredrick W. *Intellectual Foundations of China*. New York: Knopf, 1971.

Muir, William. *The Life of Mohammad from Original Sources*. New York: AMS Press, 1975.

Munro, Donald. *The Concept of Man in Early China*. Stanford: Stanford University Press, 1969.

Nandy, Ashis et al. *Creating a Nationality: The Ramjanmabhumi Movement and Fear of Self.* Oxford: Oxford University Press, 1996.

Nederman, Cary J. *Worlds of Difference: European Discourses of Toleration, c. 1100–1550.* University Park: Pennsylvania State University Press, 2000.

Nelson, Benjamin. *The History of Usury: From Tribal Brotherhood to Universal Otherhood.* Chicago: University of Chicago Press, 1969.

———. *The Idea of Usury.* Chicago: University of Chicago Press, 1969.

———. "Self Images and Spiritual Directions in the History of European Civilization." In *On the Roads to Modernity: Conscience, Science and Civilizations,* edited by T. Huff. New Jersey: Rowman and Littlefield, 1981.

Nirenberg, David. *Communities of Violence: Persecution of Minorities in the Middle Ages.* Princeton: Princeton University Press, 1996.

O'Donovan, Oliver. *Desire of the Nations: Rediscovering the Roots of Political Theology.* Cambridge: Cambridge University Press, 1999.

Paine, Thomas. *The Rights of Man.* New York: Doubleday, 1961.

Parkes, James. *The Conflict of the Church and the Synagogue: A Study in the Origins of Antisemitism.* New York: Athenaeum, 1969.

Perry, Michael J. *The Idea of Human Rights: Four Inquiries.* Oxford: Oxford University Press, 2000.

Pocock, J. G. A. *The Machiavellian Moment.* Princeton: Princeton University Press, 1975.

Popkin, Richard. *The History of Skepticism from Erasmus to Spinoza.* Berkeley: University of California Press, 1979.

Ravitzky, Aviezer. "The Question of Tolerance in the Jewish Tradition." In *Hazon Nahum: Studies in Jewish Law, Thought, and History,* edited by Y. Elman and J. S. Gurock. New York: Yeshiva University Press, 1997.

Remer, Gary. *Humanism and the Rhetoric of Toleration.* University Park: Pennsylvania State University Press, 1996.

Rimbaud, Arthur. *Une saison en enfes, Illuminations.* Paris: Gallimard, 1973.

Rokeah, David. *Jews, Pagans and Christians in Conflict.* Jerusalem: Magnes Press, 1982.

Rousseau, Jean-Jacques, and Johann G. Herder. *On the Origin of Language: Two Essays.* Translated by A. Gode and J. H. Moran. Chicago: University of Chicago Press, 1990.

Sachedina, Abdulaziz Abdulhussein, and Joseph Montville. *Islamic Roots of Democratic Pluralism.* Oxford: Oxford University Press, 2000.

Schluchter, Wolfgang. "The Paradox of Rationalization: On the Relations of Ethics and the World." In *Max Weber's Vision of History, Ethics and Method,* edited by G. Roth and W. Schluchter. Berkeley: University of California Press, 1979.

———. *The Rise of Western Rationalism.* Berkeley: University of California Press, 1981.

Scribner, Bob. "Preconditions of Tolerance and Intolerance in Sixteenth Century Germany." In *Tolerance and Intolerance in the European Reformation*, edited by O. P. Grell and B. Scribner. Cambridge: Cambridge University Press, 1996.

Seligman, Adam B. *Modernity's Wager: Authority, the Self, and Transcendence*. Princeton: Princeton University Press, 2000.

———. "Review of *The Idea of Human Rights* by Michael Perry." *Human Rights Review* 1, no. 3 (2002): 140–44.

Sennett, Richard. *The Fall of Public Man*. New York: W. W. Norton, 1992.

Shatz, David, Chaim I. Waxman, and Nathan J. Diament, eds. *Tikkun Olam: Social Responsibility in Jewish Thought and Law*. Northvale, N.J.: Jason Aronson, 1997.

Shurkin, Michael. "Decolonization and the Renewal of French Judaism: Reflections on the Contemporary French Jewish Scene." *Jewish Social Studies* 6, no. 2 (2000): 156–76.

Smith, Adam. *The Theory of Moral Sentiments*. Indianapolis: Liberty Press, 1982.

Stanton, Graham N., and Guy G. Stroumsa, eds. *Tolerance and Intolerance in Early Judaism and Christianity*. Cambridge: Cambridge University Press, 1998.

Steiner, George. *After Babel: Aspects of Language and Translation*. Oxford: Oxford University Press, 1998.

Stone, Suzanne Last. "Sinaitic and Noahide Law: Legal Pluralism in Jewish Law." 12 *Cardozo Law Review* 1157 (1991).

Swartz, Benjamin. "Some Polarities in Confucian Thought." In *Confucianism and Chinese Civilization*, edited by A. Wright. Stanford: Stanford University Press, 1964.

Taylor, Charles. *Human Agency and Language*. Vol. 1. Cambridge: Cambridge University Press, 1985.

———. *Sources of the Self*. Cambridge: Harvard University Press, 1989.

Taylor, Miriam, *Anti-Judaism and Early Christian Identity: A Critique of the Scholarly Consensus*. Leiden: E. J. Brill, 1995.

Tisdall, W. St. Clair. *The Original Sources of the Qur'an*. London: Society for the Promotion of Christian Knowledge, 1911.

Torrey, Charles. *The Jewish Foundation of Islam*. New York: Jewish Institute of Religion Press, 1933.

Toulmin, Stephen. *Cosmopolis: The Hidden Agenda of Modernity*. Chicago: University of Chicago Press, 1990.

Troeltsch, Ernst. *The Social Teachings of the Christian Churches*. Vol. 1. New York: Harper and Row, 1960.

Turner, Victor. *Dramas, Fields, and Metaphors: Symbolic Action in Human Society*. Ithaca: Cornell University Press, 1974.

———. *The Ritual Process: Structure and Anti-Structure*. New York: Aldine de Gruyter, 1995.

Tuveson, Ernest. *The Imagination as a Means of Grace: Locke and the Aesthetics of Romanticism*. Berkeley: University of California Press, 1960.

————. *Redeemer Nation: The Idea of America's Millennial Role.* Chicago: University of Chicago Press, 1968.

Unamuno, Miguel de. *Tragic Sense of Life.* New York: Dover, 1972.

Vaughan, Larry. *Johann Georg Hamann: Metaphysics of Language and Vision of History.* New York: Peter Lang Publishing, 1989.

Voeglin, Eric. *New Science of Politics.* Chicago: University of Chicago Press, 1952.

————. *Order and History.* Vol. 1. Baton Rouge: Louisiana State University Press, 1954.

Walzer, Michael. *On Toleration.* New Haven: Yale University Press, 1997.

————. *Thick and Thin: Moral Argument at Home and Abroad.* Notre Dame: University of Notre Dame Press, 1994.

Weber, Max. *Economy and Society: An Outline of Interpretive Sociology.* Berkeley: University of California Press, 1986.

————. *The Protestant Ethic and the Spirit of Capitalism.* New York: Scribner and Sons, 1958.

Weld, Thomas. "Preface." In *A Short Story of the Rise, Reign, and Ruin of the Antinomians, Familists, and Libertines That Infected the Churches of New-England,* edited by J. Winthrop. London: Tho. Parkhurst, 1692.

Wellhausen, Julius. *Reste arabischen Heidentums.* Berlin: De Gruyter, 1961.

Wensinck, A. J. *Mohammed en de Joden te Medina Muhammad and the Jews of Medina).* Translated by Wolfgang Behn. Freiburg: K. Schwarz, 1975.

Williams, Bernard. "Toleration: An Impossible Virtue?" In *Toleration: An Elusive Value,* edited by D. Heyd. Princeton: Princeton University Press, 1996.

Winter, J., and D. Joslin, eds. *R. H. Tawney's Commonplace Book.* Cambridge: Cambridge University Press, 1972.

Yuval, Israel Jacob. *"Two Nations in Your Womb": Perceptions of Jews and Christians (Hebrew).* Tel Aviv: Am Oved, 2001.

ADAM B. SELIGMAN is professor of religion at Boston University